Single Women

On the Margins?

Tuula Gordon

NEW YORK UNIVERSITY PRESS
Washington Square, New York

Copyright © Tuula Gordon 1994

All rights reserved

First published in the U.S.A. in 1994 by
NEW YORK UNIVERSITY PRESS
Washington Square
New York, N.Y. 10003

Library of Congress Cataloging-in-Publication Data
Gordon, Tuula.
Single women : on the margins? / Tuula Gordon.
p. cm.
Includes bibliographical references and index.
ISBN 0–8147–3063–9 (cloth) — ISBN 0–8147–3064–7 (pbk.)
1. Single women—Cross-cultural studies.   I. Title.
HQ800.2.G67   1994
305.48' 9652—dc20   93–36034
                                                         CIP

Printed in Hong Kong

Contents

Acknowledgements	vi
Introduction	1
1. From spinsters to singles	9
2. Individuality, autonomy and women	25
3. The making of a 'single woman'	38
4. Excursion into the public sphere	65
5. Excursion into the private sphere	84
6. Partnerships and sexuality	106
7. On being single	128
8. Independence	159
9. Marginality	178
Appendix: the interviewees	199
Notes	202
Bibliography	207
Index	218

Acknowledgements

First I want to thank all those single women who so generously agreed to be interviewed and made this study possible. It was a pleasure to meet all of them. The Finnish Academy financed the research and provided a grant which secured a leave of absence from teaching for a year. During the researching and writing of this book the Department of Sociology, University of Helsinki has been my base. While conducting my research in the San Francisco Bay Area, I was based at the Elizabeth N. Bain Research Center, University of California, Berkeley. I would like to thank Elizabeth Abel and Arlie Hochschild for their help in organising my stay. Anneli Anttonen and Jorma Sipilä offered support and help in a number of ways during that period. Margo, Peter, Tom and Rob Clarke were always hospitable and fun during my research visits to London. I am grateful for all the discussions I have had with many people concerning my research. Many thanks to all who read and commented on sections of my manuscript: Leena Alanen, Betsy Ettorre, Anneli Anttonen, Janet Holland, Elina Lahelma, Eero Lahelma, Sari Näre, Minna Salmi, Leila Simonen, Jorma Sipilä and Ritva Uusitalo. Sinikka Aapola read through the entire typescript and made valuable comments. Our discussions during the period we worked together (Sinikka was my research assistant) were important to me. I am grateful for her contribution and support. A number of people and organisations assisted me in finding interviewees; although I shall not name them, in order to safeguard the anonymity of the interviewed women, I should like to express my sincere thanks. Jo Campling, my editor, has always been ready to help when needed. When I was 19 and about to leave home, I met Dougie Gordon. Consequently I have no experience of singleness. I could thank Dougie, Mikko and Janne for lots of things, but in the context of this book I want to thank them for keeping existential angst at bay. Dougie Gordon also read through the entire manuscript.

TUULA GORDON

Introduction

Single women have been stereotyped as old maids who were unable to 'get a man', and as modern city singles who have not wanted a man. These stereotypes form a 'fiction' of single women, which shapes the reality that heterogeneous single women have to contend with. The two stereotypes represent continuities and changes in the position of women without male partners. Historically, in cultural representations, women have been defined in relation to men. Men provide the norm, the normal, the absolute; they are 'true' autonomous individuals. Women are, in this framework, 'the other' (De Beauvoir, 1972). Romantic love, partnership, marriage and motherhood form the cultural context of women and resonate in representations of them. They form a framework within which personal lives and subjectivities are constructed. Locating themselves outside families provides opportunities for women, but also places them in a contradictory and difficult position. Historically women alone have been placed along the continuum of nun/prostitute (Chisholm, 1987); yet it is possible that single women today have more independent possibilities in the context of diversification of family forms, and increased flexibility in the social construction of gender. I have attempted to explore whether single women are 'marginal'; if so, how is their marginality constructed, maintained and challenged? I shall focus on both the possibilities and the limitations single women experience in organising their lives.

My previous research and theoretical concerns led me to study single women. Work I have done on progressive education (Gordon, 1986, 1988), gender and education (for example Gordon, 1992; Gordon, Lahelma and Tarmo, 1991) and feminist mothers (Gordon, 1990) contained an interest in human agency: to what extent can people construct alternatives in given structural, cultural and personal circumstances? When I started this study on single women, I wanted to find out how they have constructed their lives in the context of prevailing notions

2 Single Women

about femininity, and how they have dealt with pressures towards marriage and maternity. In order to explore whether single women are marginal 'others' I interviewed 72 women in London, the San Francisco Bay Area and Helsinki. I chose places with different societal frameworks, but in all of which living as a single woman should be relatively easy (Chapter 2). The women come from different backgrounds; in analysing the interview data I have had to deal with heterogeneity and diversity. This is a cross-cultural study, not a systematic, comparative study in a traditional sociological sense. It is an analytical narrative based on interviews, and an attempt to explore the empirical applicability of theoretical discussion on the 'individual' as a masculine construction. Conceptions of sexual difference underpin the analysis.

Amazons

The myth of the Amazons probes sexual difference, and is an interesting metaphor for single women. The Amazons in ancient Greek stories were a nation of women warriors, who brought up only female children; the boys were either sent away or slain. The Amazons did not marry, they controlled their own offspring and they were 'outside' society. They were the counterparts of Greek heroes – brave and respected fighters (Kirk, 1987). According to the lore they removed one breast in order to facilitate the use of weapons. Their warcries were said to induce great fear. The Amazons were always eventually defeated, but their conquerors often experienced ambivalence. Their queen, Penthesilea, was killed by Achilles, but, when he saw her beauty and youth, he regretted his victory. Theseus fought against the Amazons, and took their queen Antiope with him as his captive.[1] The Amazons then entered Athens, metaphorically coming 'inside' society, and a battle was fought, which they lost.

Women could be brought into the Athenian society only through marriage. The weak point of the Athenian patriarchy was the need for women to produce sons. This weak point was evident in dissatisfaction expressed by Athenian women (Kirk, 1987). The Amazons flouted feminine ideals: 'Marginal and ambiguous, Amazons were either killed or made into proper women through marriage' (Kirk, 1987, p. 31). But the imagery of the Amazons shifted over time. In the seventeenth century, Kirk notes, the image was applied to sexually frustrated and 'excessively' independent women; Amazonism has remained 'the universal male nightmare'. Some feminists have revived positive images of Amazonian matriarchy at war against patriarchy; they were building their own social ideal, close to nature. Warner's study (1985b) of the use of the female form notes, for example, the adoption of Amazonian iconography by singers such as Toyah Willcox and Kate Bush.

I read Ilse Kirk's article about the images of Amazons when I started my research, during which I encountered the imagery on countless occasions, connected to single women in particular, and to women who challenged conventions in general. The Amazonian lore contains a number of interesting features: there are shifts in aspects of the lore that were emphasised historically, as there have been shifts in the way single women are viewed, stories about Amazons contain stereotypes which are both negative and positive. Amazons, like single women, raised questions about boundaries in their marginality and anomaly; they have been the subject of many fantasies and transformations. The Amazon has been incorporated into the iconography of Liberty (Warner, 1985b p. 292). The female wildness in breaking conventions has been utilised in images of liberation, but it is subverted: women are associated with nature, whilst men, endowed with reason, control culture. The association of women with otherness is reproduced and confirmed.

The Amazons were considered a new, third sex. Similarly single women in the nineteenth century were called 'hermaphrodites' and 'mannish maidens' as well as 'amazons' (Chambers-Schiller, 1984). Historical examples of positive stereotypes can also be found: Wheelwright (1989) refers to a British female soldier, Christian Davies, who was admired as an example. 'He' received letters from women containing phrases like 'the Amazonian race begins again' (Wheelwright, 1989, p. 14). The 'Amazon' has connected sex/gender to 'race' in many ways. Black women have been negatively labelled, amongst other stereotypes, as Amazons, invoking images of matriarchs who dominate and emasculate black men (hooks, 1982; Wallace, 1990).

The metaphor of the Amazon, and its many appearances in the context of discussion and debates about single women, indicates the usefulness of considering the meaning and boundaries constituted around sex/gender. Single women have defied definition because they are not formally connected to men (except their fathers); if 'woman' is the 'other' in relation to 'man', is single woman a 'woman' at all, or a representative of the 'third sex'? The threat and challenge of the

4　Single Women

Amazons has been subverted by their donning of the male guise (Warner, 1985b, 1983; Wheelwright, 1989). Their challenge assumes a masculine character, and they remain unassigned in the structure of the cultural terrain; they are contested characters with ambivalent sexuality.

The third sex?

Emily Blackwell was an American single woman (1826–1911) who completed her medical education and was an influential figure in her field. She wrote to Susan B. Anthony about her inclination to 'assume a man's dress and wander freely' (Chambers-Schiller, 1984, p. 67). In between the binary opposition between 'women' and 'men' there exists a grey area where the sexual difference is blurred by the existence of hermaphrodites, transsexuals, transvestites, gender blenders (Devor, 1989), cross-dressers (Wheelwright, 1989) and androgynous individuals. The constitution of gender is a contested and complex process considered by many theoreticians (Riley, 1988; Meese, 1986; Butler, 1987, 1990; Cocks, 1989; Spelman, 1990; Eisenstein, 1988; Woodhouse, 1989, Devor, 1989; Kessler and McKenna, 1978; B. Davies, 1989 and so on.). For my purposes here the main feature is the challenge of the concept of the existence of two sexes; Devor for example sees gender as a continuum rather than as a bipolarity. I shall explore the constitution of sex/gender further in Chapter 2, where I discuss individuality, and 'woman' as an individual. Here I am interested in women who have, like Blackwell, assumed the male guise in order to escape some of the restrictions on women. But the possibilities are circumscribed. Sexual inversion disrupts sexual difference, but also serves ultimately to clarify it (for example, Wheelwright, 1989; Warner, 1983, 1985b). Wheelwright studied women who had signed on as soldiers, and concluded that these women became brave *soldiers*, not brave *women*. Many became so immersed in their male identity that for them women became the 'other'; they were 'one of the boys' and proved that to themselves and those around them over and over again.

A particular challenge of cross-dressing is connected with relations of these 'men' to other women. Silverstolpe (1989) has studied trials of Nordic women who have married (women) as 'men'. They were considered to have acted against the church, the state and the natural order. Greenblatt (1986) discusses the case of Marie le Marcis who in 1601 wanted to marry a woman. She changed her name to Marin, dressed as a man and stated 'his' intention to marry, thus creating a public scandal. After Marin had been tried and condemned to be burnt alive 'he' was examined by a doctor interested in hermaphroditism and was released on the basis of the testimonial of the doctor. The court records indicated that no conclusion about the sex of Marie/Marin was reached. This case, Greenblatt argues, encoded a paradox in the way sex was interpreted at the time. All individuals were thought to contain both female and male elements – there was only one sexual structure, visible in men, and hidden and inverted in a women. Underlying the understanding of sexual difference was the conception of a woman as a defective man. A male had to establish himself as a 'man' by separating himself from the female.

Conceptions of what a 'woman' is, and how sexual difference is constituted, have undergone alterations since the case of Marie/Marin. The development of Western democracies required thinking about 'woman', who had become, by now, more distinct from a 'man'. For women to be enfranchised and thus assume citizenship, they had to be rehabilitated. Riley (1988) argues that the production of a new 'social' sphere between the public and the private in the nineteenth and early twentieth century offered a possibility of doing so. Female goodness could be exercised in philanthrophy, improving the circumstances of the poor and thus sowing the seeds of the welfare state.

In feminist analyses of the relationship between body, sex and gender, bodies are considered as sites of culturally constructed gender meanings. The body, Butler (1990) argues, is a variable boundary, and gender is not a stable identity; it is performative. Butler reads the work of Monique Wittig in terms of analysing and challenging the need for the body to become a cultural sign. Or, as Meese (1986) puts it, Wittig creates Amazons who refuse to be women, but who do not mirror men.

Single women in history

The discussion on the ambiguity and ambivalence surrounding sex/gender may seem to wander far from the subject of single women, but conceptions of what a 'woman' is have been important in shaping the possibilities and limitations of single women in constructing their lives. I shall consider two prominent women in history: Joan of Arc and

6 *Single Women*

Elizabeth I. Both women tapped the ambivalence around sexual difference, and both of them were single.

Joan of Arc

Marina Warner states in the prologue of her study of Joan of Arc that

> she is a universal figure who is a female, but is neither a queen, nor a courtesan, nor a beauty, nor a mother, nor an artist of one kind or another, nor – until the extremely recent date 1920 when she was canonized – a saint. She eludes the categories in which women have normally achieved a higher status that gives them immortality, and yet she gained it. (Warner, 1983, p. 26).

Joan of Arc was born in 1412/1413 and burned at the stake in 1431. Her presence and activity influenced the course of war between England and France. She inspired Charles of France and became a heroine in battle. Soon after she was subjected to an inquisitorial trial and was found guilty of insubordination and heterodoxy. Of particular interest here are two features of Joan of Arc: her cross-dressing and the context of the lore of the Amazons within which her heroism combined with her status as a young virgin.

Joan of Arc illuminates the sexual difference, both in its limitations and its possibilities. She was a young woman, a virgin, who lived as a man; thus she ignored what is 'natural' for a 'woman' and crossed boundaries. Joan dressed in handsome male clothes and carried arms, without pretending to be a man. Did she represent a third sex? Whilst defying men on a personal level by assuming their functions, on a social level Joan of Arc assumed some of the status accorded to men. Thus, Warner argues, she paid homage to the male sphere of action. But Joan did not only dress in men's clothes; she dressed as a knight, challenging social hierarchy and advancing her own mobility. Joan did not accept the limitations imposed on a woman, nor did she accept those imposed on a peasant.

Later Joan became associated with the Amazons, and was given her name; the arc refers to the amazonian bow.[2] Joan was compared to Amazon queens such as Penthesilea. Warner concludes, however, that the Amazons, in assuming male skills, rejected the feminine, as symbolised by the severing of the breast, but, as noted above, the Amazonian lore underwent many transformations in history. In the case of Joan a new softness was added: it was emphasised that she never took pleasure in battles. Joan, though seen as an Amazon, independent virgin, was utilised in versatile ways, depending on the cause for which she was claimed as a symbol. The figure of Joan was part of the process whereby Amazonian lore became incorporated in the figure of Virtue (Warner, 1985b). Warner concludes that the story of Joan has been told by using a lexicon of available female types, because we find it difficult to step beyond our inelastic classification systems.

Elizabeth I

When Elizabeth I inspected English troops at Tilbury in 1588, she wanted to emphasise the courage needed because of the threat imposed by the Spanish Armada. She was dressed in a male costume. Marcus (1989) has analysed Elizabeth I as the daughter of Henry VIII; Elizabeth I was better able to erase the stigma of daughterhood than her sister Mary I. Marcus refers to Elizabeth's 'Amazonian attire' and quotes the speech in which she stated that 'I have the body of a weak and feeble woman, but I have the heart and stomach of a king' (p. 409). Elizabeth did not often don the male apparel in actuality, but she did so symbolically through language. She used the concept of the King's Two Bodies, a concept in English law which refers to the simultaneous earthly and immortal beings of the king. Whilst Elizabeth's 'body natural' was that of a woman, her 'body politic' was that of a king. She ignored wishes that she should marry, claiming that she, as a husband, was married to her kingdom. By referring to imagery of the Virgin Mary she proclaimed herself a mother of the nation at the same time. Elizabeth developed herself into a successful ruler by being both the king and queen and by managing to incorporate her father's authority. Her emphasis on continuity with him ensured her legitimacy as a monarch.

I have discussed Joan of Arc and Elizabeth I for two reasons: the analyses of Warner and Marcus connect both to Amazoniasm, cross-dressing and ambivalent challenges to sexual difference; also they are both prominent historical figures who are single women. Many discussions on 'singles' today refer to a *modern big city phenomenon*. It is useful to remember the long history of singleness of women, to consider the transformations in the position of single women and shifts in attitudes to them. In Chapter 1, I shall consider the position of single women in the nineteenth century, in the 1950s and in the 1980s. This will form a background for my analysis of the changes and continuities in the lives of single women today. I shall explore what happens when women do not try to evade pressures they experience by cross-dressing and concealing their bodies; when, instead of donning the male disguise, they attempt to assume the status formally open to all in modern Western democracies – that of a citizen as an 'individual'. 'Individuality' as gender specific is explored in Chapter 2. I begin the exploration of the lives of single women interviewed in Chapter 3. Chapters 4 and 5 consider single women zigzagging between oppositionally represented private and public spheres, focusing on work and homes, respectively. In Chapter 6 their views on, and experiences of, marriage, partnership and sexuality are explored. In Chapter 7, pleasures and gains, as well as difficulties and tensions of singlehood, are discussed. In Chapter 8 the individuality of single women is explored by considering independence/ dependence. In the final chapter, the marginality of single women is returned to; by this time the question has become more complex: processes of marginalisation *and* integration shape the social locations of single women.

1

From spinsters to singles

I shall consider the position of unmarried women in Britain, the USA and Finland in the nineteenth century, in the 1950s and in the 1980s in order to illustrate some of the continuities and changes in their lives. The overview is necessarily cursory – changes in the position of women hinge on complex sets of developments – but some of the shifts are illustrated.

Spinsters in the nineteenth century

Women's relationship to the state was mediated through men in Western democracies in the nineteenth century. They had no citizenship rights and no suffrage, and did not control property if they were married. In Britain the 1851 census established that there were one million unmarried women of 25 and over (Anderson, 1984). The proportion of unmarried women rose throughout the nineteenth century, with almost 15 per cent of 50-year-old women unmarried by the end of the century (Watkins, 1984). There were more spinsters than bachelors and more widows than widowers; demographic imbalances were due to the higher death rate of males, male emigration, service in armed forces and colonial service (Jalland, 1988). The 'spinster problem' was widely debated. A solution was suggested in parliamentary debates: the redundant spinsters should be shipped to the Antipodes where they were wanted (Jeffreys, 1985, p. 87). In America the number of spinsters increased throughout the nineteenth century. For example, 7.3 per cent of women born between 1835 and 1838 and 11 per cent of women born between 1865 and 1875 were spinsters. Parallels to British social attitudes were illustrated by suggestions that 'surplus' women should be shipped to

Oregon and California, where the population was predominantly male (Chambers-Schiller, 1984). In Finland there was a similar proportion of unmarried women to those in Britain, but numbers of unmarried women continued to rise sharply until the 1940s (Ritamies, 1988). Finland was a Grand Duchy of the Russian Empire; spinsters became more integrated into the society as part of a national project – no obvious places to ship them to were thought of. Attitudes to spinsters are illustrated by Sara Wacklin, who wrote perceptively about women's lives. Of a spinster teacher, Wacklin writes that she had avoided the submissive state of marriage, as no man had tried to persuade her otherwise.[1]

Among upper- and middle-class women the separation between the spheres of the sexes was rigid in all three countries. Spinsters as well as married women were largely restricted to the domestic sphere. At home, spinsters were engaged in household management, caring for aging parents and childminding. They also acted as surrogate wives for widowed fathers or unmarried brothers. Many families had one unmarried daughter; there was a family strategy of keeping one daughter at home to ensure, in the absence of the welfare state, the well-being of the parents (Watkins, 1984). The role of spinsters at home was ambivalent, and there was little recognition of their needs and interests and of their individuality.

The dominant conception of 'woman' centred around reproduction and marriage. Women who did not pursue this path were considered pitiful creatures and had to struggle with the effects of this characterisation. Beatrice Potter lamented the unhappy position of an unmarried daughter, which presented difficulties even 'for a strong woman'. She was fearful of the harmful effects of spinsterhood, for example of developing abnormal masculine qualities (Jalland, 1988, p. 257). Anne Thackeray, the daughter of W.M. Thackeray, argued that a profession would be preferably to mending clothes (Hill-Miller, 1989, p. 366). Her father, in the absence of sons, apprenticed her to his profession of writing, but at the same time treated her as a 'surrogate wife'. He wrote to her: 'I intend when I am dismal that you shall console me if you can and I must tell you musn't I?' (Hill-Miller, 1989, p. 369). Anne Thackeray did not marry until after her father's death. She became a writer, and her novels explored the themes of women struggling to free themselves of dependence on protective male figures and of the conflict between a conventional and an unconventional woman.

Outside the home, upper- and middle-class single women were to pursue the arts, help the poor and so on. Towards the end of the century they started entering professions. Vicinus (1985) studied spinsters who pioneered new public roles for women in Britain by establishing separate communities such as settlement houses, church communities and women's colleges for them. The thinking about separate spheres framed the efforts of these women. The new communities were structured very much like families. Personal ambitions of women residing in them had to be presented as self-sacrifice; for example, settlement workers upheld family and home in their work. From mid-century onwards the numbers of colleges for women and boarding schools for girls increased. The boarding schools were based on strict discipline, in an effort to emphasise the ability of women to behave in a rational, professional fashion. Paradoxically, autonomy and individuality were to be achieved through strict regulation. Strong self-control could provide freedom for women in a context where so many external constraints operated. The pioneers used the idea of separate spheres to support their endeavours to empower women.

The story of spinsters told by Chambers-Schiller (1984) is about women trying to establish autonomy, individuality and independence in their own right in the USA. They relied on prevalent conceptions of women; 'the cult of single blessedness' emphasised the superior moral qualities of women and correlated this with their weaker sexual drive. But independent status was limited for women, and the pioneers discussed by Chambers-Schiller experienced difficulties and conflicts. Their achievements could not match their dreams. The emphasis on reproduction meant that women were very much equated with their bodies: psychoneurotic illnesses were therefore common. The notion of women's spirituality and self-sacrifice led to a denial of personal needs and somatisation of discontent.

Jalland (1988) found three types of spinsters in Britain: dutiful daughters, who accepted prevailing notions of femininity; desperate rebels who tried to escape the restrictions of their position in destructive ways such as invalidism, use of drugs and so on; and 'new women', who attempted to transcend the stereotype of the spinster as a failure. In women's movements in all three countries a large proportion of activists were single. Restrictions on the lives of married women were considered not to offer sufficient opportunities for independence; spinsterhood was necessary for autonomy.

Anderson's (1984) study of the residential situation of spinsters in Britain indicates that they lived in employers' households (as servants), with relatives, as heads of households or in institutions. The proportions of spinsters in these categories varied a great deal for different age-groups. Only 16 per cent of unmarried women aged between 35 and 44 were heads of households, though this figure increased for older spinsters. Davidoff and Hall (1987) refer to strains that lack of autonomy in housing caused unmarried women (p. 358).

The lives of working-class women were filled with material hardships. Anderson's (1984) analysis of data from the British census of 1851 indicates the difficulties experienced by unmarried women in obtaining suitable employment to guarantee financial independence. Unmarried women mainly worked as servants resident in their employers' homes and in domestic production. Women's entry to the labour market was difficult because only a narrow range of jobs were considered suitable, and training was not usually open to them. As they aged, an increasing proportion of women became dependent on the state or charity and were in receipt of Poor Relief (Anderson, 1984).

Finland was a predominantly agrarian society throughout the nineteenth century. The participation of women in agricultural work was high;[2] the low level of technology meant that large numbers of people were needed to carry out the necessary work. When industrialisation began, unmarried women in particular entered paid employment early in large numbers (Pohls, 1990). Women's entry into paid employment did not free them. Finnish women worked not so much out of choice, but in order to survive (Pohls, 1990; Markkola, 1990). They received low wages and conditions of employment were unregulated; they became a significant reserve for expanding industries. The spinster problem in Finland was solved out of economic necessity by facilitating the employment of unmarried women so that they would not be a liability. Pohls argues that women's achievement of important political and civil rights at least partly reflected this same concern. Women in Finland obtained universal suffrage in 1906, as compared to 1918 in Britain and 1920 in the USA.

In the United States unmarried women gradually entered the labour market in the new industrial centres developing from the beginning of the century; 'But no matter what her age, work, or position in the world, the unmarried female was seen (as were all women) in a family context' (Chambers-Schiller, 1984). The position of black women was determined by slavery and colonialism. Racism and sexism framed their oppression. Whilst white womanhood was idealized, black women were forced to assume a 'masculine' role by doing hard physical work without male protection. Black women were sexualised and assaulted.

On the one hand they were seen as temptresses, on the other hand they were used for breeding new slaves (hooks, 1982). It was in the interests of white women to condone the sexualisation of black women and maintain the monopoly of female virtue themselves. The sexual exploitation of black women continued after slavery; the slave system had shaped their social status (hooks, 1982). Their economic exploitation continued too: the majority of them did not manage 'to escape from the fields, from the kitchen or from the washroom' (Davis, 1982, p. 85). All unmarried women, in whatever context, were located on the borders of the gender system. They were incorporated, but at the same time their existence provided a challenge and a threat. This is evident in conceptions of spinsters as a problem, because they were unable to pursue 'natural' womanhood, and in the necessity of black women to work like men whilst they were considered to represent the sexual depravity of women.

Birkett's (1989) study of Victorian lady explorers illustrates the intertwining of sex, class and 'race'. These women wanted to escape the restrictions of Victorian society; they had a strong need to break the boundaries set for them. They were impressed by the contrast between the circumscribed lives of their mothers and sisters and the space and freedom enjoyed by their fathers. In their travels they wanted to avoid colonial communities, where they were constructed as 'women' with the cultural trappings of home. Outside these settlements they were not measured against white men, but against subjected and colonised people. They were called 'gentlemen' and 'sirs', and exploited the sexual ambiguity. May French-Sheldon explained how she just had to 'put my head outside of my tent flap any hour of the day or night and call "Boy!" constantly back would come the answer, "sabe"!' (Birkett, 1989, p. 117).

The women explorers wavered between representing a third sex and men. Racism made travelling possible for white women and gave them the power of personhood and individuality in a colonial context. The complex layering of otherness is indicated in their relations to non-white women and men, and in the way they were defined in their own society. When the travellers returned home, they were relocated as 'women'. Their biographies were represented in terms of feminine duty and their personal ambitions were ignored. It was emphasised that they were not amazonian, though they were at times represented as 'new women'; because of the way their experiences had been shaped, they were not pleased with the image. They experienced difficulties in British society. For example, the Royal Geographical Society was reluctant to accommodate them without a male through whom they could be identified and classed; An amendment was put forward to 'exclude the third sex'. In 1913, however, they were admitted. These women travellers struggled hard to escape restrictions imposed upon them, but the possibilities were framed with limitations, and their success was, unsurprisingly, partial.

That spinsterhood increased during the nineteenth century among upper- and middle-class women was clearly due to 'pushes' and 'pulls' (Stein, 1978). For example, proportions of unmarried women rose because of demographic imbalances, but an increasing number of women thought that spinsterhood offered them more freedom. This applied to women in Finland too (see Jallinoja, 1983) although less information and fewer studies are available.

Towards the end of the nineteenth century shifts were taking place in the position of women. Unmarried women were partly influential in bringing about changes. Spinsters, in their philanthrophical work in Britain, the USA and Finland, laid the foundations of the welfare state, which eased the position of unmarried women. The developing welfare state provided public employment for women and released them from some of their tasks in the private sphere. Spinsters formed the backbone of feminism in the late nineteenth and early twentieth century. They fought the conception of women as appendages to men and campaigned for educational and employment opportunities for women in all three countries (see Vicinus, 1985; Chambers-Schiller, 1984; Jallinoja, 1983). They also organised themselves against male use of prostitution and challenged conceptions of male sexuality. They used the superior moral purity attributed to women in these campaigns (see Jeffreys, 1985).

There were also developments which eroded the achievements of these women and the basis from which they conducted their work. An important one was the sexualisation of women. Sexualisation has been a constant theme in conceptualisations of 'woman', but there have been historical variations. Black women were already sexualised, as discussed above. Vicinus argues that sexualisation was a sub-text in the attitudes to women's communities she analysed. But as long as it remained a sub-text, these women could form sub-cultures of friendship, psychic love and mutual support. With the sexualisation of women's bodies the emphasis on conceptions of femininity did not merely centre on reproduction and incompleteness of women outside marriage and motherhood; it was also claimed that 'healthy', 'normal' adult women needed sex and particularly intercourse in the context of marriage.

Spinsterhood came to be seen as a sexually as well as a socially deviant state. Extension of female autonomy was considered a threat by institutions such as the church, the university and medicine (Chambers-Schiller, 1984). It was argued that women not engaging in sex with men acquired characteristics of men. Medical theories about the decay and disease of 'unused' reproductive and sexual organs were developed (Chambers-Schiller, 1984; Martin, 1987). Women's homoerotic friendships came under scrutiny. They were seen to undercut the family. This affected the way in which women in their independent communities were viewed (Vicinus, 1985), and a support for the development of women's public roles was undermined (Vicinus, 1985; Delamont, 1992). Notions of complementarity between women and men were strengthened; female sexuality was constructed as complementary to men's (Jeffreys, 1985). Sexologists of the late nineteenth century also began to categorise lesbianism. Stereotypes of spinsters and lesbians overlapped and caused alarm.

Unmarried women in the 1950s

During the twentieth century women's lives have become more varied and their options and opportunities have increased, but there is no simple picture of steady improvement. The sexualisation of women continued with the advent of Freud and psychoanalysis and the sex reform movement. The women's movement subsided. The emphasis on marriage and motherhood as the major, 'natural' vocation for women continued. Conceptions of sexual difference and familial ideology containing notions of separate spheres for women and men solidified.

The decade of the 1950s, Stacey (1990) argues, was an aberrant period, with the culmination of 'the family' preceding its imminent decline. 'The family' referred to a male breadwinner, female housewife and children. Proportions of unmarried women had declined in America, Britain and Finland (though in Finland the proportion of unmarried women increased until the 1940s). Marriage and motherhood defined women, and their place was seen to be in the home. Spinsters were pitied as old maids. This is evident both in popular culture and in research of that period. The author of a book attempting to shed light on the psychological and social aspects of the status of single women stated:

[This book] cannot give any adequate answers to the single woman's outstanding questions – 'Why am I to be husbandless and childless? How can I lead this unnatural life with some measure of fulfilment?' It cannot offer to banish any of the frustrations, depressions, restlessness, which come from such a disastrous denial of a woman's natural rights to biological and psychological completion. (Smith, 1951, p. vii)

The single woman, Smith concludes, 'is isolated and frustrated, and therefore forever incomplete' (1951 p. 127). The idea of women and men being complementary remained significant in structuring gender relations.

The housewife and mother was portrayed in a positive way: that was what a 'woman' is; women not attached to a husband were remarkable in their invisibility. But conformism to ideals of femininity was not as total as accounts of this period emphasise (Baker, 1989). Women did not always live in the way in which they were portrayed. Under the veil of happiness there were frustrations, captured in the 1960s by Betty Friedan as 'the problem with no name'.[3] The developing welfare state and education provided women with greater opportunities and an increasing proportion of women entered the labour market. Particularly in Finland the participation of women in the labour market was consistently relatively high.

The tensions posed by the realities of women's lives and popular representations of them were partly solved by the concept of 'dual roles'. Women's labour was necessary and the 'dual role' facilitated the possibility of women working outside the home, whilst being wives and mothers constituted their main, 'natural' role. This was also applicable in Finland where, although full-time motherhood was less typical than in Britain and the USA, working outside the home was considered of secondary importance in cultural and ideological conceptions of femininity (Pohls, 1990; Sulkunen, 1989). The contrast between representations of women and familial rhetoric about them, and the lives that women were leading, was strongest in Finland.

Constructions of femininity contained, besides an emphasis on motherhood, notions of romantic love. Women who questioned marriage were seen to be suffering from a masculinity complex (Baker, 1989). Feminism was associated with singlehood and childlessness. Marriage was seen as a salvation. Romantic love was the available acceptable form for girls and women to express their sexuality. Sexuality was understood in terms of complementarity and sexuality in the context of romantic love positioned women within sexual difference. Studies of romantic fiction for adolescent girls in the 1950s indicate that girls were portrayed as passive spectators (Christian-Smith, 1988; Outinen, 1992). Christian-Smith, in her analysis of the 'code of romance' in adolescent romantic fiction, noted that smart girls exhibited their intelligence with care and attained power and status through obtaining boyfriends and husbands, thus locating themselves in subordinate relations to men. But it is mistaken to view the past by assuming that women lacked a sense of agency (Carter, 1988). Women were aware of the conflicts between the images of the happy family and their own experiences. These contradictions were actively negotiated. Carter analyses problem-page letters as expressions of ambivalence. The replies to these letters attempted to channel writers' misgivings into given familial patterns.

Stereotypes of unmarried women form a 'fiction' to which single women have to relate. Baker's (1989) analysis of women's fiction during the 1950s indicates that the writers, whilst not making single women particularly visible, were clear about the dilemmas women faced. If they did not want to be 'old maids' they had to make compromises in the standards they expected from their husbands and marriages. Baker discerns themes contained in the 'old maid' stereotype: unmarried women have either been rejected or they have been unable to receive sexual love because of their inadequacies and abnormal tendencies. The sub-text is a fear of autonomous women who, by their existence, threaten notions of sexual difference and complementarity. If they remain on the 'outside' they, like the Amazons, pose a threat of coming 'inside' and disrupting gender relations and challenging the subordination of women. Some women writers during this period did not accept the stereotype and wrote about women who made the best of singlehood and those who had made a choice to remain unmarried. Problems confronting such women were considered: their loneliness and their need for intimacy. Single women were often presented as being on the edges of men's world, but Baker also found heroines who were powerful, autonomous individuals.

When we consider the three countries included in my study of single women, Britain represents a 'middle' case. Finland had a higher proportion of single women, more women participated in the labour market and the ideology of marriage and motherhood as woman's 'natural' vocation did not receive as strong emphasis in Finland. Women had worked hard in agricultural labour and, as the process of industrialisaton began, they entered public employment relatively early in relatively large numbers. In the United States the proportion of single women was than in Britain. In terms of the culture of femininity and true womanhood, American women were presented a stronger version than British women (see Baker, 1989), but the situation in the USA was not simple either. Black women were excluded from the representations of true womanhood. They had to work out of necessity to keep their families and were labelled as Aunt Jemimas, Sapphires and Amazons (hooks, 1982). Because of institutionalised racism the positions of white and black women cannot be collapsed into one. The intersections of sex, class and 'race' framed women's locations and also affected the way forward that they might wish to pursue: 'When the middle class white woman said "I want to work", in her head was a desk in the executive suite, while the black woman saw a bin of dirty clothes, someone else's dirty clothes' (Wallace, 1990, p. 126). Emphasis on 'the individual' has been particularly strong in the USA; women sought to counter pressures of conceptions of femininity by striving for individuality.

The 1960s were a period of considerable social, cultural and economic change, when changes which had already begun and the tensions and ambiguities underlying the apparently unified representations of the 1950s erupted (Stacey, 1990). But there are important continuities. The dual role of women is still a powerful ideological device today. Girls in the 1950s grew up in a period of hope (Heron, 1985). In all three countries they had images of women working during the war behind them. The welfare state expanded their opportunities and the education system increased their possibilities of grasping those opportunities. As women were needed in the labour market, their participation was encouraged, but considered temporary, or at least secondary to their main role as wives and mothers at home. But women entered the labour market in increasing numbers, and stayed there.

Single women in the 1980s

The position of single women in the 1980s must be placed in the context of shifts in family forms. Research has pointed to the elusive nature of 'the family' (Barrett and McIntosh, 1982; Thorne and Yalom, 1982; Segal, 1983; Gittins, 1985). Gittins suggests that it is more useful to talk about 'families' rather than 'a family', but it is still difficult to arrive at an unambiguous definition. 'Family' is both a pervasive ideology and an historical creation. The concept of the family developed with the industrial bourgeoisie, and its original meaning referred to the authority of the *paterfamilias*. Gittins argues that implicit in the concept of the Western family is a notion of male dominance based on paternal authority and power. Gittins (1985) and Barrett (1980) note that a crucial element of familial ideology is the dependence of women on men. The family is a site containing sexual division of labour, within which gender differences are constructed and embedded in our subjectivity in such a way that 'family', as well as 'women' and 'men' appear natural. The ideal marriage is still predicated on notions of complementarity between women and men. This complementarity is now expressed in terms of an equal, companionate partnership.[4] But as the kind of equal relationship of an ideal marriage is the experience of a privileged few, 'family' is challenged and criticised by feminists. Family is considered central in the subordination of women; inequalities are structured within it and altered practices are unlikely to be significant. But analyses of family/household forms and familial ideologies are problematic (Bhavnani and Coulson, 1986) if they do not take into account oppressive state practices vis-à-vis black families. Families are a source of support and resistance against racism among black people and other ethnic groups (Bhavnani and Coulson, 1986; Garcia, 1988; Glenn, 1986; Collins, 1990). Family studies have used the white middle-class family as a yardstick of normality. Understanding of 'the family' becomes considerably more complex when other types of family formations are considered (Zinn, 1990; Collins, 1990). Many ethnic groups have faced structural constraints in establishing families, and the diversity of family life among them is an indication of adaptability and flexibility (for example, Taylor, Chatters, Tucker and Lewis, 1990). For women the picture is even more complicated. Whilst the family is a source of support against racism, which oppresses them, inside the family they have to struggle with sexism (Glenn, 1986; Garcia 1989; Zavella, 1987). The significance of family as a source of support is not dependent on having a family of procreation; the support can be provided by the family of origin.

It is important also to consider *familism* (Barrett and McIntosh, 1982), the way in which society and the welfare state are organised with the family as a basic unit, despite the ideology of individualism and the formal construction of societies as consisting of equal individuals as citizens. Barrett and McIntosh talk about 'familialisation' of society. Philanthrophic work of women in the nineteenth century was brought under the bureaucratic control of the state. Services provided by the welfare state contain assumptions about families and the roles of women within them. Donzelot (1980) referred to government through families. Women in particular are subjects of this regulation, but in different ways. Working-class white women and black women are 'the other', constituted as subjects to be monitored and controlled. Middle-class women in the caring professions participate in this regulation and through their work contribute to the possibility of maintaining democratic fictions about autonomous abstract individuals (Walkerdine and Lucey, 1989). Though women in Nordic countries have been more inclined to view the state as their ally rather than their enemy, and though familism is argued to be less inbuilt in state policies (Julkunen, 1990, 1992; Simonen, 1991), women are nevertheless subject to state regulation both as recipients of services and as public sector employees. That they may develop the content of their work in diverse ways does not alter the framework within which their jobs are located.

The way we analyse 'the family' has implications for a study on single women. If 'the family' is a basic unit of society, and ideological representations and state practices reinforce the rhetoric around the family, then, whilst women and children may be oppressed *inside* families, those excluded from families may be oppressed *outside* them because of their very exclusion. Thus being outside familial structures contributes to the marginality of single women. But if the family is crucial in regulation it is possible that remaining outside family structures nevertheless provides single women with more possibilities in negotiating their 'careers' and with more freedom from some aspects of the sexual division of labour. This may be one reason for single women to be considered an anomaly. The circumstances of the lives of large numbers of people do not conform to the familial ideology; people live in a range of different types of households. Hence single women, as part of a heterogeneous group increasing in number may experience a greater degree of scope for constructing their personal lives.

The starting-point of this study on single women, then, is that there are contradictory aspects in the construction of their location in society, and that the tensions between ideals and reality may be such that opportunities for various ways of constructing their lives are possible. Hence I shall explore whether marginality and anomalty are eroded by diverse social changes occurring in modern Western societies.

The conception of the nuclear family predominant particularly in the USA and Britain, though less so in Finland, presented men as breadwinners and women as housewives. This is countered by a range of changes: dual career families, delayed marriage, delaying having children, voluntary childlessness, divorce, serial monogamy, cohabitation, 'open marriage', communal living, single parent families, one-person households, gay and lesbian couples and singles (see Macklin, 1980). Research has indicated increasing tolerance for people choosing a range of options and living in diverse ways (for example, Thornton, 1989). Single people are not necessarily alone and lonely. Though difficulties of single women in organising their lives have continued well into this century (Allen 1989), today single women fare better and the group with greater difficulties seems to be single men who experience problems related to physical and emotional health. There are class differences, however. Middle-class, educated, professional women still find it easier to see singleness as an option; for working-class women the choice entails more difficulties (Allen, 1989; Cooney and Uhlenberg, 1989). Though there have been changes in attitudes, Thornton's (1989) research indicates that, whilst people have become more tolerant of other options, their own futures are largely conceived in terms of marrying and having children.[5] Singleness is a more acceptable option, but it does not necessarily appear an attractive one. Moreover the liberalisation of attitudes has reached a peak, and the discourse of the 'New Right' has been channelling conservative opposition to changes in families and has attempted to resolidify the sexual difference (see Faludi, 1992).

Research indicates both pressures for continuity and scope for change. I shall be asking whether and how single women are marginalised; is the marginalisation of single women decreasing in the context of social transitions; what are the spaces for autonomy, independence and choices; is 'otherness' and the idea of 'complementarity' of the sexes disrupted? I shall focus on negative and positive stereotypes about single women: has there been a shift from old maids who could not get a man to swinging singles in cities who do not want one?

The problem of categories

Reviewing statistics and studies on single women and men is complex. Statistics are usually compiled on the basis of categories 'single', 'married', 'divorced' and 'widows'. In 1988, 23 per cent of women aged 15 and over in the USA were single; in England and Wales 23 per cent of women aged 16 and over were single; and in Finland 28 per cent of women aged 15 and over were single. The increase of singles has been rapid in the USA. In Britain and Finland the recent increase has been more even. For example, in Britain in 1970, 19 per cent of women aged 16 and over were single; in the USA in 1970, 14 per cent of women aged 18 or over were single. Of women aged 35–9, 9 per cent in USA, 8 per cent in England and Wales, and 15 per cent in Finland were single.[6] The increase of singleness is largely due to an increase in the number of young singles, as age at first marriage has increased in all countries. The median age at marriage for women was 24.5 in Finland and 23 in USA in 1985.[7] Singles include those who cohabit, hence information on the basis of the category 'single' is misleading. Especially in the Nordic countries the position of a cohabiting couple with joint children has been brought close to the position of a similar married couple. The higher proportion of single women in Finland is partly due to the greater incidence of cohabitation there: 19 per cent of single women aged between 16 and 64 cohabited in Finland in 1985. In Britain, 15 per cent of single women aged between 18 and 49 cohabited in 1984/85. In the USA, about one-sixth of single women aged between 25 and 34 cohabited in 1987/88.[8] The percentages of divorced women in 1988 were as follows: USA, 8.4 per cent; England and Wales, 6.2 per cent; Finland, 7.6 per cent. About half of Finnish women and under 60 per cent of women in the USA and England and Wales were married in 1988.

Clear information on the proportions of single women, unmarried or divorced, and not cohabiting is difficult to obtain, if one is interested in singleness as a lifestyle of women in general. Studies on single women have tended to solve some of these problems by considering 'never-married women' (Allen, 1989; Simon, 1987; Adams, 1976). This category includes women aged 50 or over; hence women included in these studies have lived in different circumstances from those who are constructing single lives today in the context of social changes going on in Western societies. Further, the category of 'never-married' contains an assumption that marriage is the norm and singleness is deviant, and can only be confirmed in later life.

Assumptions and presuppositions

Research on single women seems rife with assumptions of deviance. These assumptions colour studies even when they attempt to show that stereotypes about 'old maids' are not applicable; the claims that single women are in fact well- adjusted, resourceful people have an air of testimony about them. The more patronising assumptions can be illustrated by the following:

> though denied a husband and children, a woman may nonetheless achieve a satisfactory personality integration and become a useful, happy participant in society. (Luther, 1968, p. 478)

As well as studies which set out to show that single women are not miserable, there are studies which set out to show that they are more than fine.

> many [single people] manifest a particular interest in events and experiences pertaining to the mind and imagination and that, in the final analysis, they allocate higher priority on their value scale than other social transactions that pivot around emotional relationships. (Adams, 1976, p. 123)

Emphasising that the number of singles is increasing, and that they are resourceful and resilient, masks many aspects that need to be considered when studying single women.

Conclusion

Although the proportion of the unmarried has increased, it is useful to remember that this recent increase was preceded by a decline. A great increase has occurred in the proportion of one person households, but the largest group of women in this category consists of widows.

Professional women tend to delay marriage and childbearing, and those who remain single are more likely to have made a positive choice to do so. For working class women the choice may be more complicated. Allen's (1989) study of never-married working-class women indicates that the practice of having one daughter stay at home and look after the household and the elderly, dependent relatives has continued from the nineteenth to the twentieth century. Whilst there is a growing emphasis on single women as autonomous and independent, there are those who are closely bound to their families of origin and whose personal options have been limited by their responsibilities. Simon's (1987) study indicated that pressures towards marriage and maternity among black women are different; they are urged to study and get a good job in order to break out of the economic vulnerability of their families of origin. Familism assumes different dimensions for black people. Though there are aspects of singleness that affect all women in that category, we also have to take into account diversity and heterogeneity among them.

The discussion so far has indicated that women have striven to establish their autonomy and independence, and have encountered difficulties in doing so. Proportions of single women have increased again since the 1950s, but caution is necessary when drawing conclusions from statistical information about women. Before proceeding with the examination of the position of single women, I shall consider citizenship and individuality in order to clarify how women are constructed as 'the other' and how women not defined in relation to a man may be marginal.

2

Individuality, autonomy and women

Relational individuality of women

Western democracies required the development of the modern, absolute individual, upon whom citizenship rights could be conferred. Meanings attached to 'the individual' have changed in emphasis. Williams (1961) notes that in medieval society an 'individual' was defined by his membership of a group. In the modern usage the individual has been abstracted from social relations; an individual is a separable entity whose formal rights as a citizen are ensured by the state. The social contract between equal individuals is the premise of the development of Western democracies. 'Individuals' became citizens through a voluntary contract to maximise their self-interest. The contract centred around the rights of men (see Yuval-Davis, 1991; Pateman, 1988; Bellah *et al.*, 1988). The 'individual' is a masculine construction which marginalises some groups as 'others' within structures of power.

In the nineteenth century, women were 'outside' the state, without citizenship rights (Chapter 1). Women have now obtained political citizenship, but they have not become 'individuals' equal to men except in the formal sense. In the abstract 'an individual' is presented as gender-neutral; historically, however, an 'individual' is gender-specific. The structures, discourses and practices centring on 'the individual' have constructed women as 'the other', whilst men have provided the norm and the normal. But it has never been possible to keep women outside 'individuality'. The conduct of Joan of Arc in her trials indicated that she believed in the primacy of individual conscience (Warner, 1983). Spinsters studied by Chambers-Schiller (1984) and Vicinus (1985) struggled to assert their autonomy and sought to be recognised as individuals, while remaining female persons. That is, they wanted to become individuals as women, not as 'men', which has been the more instant solution adopted by some women who have tried to escape restrictions imposed upon them by assuming male privileges; examples of cross-dressers, female soldiers and Victorian women travellers have been used above.

A myriad of structures, discourses and practices centre on 'the individual (see Gordon, 1992). Structurally individualisation is constituted through state practices and the social division of labour. It is rooted in material practices and appears to be 'natural' rather than social and contingent. Individuals are also culturally constructed through *individualism*, which has acquired meanings ranging from independence and self-reliance to self-interest and normlessness (Lukes, 1973). Individualism is a doctrine of human rights (Abercrombie, Hill and Turner, 1986). *Individuality* is used to refer to personality and incomparability of individuals (Abercrombie, Hill and Turner, 1986). The concept of 'the individual' embodied in 'individualism' and 'individuality' is based on a conception of *absolute individuals* who are not located in particular social relations. Such individuals are characterised by a unitary construction of personal consciousness. This interpretation has been challenged by conceptions of *subjectivity* which emphasise that social identity is non-unitary, contradictory and fragmented, and located in material and ideological social forms (Henriques *et al.*, 1984).

'Individuals' are gender-specific; gender relations cut across the structural processes of individualisation, cultural individualism and construction of subjectivities. The achievement of legal, civil and political rights by women has been out of step with men. It is not simply a question of women assuming such formal rights later than men: the social contract is based on the construction of sexual difference. Pateman (1988) argues that the social contract presupposes a sexual contract, based on the domination of women by men in the natural sphere. The social contract created a cultural sphere above this natural sphere. For political theorists the primary location of women was in the state of nature; for men there was a rational separation between the state of nature and the state of culture. Sexual difference is maintained by a range of binary oppositions, which are connected to the distinction between the state of nature and the state of culture: mind/body, reasons/ emotions, rationality/irrationality, abstract/concrete, objective/subjective, public/private, independence/dependence, masculine/ feminine, male/ female, man/woman.

The state of culture is the 'natural' habitat of Western white, heterosexual, able-bodied males, who represent hegemonic masculinity (Connell, 1987). Gender, class and 'race' intersect in the production of otherness. White women, women and men of colour, disabled women and men and working class men are on the margins of norms and normality constructed in locations of power along the axes of hegemonic masculinity. The modern state is characterised by institutionalised racism (Yuval-Davis, 1991): the social contract is built on colonial constructs of black people (Pateman, 1988) who are also located in the state of nature. Reason, rationality and objectivity are the attributes of privileged white men. It is, then, difficult for members of other groups to fill the space and contours of 'the individual' and thus assume full citizenship in its political, economic and social aspects.

The distinction of the state of nature and state of culture is based upon the sexual difference, an important facet of which is the division between the mind and the body. Gatens (1988) argues that the birth of the human subject and of the modern body politic presupposed each other. Women's bodies do not leave the state of nature and they acquire different meanings than bodies of men. The sexualisation of women's bodies was discussed in Chapter 1. The relationship between mind and body is not construed in the same way for women and men; the latter can subject intrusions of their bodies to control of their minds (Gatens, 1988). Women's bodies are seen as more anarchical and dangerous; women are less able to control their bodies. Their bodies also evoke desire, which tendentially erodes the distinction between mind and body, and spells danger to men, whose bodies are less associated with flesh, corporeality and irrationality. Women's bodies threaten the reason and rationality of men (Warner, 1985b; Theweleit, 1987, 1989). This pits women against rationality, which is connected to conceptions of individuals as absolute, separate and unitary. Warner's (1985b) analysis of the female form as an allegory illustrates connections between absolute/relative and men/women distinctions:

> men are individual, they appear to be in command of their own characters and their own identity, to live inside their own skins, and they do not include women in their symbolic embrace ... But the female form does not refer to particular women, does not describe women as a group, and often does not even presume to evoke their natures. (p. 12)

The bodies of women and men acquire different meanings, and the relationship between mind and body is differentially construed for them.

Women's bodies have been subjected to legal control, which curtails their autonomy, independence and self-control. Women's rights to bodily autonomy and to reproductive control have been important aspects in their campaigns for social citizenship and individuality. The New Right critique of such campaigns is based on the reassertion of sexual difference as natural and enshrined in the nuclear family with its gendered division of labour. 'Difference', rather than 'discrimination' explains the position of women inside and outside the family (Eisenstein, 1988).

Construction of absolute/relative individuality

Women, according to discourses around sexual difference, are *complementary* to men. The characterisation of this complementarity has shifted historically. Today the emphasis is on partnerships between equal individuals. Feminists challenge these liberal conceptions with studies which indicate that the reality of sexual relationships, marriage and the family does not tend to match the rhetoric of symmetry in complementarity. Negotiations within families occur in weighted relations of power. Feminists have challenged the notion of complementarity and have theoretically questioned the sexual difference in terms of a bipolar opposition 'woman'/'man'. This critique has political implications: Cynthia Cockburn argues that genuine independence for women means achieving a situation where they can be 'complete without a complement' (Cockburn, 1988).

How is relative/absolute individuality constructed and reconstructed? Psychoanalysis has challenged notions of a unitary self and 'radically undermines notions about autonomy, individual choice, will, responsibility, and rationality' (Chodorow, 1986). Psychoanalytic theories portray different ways girls and boys resolve the Oedipus complex. Boys, in order to become 'men', must separate themselves from their mothers, whilst girls maintain an identification with the mother and thus remain in an emotional triangle (Chodorow 1978, 1986). This contributes to the construction of absolute and relational individuality. Masculinities are based on maintaining separateness from others. Masculinity cannot be a state that is achieved; it has to be proved over and over again in contest and competition (Brittan, 1989; Connell, 1987; Chapman and Rutherford, 1988). Whilst masculinity confers status, power and privileges, it also takes its toll, as is evident in a range of problems related to behaviour patterns of men, particularly those who are located in subordinated masculinities. This is manifested in emotional and physical illnesses, alcohol and drug use, suicide and violent crime (see Segal, 1990). Chodorow argues that we should shift from rigid notions of autonomous separateness towards relational individualism; the self is conceptualised as social and connected. I find Chodorow's analysis persuasive. The most pertinent criticism centres on her treatment of gender in isolation from other hierarchies. She places mothering in a social context, but does not acknowledge sufficiently different mothering practices in the context of racism and classism as well as sexism (Spelman, 1990). Her analysis is nevertheless useful when thinking about tensions in femininity/masculinity, and in relatedness/separateness. Gilligan (1982) in her study of morality explored the themes of separateness and connectedness, and different ways in which women and men tend to experience these. In individualism the self is defined in terms of separation. Women, more typically, see their own individuality in relation to others. Gilligan illustrates this by discussing two 11-year-old children, Jake and Amy:

> Describing himself as distinct by locating his particular position in the world, Jake sets himself apart from that world by his abilities, his beliefs, and his height. Although Amy also enumerates her likes, her wants, and her beliefs, she locates herself in relation to the world, describing herself through actions that bring her into connection with others, elaborating ties through her ability to provide help. (Gilligan, 1982, p. 35)

Gilligan's analysis is interesting in its interpretation of different 'voices' in relation to connectedness and separateness. Her methods and conclusions are open to criticism though (see Kerber *et al.*, 1986). She does not appear to problematise social relations that cut across gender and I find traces of American middle-class individualism (see also Bellah *et al.*, 1988) in her work

I have explored structural, cultural and psychic constructions of 'the individual', and the rhetoric and discourses round 'individualism' and 'individuality' for well over a decade, yet there is always something about the concept that is elusive and difficult to grasp. It is too easy to slip into abstract ruminations, the exact relevance of which is not always easy to demonstrate. The word 'individuality', Hamacher (1986) claims, is spoken 'with a forked tongue'. Butler (1990) characterised gender as performative. Individuality can be treated in the same way. As absolute it is always in the process of becoming but, as with salvation, it is yet to come and we have to work at establishing it through display. Despite these difficulties I have found that disentangling 'the individual' has been useful in constructing empirical and analytical understandings around education and schooling. I this study on single women I try to explore the gender specificity of individuality through the lives and perceptions of women who are not located in marriage, which is 'the main agency for gendering women' (Chandler, 1991, p. 172).

If single women challenge boundaries of sexual difference and if nineteenth century fears of a 'third sex' have modern manifestations, then how do they experience the boundaries around their own person? Studies of spinsters in the nineteenth century have indicated conflicts and difficulties of middle- and upper-class spinsters in establishing themselves as autonomous. Working-class white women and black women, and women engaged in heavy agricultural labour experienced such hardships that there must have been little space for conscious struggle for autonomy. But they were constructing autonomy through their day-to-day lives, if not out of choice, and if not in ways that would have brought independence closer to them in their own lifetime.

Charlotte Brontë's *Shirley*, first published in 1849, reflects on the position of women. Caroline, assuming that she is not going to marry, asks what she should do 'to fill the interval of time which spreads between me and the grave?' She continues:

> I shall not be married, it appears ... Till lately I had reckoned securely on the duties and affections of wife and mother to occupy my existence. I considered, somehow, as a matter of course, that I was growing up to the ordinary destiny, and never troubled myself to seek any other; but now, I perceive plainly, I may have been mistaken. Probably I shall be an old maid ... What was I created for, I wonder? Where is my place in the world? (Brontë, 1974, p. 190)

Shirley was less shy and retiring. When the two women decide that it is necessary to organise aid for the poor in the local village, Shirley sets out to enlist the financial help of men. In order to do so she adopts a habit of crossing the sexual difference, not in clothes, but in language. She addresses Dr Boultby:

> you must regard me as Captain Keeldar today. This is quite a gentleman's affair – yours and mine entirely, Doctor ... The ladies there are only to be our aides-de-camp, and at their peril they speak, till we have settled the whole business. (Brontë, 1974, p. 273)

Shirley referred to herself as a gentleman in situations where the assumption of a male role conferred more prestige and authority on what she was trying to accomplish. More typically women strive to establish autonomous individuality as *women* without donning the male apparel in speech, symbolism, dress or actions.

Development of the individuality of women

Women could not be kept completely outside 'individuality'. Several developments led to them gaining the position of an individual, even though their individuality is characterised by relativity rather than absoluteness. The contribution of *religions* has been important (Abercrombie, Hill and Turner, 1986). As early as the fifteenth century, Joan of Arc challenged conventions with determination, with the ideal of the primacy of individual conscience as her support (Warner, 1983). In the nineteenth century various radical religious sects provided opportunities for women in their emphasis on the direct relationship between God and the individual. Chambers-Schiller (1984) cites the Quakers and Antinomians. These sects provided larger roles for women, and included high proportions of spinsters. In Finland a religious revivalist movement gathered momentum at the end of the eighteenth century and continued spreading in the nineteenth century (Sulkunen, 1990). It emphasised individual conviction and voluntariness, and broke with traditional hierarchies. Participation required personal decisions. In these movements a new conception of individuality emerged, affecting also women who participated.

The phenomenon of *courtly love* also encouraged conceptions of women as 'individuals' (Turner, 1984). Patriarchal family structures during this period granted inheritance to the first-born sons. Thus second and subsequent sons occupied an ambivalent position in establishing their status and masculinity, with fewer privileges and material advantagers than their older brother. These younger sons had time and space on their hands, and were active in the development of courtly love, whereby men would address their passionate admiration to a chosen woman, typically a married one. In this process unique qualities were attached to women; they were not merely seen as family property.

The expanding *educational opportunities* for women enhanced their possibilities of developing individuality as pupils and students, and as teachers. As early as 370 AD the Greek mathematician and philosopher Hypatia taught in a university in Alexandria (Miles, 1989). In Italy in the fifteenth century Christine de Pisan was a learned scholar and an advocate of women's right to education (Miles, 1988; Riley, 1988). Before institutional educational opportunities were open to women, there have always been those whose background has made it possible for them to engage in private study. Pursuit of educational opportunities was a crucial goal of nineteenth-century women's movements in America, Britain and Finland. Knowledge was considered empowering in the pursuit of female autonomy. As women entered formal education, they fought for the right to reach higher educational levels and also worked to broaden the content of learning available to them.

These pursuits were not without difficulties. Hostile reactions related to the maintenance of male privileges were strong. A conceptualisation of women which connected them with reproduction was invoked. Women's and men's social roles were grounded in nature through the differences in their bodies (Martin, 1987). In the nineteenth century women were thought to require a great deal of energy to keep their reproductive functions in operation. Studying and intellectual endeavours in general were likely to produce infertile women, as the blood circulated into their heads, away from their reproductive organs: 'During the crisis of puberty...there should be a general relaxation from study, which might otherwise too forcibly engross the mind and the energies required by the constitution to work out nature's ends' (quoted in Jalland, 1988, p. 8). This kind of argument was used to oppose too rigorous learning for women; it militated against notions of what 'a woman' was.

The efforts to push back the boundaries by *individual women*, such as women travellers (Chapter 1) influenced the way in which women were seen and the way in which they saw themselves. *Feminists* campaigned for rights of women. Not only were their achievements significant, but by their own conduct and example they challenged notions of womanhood. A large number of feminists were single women (Vicinus, 1985; Jeffreys, 1985; Jallinoja, 1983).

Industrialisation affected the position of women. It altered family structures and household constitution, and eroded the authority of the father in the family, as areas of private lives came under increasing state control. Geographical mobility also facilitated the construction of more autonomous lives by women. Women's labour became necessary, though their entry to the paid labour market was ideologically resisted as eroding the separation of the spheres of women and men into private and public. When opportunities for employment outside the domestic framework increased, it became easier for women to control their own lives, either inside or outside marriage and motherhood. The advent of the welfare state was also important in providing jobs for women on the one hand, and releasing them from some of their domestic responsibilities, on the other.

All these developments contained tensions and contradictions, and offered both possibilities and limitations for women. Social control is never all-pervasive and completely successful. Women have always conducted their lives in broader terms than they were supposed to do by current regulation, and also than they were assumed to be doing. Besides feminist movements which have been more visible and rebellious, women have resisted in their day-to-day lives, through their day-to-day activities. Most of the time they have done so without opportunity or inclination to **articulate** ways in which they have expanded their areas of operation or digressed from paths assigned to them. I shall explore women as 'individuals' through discussions on dependence, independence and interdependence in Chapter 8.

Marginality

I have one more task to accomplish in outlining the background and framework of this study, before turning to women I interviewed. I had been interested in single women for several years. When I started to plan this work more systematically, I thought of the title, 'Single Women: On the Margins?', in the early stages. I wanted to explore whether women without husbands or male partners were defined as 'the other' and, in representations and in lived experiences, were pushed to the margins of familist societies. I still consider these important and interesting questions. But I also became aware of the complexity of the term 'marginality'. It is widely used in political speech, theoretical work, cultural studies and in 'everyday' talk. But it is precisely used as a *term* rather than a *concept*: it does not predicate analysis and explanation – it is something that is usually evoked without much further consideration.

The term 'margin' is really a spatial one. It is connected to the centre/periphery analysis in geographical and social scientific studies. Shields (1991), in his study, *Places on the Margin: Alternative Geographies of Modernity*, connects conceptions of marginality to High/Low distinctions, where Marginal is the other. Thus the spatial becomes a metaphor; marginal is at the edge of the civilisation, but this edge is no longer necessarily a place. What had bothered me with my question about marginality was the idea that there might be a centre, and the further you are located from the centre, the more marginal you are. This is simplistic, mechanical and deterministic and not how I understood the operation of power, yet I was reluctant to give up the term 'marginal', because it had usefully guided some of the questioning in my research. I began to understand that centre and margins exist side by side and overlap. Thus there are no clear, solid boundaries between them, but an ongoing process of fluidity and interaction. Shields argues that marginality has become central. Liberalism in Western democracies has, in its emphasis on plurality, given space for the existence of differences, of alternatives. Marginality is not necessarily subversive; marginality can be incorporated. Marginality can be a negative vantage point. Sexual inversion, it was argued above, strengthened as well as challenged sexual difference. If marginality is defined in terms of a challenge to the centre, and being what the centre is not, marginality may strengthen the centre, whilst contesting it.

Seeing marginality as not a place but a tendency, and an intertwined tendency at that, made the question of the marginality of single women very interesting. They could move in and out of marginality, or be marginal and not-marginal, or define their marginality in different ways – of two women in similar positions one might consider herself marginal, the other might not. Asking questions in terms of marginality entails some difficulties. Naming some groups as marginal may reinforce their very 'marginality'. Thus my asking if single women are marginal may inadvertently contribute to their continued marginalisation, which is not my intention. My aim is to explore processes that both produce and erode marginality. The different places in relation to marginality occupied by the women I interviewed, and the different perceptions they have of their situations, serve to challenge simplistic notions.

The countries in the study

Britain, the United States and Finland have many similarities as industrialised Western democracies. In broad terms, they all have similar marriage patterns (Wakil, 1980). But there are interesting differences between them, which frame the study of single women. Proportions of single women in these countries are roughly similar, but Finland has consistently had more single women than the USA or Britain. The majority of Finnish women are in full-time paid employment. The organisation of public childcare has ensured their entry into the labour market. A smaller percentage of women work in the USA and Britain, where part-time work is more common. The USA has, during the twentieth century, had a lower percentage of single women than Britain or Finland, but the number of unmarried women has increased there rapidly, and has now reached British proportions.

The welfare state is important for single women. Allen (1989), in her study of American working-class single women born in 1910, emphasises their increased dependence on public welfare; middle- and upper-class members had been able to resort to the private sector. Thus the dependence of the working class on the state increased. The welfare state is widely criticised in the United States. Britain organised an extensive welfare state system after the Second World War which has been weakened since the early 1980s by Conservative Government policies of privitisation and cuts in public spending, but it is still more solid than the American model, where many areas that are considered to be public responsibility in Britain and Finland are privately organised.

Finland has had a strong, Nordic-type welfare state. Compared to Britain and USA it is a more homogeneous, social democratic society, where the Russian tsarist bureaucratic heritage and the modern welfare state have combined in an emphasis on public responsibility for the welfare of all citizens, an ideology of equal opportunity, emphasis on consensus and regulation of citizens. A combination of conservatism and liberalism prevails in the USA and Britain. Free market thinking is strongest in the United States, but Britain has been moving closer to the American model. Finland has also shifted to the right recently, and this, combined with the present recession, has led to a review of the welfare state. It is not yet clear how fundamental will be the effects of the present cuts in public spending on the structure of the welfare state.

There are differences in the theoretical and political approaches to the welfare state. Particularly in the USA the welfare state has been criticised for controlling women and tying them to nuclear families. More recent work has emphasised the role of women in developing the welfare state (see Sarvasy, 1992; Brenner and Laslett, 1991; Walby, 1990). In Finland the welfare state has been seen as an ally of women; it has facilitated their entry into the labour market (Simonen, 1992; Julkunen, 1990). The term 'woman friendly welfare state' has been coined in Nordic countries. This alliance is, however, somewhat unholy in that services provided are controlled and regulated, and women are located in predominantly female sectors of public employment, and that they are under-represented at the top of hierarchies. The Nordic welfare states, it has been argued, make *social* citizenship accessible for women, though debates contain conflicting views (for example, Siim, 1987; Summers, 1989; Hernes, 1988; Haavio-Mannila *et al.*, 1985). I shall return to this discussion in Chapter 9.

The cities

The San Francisco Bay Area is thought to be a place for the search for an ideal: a niche for those with nowhere else to go. Alternative networks thrive there and different lifestyles exist side by side. I was based in Berkeley and conducted interviews there, in San Francisco, Oakland, El Cerrito and Richmond. London is a large cosmopolitan city of over eight million people. Its size affords anonymity and space for alternative cultures. London is a melting pot, where people from countless nationalities live. Where San Francisco might be the epitome of the American dream, London can be construed as a place where liberal traditions have strong roots. Helsinki is smaller and more peripheral. As a capital city it has a wide range of cultural opportunities relative to its size and population of 500 000. But possibilities for building large alternative networks are narrower. Women in Helsinki have been brought up in the context of the Finnish welfare state which has offered many (contradictory) possibilities for women. In all these cities the state of singleness can be expected to be relatively easy; the proportions of single women are higher than national averages. In 1981, 26.5 per cent of women aged 16 or over in London were single (more recent figures are not available). In Helsinki in 1988 37 per cent of women aged 15 or over were single. In California in 1988, 24 per cent of women aged 15 or over were single.[1] I have no information on the percentage of single women in the San Francisco Bay Area, but as there are more one person households there than in the remainder of the state of California, we can assume that the percentage of single women is also higher. The higher percentage of single women in Helsinki is partly explained by the greater incidence of cohabitation. In all these places diversity of family and household formations is greater than in smaller cities or rural areas, and women can be expected to be less constrained by familist ideologies.

I shall now turn to the single women interviewed and explore a range of themes in an effort to illustrate their lives and their own perceptions of their location. Do they consider themselves autonomous, do they 'fill the space of an individual', do they consider themselves 'complete without a complement', or are they marginal 'outsiders'?

3
The making of a 'single woman'

The women in the study

I interviewed women who were at least 35 years old; there was no upper limit (the oldest interviewee was 69). A total of 20 women were aged over and 52 were under 50. I chose 35 as the lower limit because these women are likely to have thought about singleness.[1] Though I interviewed women who have boy- or girlfriends, I did not include women who cohabit. Cohabitation is increasingly similar to marital relationships. I have, however, included divorced and separated women. Family studies and statistical categories tend to fix people in particular places, whereas people shift in and out of categories. I wanted my study to reflect this.

I wanted to study women who were not connected to men in marriage-type relationships, and who had no immediate dependants to care for. Therefore I had decided not to include women with children. I had concluded that having children is crucial in shaping women's lives: motherhood is an interstice which locates women within patriarchal structures and cultures, and familial ideologies – it is the context of specifying what a woman *is* (Gordon, 1990). But when I approached potential interviewees, and found out they had children, I realised that they did not think about their singleness only in connection with motherhood. The number of single women with children has increased, and it did not make sense to leave them out. Of the women interviewed, 23 had children. The single mothers did not form a homogeneous group: some were unmarried, some divorced, and the age-range of their children ranged from pre-school to adults.

I interviewed women who lived alone and those who lived in a range of settings with other people (excluding cohabitation). I interviewed women from different social classes, in different employment. The women were from different ethnic groups and nationalities: African-, Chinese- and Japanese-American, Chicana, Jewish, French, British and South African in the San Francisco Bay Area; Afro-Caribbean, Jewish, Greek Cypriot, Chilean, German and American in London; and Sami,[2] Romany Gipsy, Eastern European and Finnish–Swedish in Finland. I included lesbian as well as heterosexual women; lesbian women are always 'single' in *formal* classifications, as they are not able to marry by law. Disabled women were also included; this is an important category, because a large proportion of disabled women are single and as a group they remain invisible in most studies. I have not included women who are homeless, who suffer from extreme poverty or have current difficulties related to alcohol or drug use. This decision was dictated by 'research sensitivity': being asked to talk about personal and intimate matters starting from childhood hopes and plans and concluding by considering the future might be emotionally difficult for these women.

I found the women through various personal networks, women's organisations, trade unions and so on. I used a snowball method: I asked women I interviewed if they could suggest anybody else I might get in touch with. Initial interviewees were easier to find, but as I had set the categories of women I wanted to interview, as the interviews progressed, particular types of interviewees were more difficult to find. The method of selection is called theoretical sampling. I did 24 interviews in each area; it was not possible to construct a sample that is representative of the population as a whole. Instead I set out to cover as many types of single women as possible, given my initial categories (unmarried or divorced, aged 35 or over). My method of obtaining interviewees was not without its drawbacks; although I managed to cover a range of ethnic groups and women in a range of jobs, with different sexual orientations, the women are better educated and better paid than women on average. The difficulty with this is allayed somewhat by the fact that a large proportion of well-paid, highly educated women are single. A further difficulty is that I came across women who are connected in some sort of network; I have been less likely to reach isolated, lonely women. This problem is alleviated by variation in the type and size of networks. Overall, then, we are dealing with a heterogeneous sample. Whilst many ethnic groups are represented, about two-thirds of the women were white. Though the women have a range of occupations, from cleaner to clinical manager, the

40 *Single Women*

majority of them work in skilled occupations or semi-professions.[3] More detailed information about the women will be provided in the context of the discussion of various themes. The appendix lists the women.

The interviews

The interviews lasted two to four hours. Women in Helsinki were interviewed in Finnish. Of the Finnish interviews, 13 were conducted by my research assistant, Sinikka Aapola.[4] The interviews were recorded, except for the background information (a form filled in with the interviewee), a word association list (where the interviewees were asked for their immediate thoughts on words such as single women, single men, marriage, family, children, feminism, future) and a list of hobbies and 'Top Ten People'.[5] A post-interview sheet was used to record the immediate reflections of the interviewer and the setting, timing and the length of the interview.

The interviews were semi-structured. Some women stuck fairly precisely to the questions asked, some elaborated the points by giving examples, and some tended to tell their life stories. There was an attempt to cover all issues in all interviews, but some gaps remained, either because of the time constraints of the interviewee or because of the complex nature of the interview. The span covered was very wide, from childhood to the present day, the issues dealt with were broad, from concrete areas such as living arrangements (housing, eating, cooking, housework), work, hobbies, social and support networks, friends, family of origin, hobbies, children and so on to issues such as whether singleness was voluntary or chosen, views about attitudes to single women and single men, changes in the position of single women, questions about positive and negatives aspects of singleness, experiences of loneliness and depression and ways of overcoming these, about independence, marginality and so on. It was difficult at times to keep all the strands going in such an interview. On the whole, however, the gaps in the data are not great.

Interviewing a heterogeneous group of women presents difficulties: for example, were my questions and their answers located in different frameworks; how insurmountable was the gap? These problems were alleviated by background preparation: getting acquainted with literature on single women and on different groups of women, informal discussions with single women, and reading about methodology and experience of interviewing women. My personal experiences (of having lived in two countries and of having conducted interviews with women and men and girls and boys from different social and cultural backgrounds) has increased my interest in, and awareness of, differences. I am interested in research that *gives a voice*, though I realise the difficulties of such an approach. My aim has been that the interviews and the analysis form interlocking sets of narratives; my narrative is one of selection and interpretation, but not of silencing.

The analysis

I have sifted through information, connected or disentangled, underlined or set aside; in this process data and the theoretical framework interrogate each other. Thus 'giving a voice' is always partial and selective (see Ribbens, 1989). The data were analysed by compiling information about each interviewee on the basis of the background information, the interview, the association list and the Top Ten list. Information was also organised horizontally, across all the interviews: the association lists and the Top Ten lists were compiled and the interview contents were thematically organised – this is the main material used in the analysis. I have not attempted to explain the individual women's lives, but to look for similarities and diversities in the interviews, placing these in the context of previously available information where possible. In the process of the analysis the responses of women were studied by differentiating, for example, divorced and unmarried women, ethnic groups, different countries, and in relation to having children. Categorical differences were not found in many cases; if they were, I shall indicate that.

I have not tried to isolate singleness; I do not believe this to be possible. The traditional sociological method for doing so is to include a comparison group – in this case married women. I did not want to do that for several reasons. First, single women are usually measured against the yardstick of assumptions of 'normality' of married women. Second, the size and heterogeneity of the sample of single women would have narrowed down – it would not have been possible for me to interview 72 married women as well. Third, comparative research typically concentrates on issues which can be categorised sufficiently for comparison.

The isolation of singleness was not my aim anyway. The heterogeneous sample helps to avoid simplistic pinning down; it is difficult to make clear categorical statements, but a variety of experiences of singleness is covered. The analysis of such experiences is placed in the context of the macro-world in which they are located. My starting point is that structures and cultures do not *determine* people's lives, but form a framework within which the drama of their lives is played out. This framework poses limitations and conditions possibilities, but does not in any simple, mechananical way foreclose them. Biographical aspects are important when structures and culture are translated into a level of effectiveness in people's lives. For example, I argued above that 'individuality' is a masculine construction, but nevertheless historical and empirical processes indicate that it has not been possible to keep women outside it; the struggles of women have contributed to the pushing back of the boundaries.

Butler (1990) questions the assumption that there is a 'doer behind the deed'. I have grappled with this issue during the writing of this book. I attach importance to a sense of agency, but this is typical of Western individualism. My previous book on feminist mothers explored a sense of agency: how do people with an alternative political and ideological stance construct their lives and how do they understand them? Single women I interviewed cannot generally be characterised as conscious rebels or resisters who have tried to realise alternative ideological or political perspectives in their own lives in a considered way. But resistance is not typically articulate or intellectual. People generally do what they can to make the most of their circumstances (whatever that might mean for them personally), but they may do that implicitly rather than explicitly.

Against this background I conducted the analysis of the stories that the women told me at my instigation. My analysis can be considered another story which I have formulated from the meeting of my framework with those of the women. To analyse single women without concentrating on a specific group of them is complex; one of the women I interviewed thought it might be like analysing people with blue eyes. Coherent, categorised typologies would be a travesty of the diversity and multiplicity of my data. What it is to be single was constantly pulled apart and put together again in the process of writing this book – I hope this is reflected in the end result. I have attempted to break down stereotypes of what it means to be single both in terms of theory and practice.

Conception of self as single?

I wanted to explore whether the women thought of themselves as single. Because of the modern diversity in patterns of people's lives, perhaps singleness need not be so conscious. Simon (1987) in her study of 50 never-married women found that they tended to be unwilling to identify themselves as single. Of the women I interviewed 45 considered themselves single:

> I'm definitely single. (*Bridget*, Cal)

> Yeah. Reluctantly. (*laugh*). (*Emily*, Bri)

> I do nowadays. (*Eila*, Fin)[6]

Eight said they thought of themselves as single at times; for example:

> Sometimes. ... Things like Christmas – family things – think of myself as a single woman. But I don't go round the world thinking of myself as a single woman. There are certain occasions, when I think I am treated in a certain way because I'm single, and so then I become aware of the fact that I am single. (*Liz*, Bri)[7]

Eight women considered themselves single, but did not seem to reflect on it a great deal:

> Yes. I don't think about it much. I'm not married with a family. (*Sue*, Cal)

When asked whether they thought of themselves as single, 13 women said no. Some said they were divorced rather than single, some described how they saw themselves:

> I think I'm important to myself and I'm important to my community and to my church and I'm not a flirter, I don't put myself toward no single men or no married men. I'm just an outgoing person. (*Naomi*, Cal)

Some explained that they were generally not interested in categorising themselves or other people:

> I think of myself as a woman ... I have never thought about whether I am unmarried or married. (*Ursula*, Fin)

The responses of these women indicate both sidestepping of issues connected to singleness (as many of them later in the interview referred to differences between single and non-single women) and a desire to claim 'normality' for singleness.

Whilst the majority of women considered themselves as single, there were differences between the countries: about four-fifths of the American women, two-thirds of the British women and half of the Finnish women said yes; only one American woman and seven Finnish women said no (British women were in-between). These differences are consistent with the overall numbers of singles. Finland has most single women, so it may be easier there to sidestep the issue of singleness in terms of self-perception than it is in the USA, where the increase of singleness is more recent. Language posed some complications on this issue. In Finnish the term 'unmarried' had to be used; this term has a stronger connotation of lack than 'single' and Finnish women were therefore less likely to identify with it. Differences between the countries were more significant than whether women were divorced, separated or unmarried. Having children was not significant: these women viewed themselves more as single women who have children than as 'single mothers'.

It is interesting that the women in this study were more likely to affirm their singleness than those in Simon's (1987) study, who were born between 1884 and 1918. The women in my sample were born between 1921 and 1955. It is possible that singleness does not bear as clear a stigma as it did earlier and that it is easier to make a positive identification as single. Women in Simon's study were not interested in comparisons with other never-married women. A clearer willingness to do so among women in my sample reflects partly the influence of feminism: increased solidarity among women and an awareness of shared circumstances.

Singleness as a choice?

Stereotypes of single women represent them either as 'old maids' who could not get a man, or city singles who have not wanted one (see Chapter 7). Such popular representations raise the question of choice. About a fifth of the women interviewed have fairly unequivocally chosen to be single. I have not included those who say they made the decision in their late forties, or who said things like: 'I guess somewhere I chose – I didn't want to be married. ... Yeah, I mean I suppose I've chosen but it doesn't feel like it' (*Gwen*, Bri). I judged women to have made a choice if they said things like:

> I did choose ... to split my marriage. ... I have decided to be on my own, it's my decision ... I've been happy. (*Clara*, Bri) Or

> I've had many marriage proposals. ... In one case I had lived with the guy for seven years ... and when he proposed it sort of brought it to my mind that I didn't want to marry him and, therefore, I started considering some of the other aspects of the relationship and broke that off. So I actually chose, I think, because I think it takes a certain kind of strength in today's society to say no when someone proposes because of the fear of being a spinster or old maid, all those nasty kinds of things, at least that society casts in a nasty light. So I chose. (*Norma*, Cal)

About two fifths of women clearly stated that they have *not* chosen to be single.

> Not at all, no. Not intentional ... it's not a positive decision. I'd quite like it to be reversed very soon (*laughter*). (*Betsy*, Bri)

> [When] I was in college there was all this – just the very beginnings of a lot of divorce and sort of serial relationships. And I made some statement that I would kind of wait until things settled down a little bit and then see where, you know, where people weren't changing so easily. ... I think it was sort of a flip statement and I don't think I had any idea it would take so long. (*Rachel*, Cal)

> I have not made a decision. The circumstances have worked out that way. So that it hasn't really been my own choice, no. (*Annikki*, Fin)

'Choice' is a very complicated matter. Whilst some women clearly stated that they had made a choice, and some said they had not, many women had made 'sort of' choices, or 'half and half' or had made 'small decisions' which led to singleness, without having chosen singleness as such. But this does not mean that the great majority of the women were reluctant singles. It is easier to analyse their position by using somewhat different terms – not whether they chose to be single, but whether they were voluntary singles.

Voluntary singles?

Stein (1978) argues that it is not useful to define 'single' as an interchangeable term with 'unmarried'. 'Single' should not be regarded as a residual category in relation to marriage. Stein takes into account those who are not married at any given time. He constructs a typology of singles on the basis of elements of choice and permanence. First, 'voluntary temporary singles include younger never-marrieds, the divorced who are postponing remarriage and never-marrieds who are interested in marriage, but are not actively seeking it. Second, 'voluntary stable singles' include those who have chosen to be single, those who have not married and are satisfied with that, or those who are divorced and do not seek remarriage. Third, 'involuntary temporary singles' include people whose marriages have broken down who want to remarry, or those never-marrieds who actively seek marriage. Fourth, 'involuntary stable singles' include those divorced, widowed and never-married people who wished to marry but have come to consider singlehood as a probable permanent situation. Whilst Stein refers to elements of choice, it is clear that 'voluntary' is wider than 'choice'. Simon (1987) used Stein's typology and concluded that the majority of women in her study had chosen to be single. I think there is an important difference between having chosen to be single and being voluntary single. Whilst only a fifth have chosen to be single in my sample, I considered three quarters of them voluntary (similar to the proportion of women Simon judged to have chosen to be single). There were no differences between the countries.

Voluntariness, like choice, was not easy to ascertain in all cases.[8] The following quotations indicate why it was important to distinguish between choice and voluntariness:

> [*TG*: Have you chosen to be single?]

> Half and half. ... I think since I'm a very disciplined person it's been difficult for me to fit in relationshps. And I've had, like, three pretty good ones in my years. Um, but there, I'm a workaholic so that always takes precedence. ... I think I'm really a relationship person and I would love to be in a relationship but I just, I'm not attracted to very many people, so it's really hard for me to meet people that I want to be with and I'm very busy, so it's doubly hard. (*Maxine*, Cal)

Single women may feel positive about some aspects of singleness and negative about others. Therefore any consideration of 'choice' is filled with ambivalence.

> I don't think I've chosen to be single. It's just – well, I just happen to be. I don't think or define myself that way. ... I have not tried to get married, but nor have I decided that I definitely don't want to. You could say maybe that perhaps I thought that I might not want to get *married*, but I could live with somebody. ... I think it would be nice if I found someone with whom it would be fun to live. But it's not a sort of desperate situation that I should look for someone all the time ... I sort of feel lonely, but I get by on my own. I've learned to be quite demanding in what sort of relationship I would accept. (*Laura*, Fin)

It was quite usual for women to have chosen not to develop particular relationships, but also not to have decided to be single. They had made various small decisions at specific points; these led to singlehood. For some the realisation of their singleness was tinged with negative feelings, as described by *Lorna*, who talks about the time when she began to think of herself as single, in the context of assessing her life:

> It was as if all sorts of blinkers had been lifted off. ... How the hell did I end up in this position that I'm in? ... No proper job, no husband, no property. ... I began to realise that I'd actually picked out a path for myself which I was travelling along, and I wouldn't be able to jump across to some other kind of path. ... I never picked it out, I ... happened across it, but obviously I did pick it out. ... That was never conscious. ... What I wanted didn't seem to bear very much relation to what I'd got. (*Lorna*, Bri)

Saara reached a more positive conclusion when she began to reflect on her single status:

> I started thinking that, goodness, I've not been a victim or anything – well, OK, at all stages I have not been aware of the sort of decisions I've made, but at least partly I have wanted to become what I am. And that may have led me into a situation which is not always fun. But partly I have wanted it, so why cry over it and worry about it? ... After that life has felt much better. I sort of made it clear to myself. (*Saara*, Fin)

It was typical that women had consciously or unconsciously steered themselves in particular directions and often in their early thirties started to reflect on these. Many of them accept singleness as a preferable alternative; some still hope to form partnerships; others feel unhappy about singleness, but they are in a minority. There is also a small group of women who for various reasons thought that they were not able to make a choice.

> I get very upset whenever any man becomes very interested. I feel that I have to defend myself. ... Everybody feels that you should get married, that that's the normal thing to do. I thought until very recently that I should get married. ... You know ... maybe it's better not to try, to live with the deprivation. And I'm not sure it's a deprivation because I know so many unhappy married women and I know some very self-reliant that are happy, single women. So, in retrospect, I think I refrained from doing the wrong thing. (*Rebecca*, Cal)

A few women who stated that they have chosen to be single meant that their singleness was voluntary. For example if unmarried women say that they chose to be single in their forties, they were making the choice that was most likely available. Or they have become conscious of the way in which particular decisions they made at particular points have operated to bring about their single status.

Thirteen women were *involuntary* singles. Some of them expressed this very clearly:

> I never intended to be single. I don't particularly want to be single, I don't particularly want to be on my own. (*Liz*, Bri)

In other cases the judgement was more difficult to make:

> Lately I've begun to change, to think that maybe it's just too hard to be single in an economic sense and that if you're married you might have economic advantages in the housing market. And also it's beginning to be somewhat stressful always doing things on my own. (*Susan*, Cal)

Over two-thirds of the women were *stable*, and under a third were *temporary* singles. For example, if a younger woman said she was interested in developing a partnership, and her social life involved possibilities for meeting potential future partners, I judged her to be temporary. If a woman said she would like a relationship, but was older, said she was not looking for partners, had stringent standards of what would be acceptable in a relationship, and her social life did not seem to provide many opportunities for meeting potential partners, I judged her to be stable.

Before I talk about the divorced or separated women, I shall have to explain what I mean by separated. Some are married and not yet divorced. Others have not been married, but said they had cohabited in a marriage type relationship, and I have concurred with their judgement. One American woman said she had lived in a common-law marriage, one British woman had cohabited for a long time and four Finnish women termed their past partnerships as 'avoliitto', which is now an established term for marriage-type cohabitation. Cohabitation is more common in Finland than in the USA or Britain (Chapter 2).

Questions of choice and voluntariness for divorced or separated women include particular elements. Some would have preferred to remain married, but judged their particular marriages or unions to be unsatisfactory; here choice is relevant. It is more complicated to assess if someone has chosen to be single, if the relationship broke up at her partner's instigation and initially against her will. Some of these women later judged the break-up as positive and decided that they did not want to remarry. Such personal intentions are located in a context where opportunities for remarriage are fewer for women than men. Men tend to marry 'down': that is, they marry women younger and lower in status than themselves. Women tend to marry 'up': they marry men older and higher in status than themselves (Doudna and McBride, 1981). Demographic aspects also influence the possibilities of remarriage for women. The gap between marriageable men and women works in the favour of men at certain ages, and the potential pool of partners for women at those points is smaller.

In the scale of temporary/stable, I judged those women who were relatively recently divorced, and hoped to remarry, as temporary. This particularly applied to women who were still doing 'divorce work' (Chandler, 1991); that is, they had not yet settled into their lives after the divorce. I tried to avoid interviewing women in such situations, but whether someone is still involved in 'divorce work' is complicated, as time is not a clear indication.

Who becomes single?

The likelihood of marrying declines for women who have not married by the time they are 30. Thus those who intend to get married but postpone it are more likely to remain single the older they get. *Sue*, for example, explains that she never made a decision to be single:

> I always thought I would be married with a family, ... but every time I thought about it I thought, well, gee, I'm not ready for it. And than I got older and older and probably the last ten years or so I've started thinking, well, what's ... wrong with me? There's some reason why I'm single. (*Sue*, Cal)

Singleness can thus be age-related. In Finland the average age at first marriage is higher than in Britain and the USA, and the percentage of singles is also higher there.

People living in metropolitan areas are more likely to be single than those living in rural areas. Many of the women I interviewed who had lived in rural areas or small cities reported that they had wanted to get away. This cannot be attributed to singleness only – there are often many reasons why internal migration takes place: job opportunities are crucial.

Well-educated, professional women are more likely to remain single than other groups of women (see Houseknecht, Vaughan and Statham, 1987; Cooney and Uhlenberg, 1989). There are several reasons for this: these women are economically reasonably well placed to remain single; they have studied for a relatively long time, have postponed marriage and thus ended up single; they have concentrated on building their careers and paid less attention to relationships; as men tend to marry down and women tend to marry up, the available pool of partners has narrowed down.

There are differences in the likelihood of singleness among different ethnic groups. African–Americans and Afro-Caribbeans in Britain are more likely to be single than white women. For example, 20.9 per cent of white women aged 15 or over and 36.9 per cent of black women were single in the USA in 1988.[9] Single black women are more likely to have children than single white women in the USA and in Britain. In 1987 in the USA, 88.3 per cent of never-married white women aged 18–44 had no children; 46.6 per cent of never-married black women had no children.

The high proportion of single women among black Americans and Britons has been connected to structural constraints and demographic imbalances: there are more women than men. Because of economic deprivation and poverty fewer black men are able to provide for families than white men. Adapting to structural constraints 'leaves Black women disproportionately separated, divorced and solely responsible for their children', argues Zinn (1990, p.78). She argues that, whilst white women do not marry because of greater economic independence, black women's singleness reflects the problems of black men.

Using the distinction between choice and voluntariness, being single for black women is not necessarily a choice, but it may nevertheless be voluntary. Researchers are not consistent on this. Staples (1981) argues that voluntary/involuntary dimensions are not easily applicable when black people are discussed. But women of colour also express anger towards men and their sexism. Wallace (1990) criticises the Black Power Movement for its incorporation of Black Macho. The myth of the matriarchal black woman was perpetuated in the dominant ideology in America, but it was also taken up by black men who argued that the economic and cultural structures had emasculated them. Wallace as well as hooks (1982) criticises black male leaders who supported patriarchy and who called for women to 'complement' their men. Whilst 'matriarchal' family structures were considered to cause problems for men and children, and to hinder the achievement of equality, black women were faced with experiences of poverty and hardship. When they worked to keep themselves and their children they were labelled as Amazons because of their endurance (hooks and Wallace). Indeed, Wallace argues, there was a tendency for black men to think that, if black women were weaker, they would be stronger.

While dominant culture blamed strong black women for the reproduction of inequalities of blacks, latino machismo has been blamed for the reproduction of inequalities of Chicanos, as compared to the white population. Feminist Chicanas have criticised Chicano movements, where machismo has been considered to be an imperialist cultural tool to oppress latino men, but also a source of ethnic identity for them. Chicana as well as Asian–American feminists have criticised sexism in Chicano and Asian–American movements, while working within them against racism (Garcia, 1989; Chow, 1987). Among Chicanos and Asian–Americans the emphasis on family is stronger than among African–Americans, and fewer women in these ethnic groups are single. Hispanic families have become increasingly vulnerable to marital disruption (Vega, 1990), but familism is still significant (Vega, 1990; Paredes, 1989). Research into Mexican–American families indicates that machismo is softening, and the autonomy and independence of women is increasing (Paredes, 1989). Growing proportions of Chicanas are engaged in paid work. This has brought changes in families, but Zavella (1987) argues that, 'although women may have gained more control over family matters, their subordinated position in the labour-market ultimately preserved their vulnerable economic position relative to their husbands' (p. 170).

The complexity and variation of family formation and singleness among different ethnic groups is evident. Women from different ethnic groups I interviewed have had to deal with the racism of the wider society and sexism within their own communities. But the historical processes differ and hence black American and Afro-Caribbean women in Britain are more likely to be single than members of other ethnic groups such as Chicanas, American–Asians and British Asians. I have no clear statistical information about all the ethnic groups in this study, but, on the basis of information obtained, singleness (as being never-married or divorced) is less typical also among Greek Cypriots, the Sami and gipsies.

These patterns are reflected in the interviews. Some women were distanced from their ethnic cultures. The family history of *Sue*, a Japanese–American woman, was connected to the processes of internment during the Second World War and the subsequent resettlement. She did not grow up in a Japanese–American community, and her father actively distanced himself from his ethnic group, but her mother was more interested in maintaining connections. *Amy*, a Chinese–American divorced woman, became increasingly detached from the Chinese community after her divorce. *Rosa*, a gipsy in Finland, consciously distanced herself from her family in order to pursue her own ambitions, which were not consistent with the position of women in that culture; she subsequently built closer links again. *Mari*, a Sami woman, though 'in her heart' still a Sami, married a non-Sami man and moved away from her native community. However, many women were connected to their ethnic groups; three Chicanas emphasised close contacts with their families of origin. Black women had no need to distance themselves from their communities, as singleness is common there. I shall consider issues relating to family contacts in Chapter 5, and experiences of singleness in Chapter 7.

Highly educated women from ethnic minorities are particularly likely to be single. Women from middle-class origins are more likely to be expected to combine career and marriage, whereas for women from working class origins the crucial emphasis is on achievement and completion of education. Higginbotham (1981) concluded that only a few single highly educated black women were committed to being single, but they were not unhappy, and had become adept at coping with singlehood. Thus they had not chosen to be single, but were voluntary singles. The three Chicanas I interviewed were highly educated and came from working class origins. That they have been able to maintain close family contacts seems consistent with Higginbotham's conclusion that only middle class black women were expected to integrate careers and family.

Lesbian women are always single in terms of formal marital status, though there are lesbians who are involved in heterosexual marriages and partnerships, either because they have only recently thought of themselves as lesbians, or they have been lesbians and have become heterosexual, or they are bisexual. Out of the nine lesbian women in this study one was divorced; the rest had not had long-term relationships with men. Cohabitation is more common among lesbians than among gay men. Lesbian women in this study were chosen by the same criteria as other women, so none of them cohabited, though one had lived with a woman for a very long time, and aimed to do so in the future as well.[10]

Generally, people with either physical or mental health problems are more likely to remain single than healthier and able-bodied people. Disabled women are a group among whom singleness is very typical. The more severe the disability, the more likely they are not to marry. There are also considerable constraints in establishing varied and autonomous lives; this is very much dependent on the framework which is created by resources made available for the disabled by social services, as well as on the level and quality of support from family and friends (Lonsdale, 1990). For disabled single women the issue is not simply singleness, but also femininity, relationships and sexuality (Campling, 1981). There is a tendency to see disable single women as asexual, representing a 'third sex'.

Besides the groups mentioned above, women who are somehow 'different' are more likely to be single. Such women in my sample included two very tall ones, four 'dry' alcoholics (AA members), and women who had experienced dislocations: in addition to the ethnic groups mentioned previously, there were also one Iranian and two European women who had moved to the USA, two American women who had moved to Britain, two Chilean and one Greek–Cypriot woman who lived in Britain, one Eastern European woman who lived in Finland, four Jewish women whose families had gone through dislocations and a woman in Finland who was evacuated from Carelia during the Second World War, when the area was lost to the Soviet Union.

I have dealt with the question of who becomes single by considering various groups in relation to pushes and pulls (Stein, 1978) towards singlehood and marriage. In broad terms singleness of women is now located. But I shall try to be more specific about the 'making of a single woman'. I have not tried to explain why any particular woman is single: people's biographies are too complex for such considerations. I argued earlier that singleness cannot be isolated. Some themes, however, can be considered on the basis of the interviews. When discussing choice and voluntariness it was evident that some women have decided to be single, whilst others have floated into singlehood because of decisions they had made at various stages in their lives, or because circumstances had not been conducive to marriage. I tried to explore whether anything more could be said about becoming single by considering the childhood hopes the women remembered, messages they received from others, and by considering their families of origin, particularly their relationships to their mothers and their fathers.

Childhood hopes

When women were asked about their plans and dreams as young girls, over half said they had either wanted to get married or assumed that they would do so. Nearly half said that they had specifically decided not to get married or had not thought about their future in terms of marriage. Of the women whose future plans included marriage, some expressed this in terms of active wishes: 'My dream would have been to live in a little white house with a white picket fence and have two kids and, you know, be married for 40 or 50 years' (*Michelle*, Cal). Children often figured strongly in the plans; like Michelle, many women expressed the wish to have children first and the wish to marry second. The fairy-tale aspects of the dreams were noted: 'You were going to meet this man of your dreams and fall in love, you know. And if not with a white horse at least with a white Mercedes Benz ... the girl was found by a prince' (*Shoshana*, Cal).

More women did not plan to marry, but assumed that that was expected and that was what adult women did: 'I wasn't like one of those kids ... whose idea was to be married or have children. Although I suppose I always thought I would get married because that's what people did' (*Lorna*, Bri). Besides marriage, future plans regarding work figured quite strongly in the responses. I shall discuss these further in the next chapter.

There was a small number of women who did not remember planning their future at all. They referred either to difficult family circumstances, poverty or the aftermath of the war (in Finland). Their main concern even as young girls was a struggle to maintain their daily lives. Two said they thought they would not get married, but expressed this more in terms of regret than as a positive decision; their self-confidence was low and they thought marriage would not be an option as nobody would 'want' them. The rest stated a clear decision not to get married: 'Mainly, I thought that I want to rely on myself. Have a job' (*Kaisa*, Fin). *Carlotta* expressed strongest determination not to marry. She is a Chicana from a working class background; she is a voluntary single who chose not to marry. But she could also be considered a person who opted not to marry for structural reasons rather than out of personal preference or ideology.

> I think that it was more a matter of knowing that i order to get an opportunity for myself for a better lifestyle, I would have to ... in other words, I couldn't settle down ... and because by having a family, or getting married, or changing my status from a single person to a married person, I really had to be prepare emotionally and financially to be able to provide for a service which I take very, very seriously in terms of family. Providing for them in the fullest sense. My security, health, etc, and I never wanted to take this lightly. ... So marriage was not something that I could consider. It just wasn't. (*Carlotta*, Cal)

Carlotta is content to be single, though she does not rule out marriage or partnership in the future.

Comparison of the responses of unmarried and divorced or separated women indicates that well over a half of the unmarried women had expected to marry, but just under a half or the divorced or separated women remembered such an expectation. It may be that, especially, voluntary singles whose marriages had broken up at their instigation were likely to make sense of their current position by remembering that at some point they had not been interested in marriage anyway. Overall attitude surveys indicate that a larger proportion of young girls expect to marry than these women have done (Chapter 1). No definite conclusions can be drawn from this, as women here are reporting what they *remember* of their hopes and plans.

Messages received

Messages that women remembered receiving as young girls from parents and other significant people are potentially more illuminating. The majority mentioned education or work in the expectations or assumptions expressed by parents (38, 13 of whom said marriage had been expected as well). The kind of emphasis placed on work and education varied. Some parents expressed ambitious hopes:

> I think my father would have liked it if I were a doctor and he certainly was very disappointed when I changed from being a Math major to an English major – he encouraged on some levels of taking on something other than being a secretary or a wife. (*Frances*, Cal)

For others the main emphasis was on getting a job, and being able to look after oneself.

> They didn't understand why I didn't want to become a traffic warden or have a totally secure job that was totally boring. I just kept saying I wanted to do something artistic, and I didn't know what, and we'd have big rows. (*Gwen*, Bri)

Frances's family is white middle-class; Gwen's family is black working-class. Though academic education figured more in middle-class families, many working-class families also stressed education, and worked hard so that their daughters could receive as good an education as possible. They were less able to give concrete guidance about the content or level of education that they hoped their daughters would strive for.

Only six remembered marriage as the only goal expressed. More typically marriage was not emphasised at the expense of education or work, but it was assumed.

> They very much wanted me to be married, but they also wanted me ... to pursue a career in science or some kind of technical field where I'd make lots of money. (*Kate*, Cal)

> The emphasis was doing well at school, having a decent education and being in command of your future. Once you've got a pay packet you're in command of the future. ... And marriage was ... naturally thought to happen in its own due course. (*Valerie*, Bri)

The second largest group (23) were those who felt they had received no clear steering towards any specific goal. These will be discussed in Chapter 4. Besides parents, grandparents in particular, sometimes aunts and other relatives, and teachers were mentioned. The effects of their messages were considered both positive and negative. If they were single women themselves, their very existence made singleness seem less unusual.

Whilst some parents gave their daughters strong encouragement to pursue a course that keeps their options open, not all were able to give sufficient practical support. Parents also often steer their daughters towards safe options. However it should not be assumed that it is particularly *parents* who encourage girls to opt for a traditional feminine role. Parents do tend to be interested in the unique characteristics of their children. Those occupational groups involved with the upbringing and education of children and young people may, despite a general stance emphasising equality of opportunity or even anti-sexism, have less time or commitment to the individual children they are interacting with (Hilton, 1991). School experiences were not discussed in detail in all interviews, but it seemed that schools did not provide supportive back-up for girls who were given encouragement at home but lacked practical guidance.

A further interesting point is that parents give their daughters *contradictory* messages. They may encourage them to pursue education and emphasise the importance of economic self-sufficiency. At the same time they may pay more interest to the education of their sons, or encourage their daughters to become competent at domestic tasks or expect them to do a considerable amount of housework.

> I got these very conflicting signals all through my formative years. On the one hand, I was supposed to be very competitive, do very well in school, which wasn't trouble. I was always very good at that. But, on the other hand, a girl was supposed to be helpful to her parents and – – – they felt that since I was the only child, I was their only prop for old age. They'd had such ... such a hard time, and they were making such great sacrifices for me. Now that is now known as the Jewish mother syndrome and it's mocked and it's a good thing, you know. (*Rebecca*, Cal)

Parents consider the best interests of their children with the best means that they have at their disposal; they cannot, however, sidestep prevailing notions of femininity and of what 'a woman' is. Hence, although only a section of women expressed explicit contradictions in messages they received, I assume that implicitly such messages were more common.

Mother and father

When discussing singleness the emotional constellation of the family, the balance of power between the parents, and between the parents and the children, are significant. My interview schedule dealt with parents and I was more inclined to concentrate on the mother as a possible role model. Relationships between mothers and children have been more fully researched than those between fathers and children. In particular, little research has been conducted on the relationships between fathers and daughters; for example psychoanalysis has concentrated on the role of the mother and feminist therapy has also adopted a mother-centred approach (Sayers, 1989). This, argues Boose (1989), is because 'In the four-cornered nuclear enclosure that is at once the source for and product of Western ideologies about the family, the father weighs most and the daughter least' (p. 20). To study fathers and daughters is to study the most asymmetrically placed figures in familial relations of power. But in fact women tended to talk more about their fathers.

Fathers

Fathers tended to figure more than mothers when parents were discussed by the women interviewed, despite the fact that fathers were more absent. Nineteen fathers and eight mothers were dead, away, or away a great deal during their daughters' childhood. Seven women mentioned that their fathers had problems with alcohol; one mother was said to drink a lot. Women tended to talk more with love and admiration about their fathers than about their mothers, and more women (in my judgement) considered their fathers closer than their mothers. Women were also likely to consider fathers more 'difficult' than their mothers. The differences were not great numerically, but overall a sense of the importance of fathers was communicated. There were those who talked at length about their mothers, exhibiting either love and admiration or ambivalence and frustration, but not as much as about their fathers. An example is provided by *Peggy* (Cal). She talks relatively briefly about her mother; for example:

> I would think it was a pretty typical child–mother relationship. She was always busy, taking us somewhere or, you know, up until the time of her ... Well, she was very active in gardening and then she worked and she had this [chemical laboratory?] that she rented at home, so she was always busy. But she was just a fine mother. She, I mean, we always had well-prepared family meals and it was always a pleasant time to be together. I think it was what you might describe as normal or average.

[*TG*: Quite nice memories overall?]

Oh, yes.

[*TG*: No particular resentments?]

Oh, no, no, none at all.

Peggy talks more about her father; for example:

> My father is an extremely strong man and everything that he said is right. And he is very convincing, he's an excellent persuader, but he is very very certain of his own value of strength. And I was at odds with that a lot, so I learned how to argue, I learned how to stand up for myself, I learned how to persuade and to tolerate and cope ... I think if you talked to my three sisters that are still single, you'd find the same thing, that all of us ... we love our father very much and he's a great man. ... If new people meet him, they think he's wonderful. I mean, he is very intelligent, he has a memory that's just incredible for quotation, poetry, literature, events or whatever, but when you have to live with him day and day out, it just, it's an overwhelming personality. It's got to be done his way and that's the only way there is.

Whilst *Peggy*'s relationship to her mother was less ambivalent and contradictory, father seemed more exciting, and she, like some other women, referred to being in some ways like her father.

Many women referred to a special relationship with their father. Some fathers were protective of their daughters, but protection merged with control:

> I would say basically I'm probably Daddy's little girl. More or less, he's protective and he – – – he's distant in a way, doesn't communicate easily or very much ... I think that I really was on a certain level his princess. I mean, I think that I am caught up in father, you know that whole archetype of being the father's daughter and I don't think he ever released me, I mean, in that way. Or I never cut it off, however those two things work. (*Rachel*, Cal)

Eighteen women talked in strong, emotional terms about their fathers – about loving their father or idolising him, being a 'daddy's girl', putting their father 'on a pedestal' and so on.

Other women referred to their fathers in less affectionate, less intimate terms whilst still emphasising their significance. Their fathers were 'colourful', 'larger than life' or 'rejecting' despite the daughter's efforts; a few women said they hated their fathers:

> My father was a sort of ambivalent type. He, he was never there and it was very difficult for him to show his feelings, though he was a very emotional type. I had to try and beg for love from him, and he pushed me away when I was a child. (*Laura*, Fin)

Some fathers were distant, but even so they figured largely when daughters talked about their childhood and their parents.

> My father speaks very little. He doesn't talk much, and when he says something, he's very articulate. And he's very smart and ... he'll say one sentence that'll end the conversation. That's it. (*Sue*, Cal)

In the majority of families fathers set the tone and the framework, and thus were influential even when distant or absent a great deal.

Twenty-three women said their fathers had had a great impact on their lives, or that they were in many ways like their fathers:

> I always hated my father from a very early age. Physically I wouldn't let him close to me. ... I've sort of rejected my father and have turned out more to be like him. He's a craftsman, you see, and here I am, found myself in a position of being a craftsman without really knowing how I got there. (*Lorna*, Bri)

Alternatively they connected the types of relationships they had later with men to that they had with their father.

> It's clear why I am not married and my relationships with men don't work and what that is connected to – it comes from childhood and my relationship with my father and all that. (*Laura*, Fin)

Sue (Cal) makes similar connections between her relationship with her father and her relationships with men. She talks, for example, about a past relationship:

> [He was] sort of like my father in that he wasn't, he couldn't express affection. So I sort of thought this was like my father cause my father couldn't do that and I just assumed the guy really cared for me but just couldn't express it. And then ... physically, he was sort of like my father. You know, sort of short and muscular and no nonsense yet with a real soft spot for children and animals, that kind of thing. You know kind of a tough, tough guy exterior but inside really soft.

Tina (Bri) refers to her 'fixation' on older men: 'I just wonder whether it's coming from my problems with my father or whether it comes from him, but I definitely can't deal with younger men.'

It was significant whether daughters were allowed to, or felt that they were able to, fight back against their strong, loving, protective, colourful, difficult or violent fathers. No direct connections can be made about the influence of fathers on the single status of these women. Again, singleness cannot be isolated in such a way. Many fathers were significant, but this significance interacts with other elements, such as relationship to the mother, being an only child or only daughter, relationships between siblings, interaction between mother and father and, subsequently, a whole range of biographical events. Family interaction will be considered further in Chapter 5. Interaction with fathers in terms of struggling, fighting back, conforming, acquiescing or withdrawing will be discussed in Chapter 8.

Mothers

There were less references to mothers being influential than to fathers and only a couple of women said they were like their mothers. Fathers were talked about in colourful terms, but mothers were talked about more in terms of understanding, support, kindness and warmth, when positive descriptions were made:

> She kept giving me a lot of praise about being really smart and wonderful and she knew I could do great things and was there to help, and all that kind of stuff, so she was really encouraging. (*Norma*, Cal)

> My mum was really positive about life. She had this saying ... that that's what's happened, but let's go forward from here. I try to remember that. (*Eeva*, Fin)

Overall there was a tendency for relationships to involve more negotiations.

> I basically felt very supported. Sort of in whatever I did. I mean, I had almost no restrictions. In fact, when my friends would ask me if I could go out and do something I would, I'd make up rules because they all had rules and I never had any rules! [Giggles] ... If she was punishing me, it was usually for talking back and ... if she punished me by making me stay home I could usually talk her out of it. ... I feel very close to her, and my sister, 16 years later, felt very, very close to her, too. And not judged. If there' sanything about my mother, it was that I was too powerful for her. I mean, that part of me bothered her at times, ... getting involved in school activities, getting involved in politics, all that kind of stuff is much more my father's side. ...

Not that she criticized me but ... she ... was wary of that – – – part of me. And she certainly did not encourage me to go to school or it was – all the advice, she gave me just terrible advice regarding men, how I'm supposed to take care of them, let them win arguments, all that kind of crackpot stuff [laughs] which didn't stick very well! ... my mother was the loving caregiver who – – – she really ran the family. (*Michelle*, Cal)

Sometimes daughters felt that mothers kept them too close:

> When I was sort of feeble about going out, she'd say, 'Oh well, never mind, dear, you stay at home', you know, whereas really in a way she should have said, 'You get on out there and enjoy it.' (*Tina*, Bri)

Separation from the mother by the daughter is not easily accomplished (see Chodorow, 1978).

But mothers were also distant. There may have been many children in the family, and mothers were busy looking after them.

> With mum we didn't really discuss much. She was always concentrating on housework and all that side. And I have this image that she was always sort of tired and had headaches and something like that. (*Hanna*, Fin)

Whilst daughters talked a lot about mothers being supportive, understanding and so on, 'love' did not figure as much in the descriptions about mothers as about fathers.

> I'm sure she loved me and I know she loved me, although I didn't feel it all the time. But I know she did, intellectually, I know she did. (*Simone*, Cal)

Critical descriptions about mothers included references to them being a negative role model, aspects of pain in the relationship to the mother, the mother living through the daughter, and mothers being controlling, distant (this was mentioned as often about mothers as about fathers). Whilst fathers were colourful and influential, on the one hand, mothers were described as subordinated, oppressed, dependent, self-sacrificing and restricted:

> She has always been a devoted server of my father, in spite of the fact that she can see intellectually that if he dropped dead tomorrow she'd have a better quality life. ... She's kind, loving, generous, giving and self-sacrificing. (*Caroline*, Bri)

In a few cases the controlling influence of the mother was strongly emphasised: 'I was very much my mother's sort of servant. ... She's quite possessive ... she will just try to take something over' (*Lynne*, Bri).

Finnish women said less about their mothers, felt less close to them, less supported by them and reported less warmth towards them than British and American women. American women spoke with greatest warmth and length about their mothers, were closer to them and more understanding about them. A possible explanation is that, as singleness is more prevalent in Finland, and as conceptions of femininity tying women to housewifery are least common there, Finnish women are less sympathetic about compromises their mothers have made. The culture of femininity is stronger in America, and the increase of singleness is more recent. American women may be more understanding about the lives of their mothers because the circumstances in which compromises were made are more familiar to them.

About a quarter of interviewees described their parents' marriage as good, and about a quarter described it as bad. For the rest, either the marriages were considered to have tensions, or one of the parents was dead, or the parents were divorced or separated, or the children did not live with their parents for extended periods, or there was no information on the subject. Therefore over half of the respondents did not have an example of a happy marriage. But this cannot be directly connected to singleness. There is no comparative information about married women and direct comparison would be difficult; unmarried, separated or divorced women may be more likely to bring out negative aspects of their parents' marriage than married women, who are more likely to focus on positive aspects of their parents' relationships. There were no clear differences between divorced, separated and unmarried women. Past life histories are sifted through the present. How these single women talked about their mothers and fathers illustrates their perspectives. Overall it seems that men are interesting, contradictory, powerful, distant and controlling. Women can be distant and controlling too, but they can also be supportive, encouraging, interactive and easier to negotiate with. In relation to men there is a danger that women have to make sacrifices, accept compromises, deal with loss of control and search for power and influence.

Conclusion

No one specific type of woman is likely to be single. Singlehood is a result of a complex interaction between structural, cultural and biographical aspects. It is not likely to be a clearcut choice; however the majority of women interviewed were voluntary, if not stable singles. I shall now endeavour to illustrate lives of single women (Chapters 4, 5 and 6) before discussing their perceptions of the status of single women (Chapter 7). I shall then return to questions posed earlier: do single women 'fill the space' of an autonomous individual (Chapter 8) or are they marginal 'others' (Chapter 9)?

4

Excursion into the public sphere

Public/private

The social contract is based on a separation between state of nature and state of culture. One of the binary oppositions connected to this separation is the distinction between the public and the private sphere (Chapter 2). The public sphere is seen as the primary location of men, the private sphere as the primary location of women. Such an opposition is not self- evident or historically static and women's exclusion from the public sphere has never been complete. Feminist researchers have criticised the use of the public/private distinction (see Siltanen and Stanworth, 1984). I agree that it is not applicable to women and men as a descriptive categorisation, but it is useful as an analytical distinction. Men are still connected to the public and women to the private sphere in gender representations. Women carry the 'aura' of the private sphere with them when they enter the public sphere; the labour market is gender-segregated and women's work in semi-professions (teaching, health care, social work) and in service occupations is a continuation of jobs they do at home. Men bring the 'aura' of the public sphere to the private; they do less housework and are less involved in childcare. Public and private are connected, not distinct, and the relationship between them is complex and dynamic. Women have not accepted their confinement within the private; they have sought to challenge limitations imposed on them.

I shall explore the topic of single women in public and private spheres in two separate chapters. To avoid the complexity posed by the public/private split I had planned to concentrate first on work and then on social relationships. I was interested in how critical women were of the construction of 'work' and of 'careers'; here it was relevant to consider their political orientation. Many were not particularly interested in politics and few were activists. When analysing social relationships, including outside work activities, I realised that many women were involved in public pursuits which could not be classed as 'hobbies'. The 'public' roles of these women were not confined to work, but were constructed and mediated through a range of activities. Therefore the categories 'work' and 'social relationships' were misleading in their apparent clarity; I shall discuss them in the context of single women negotiating the public/private divide. Historically this negotiation has been important in shaping the social and cultural locations of single women. This chapter concentrates mainly on work.

The centrality of work

Where people are located in relation to the labour market is an important dimension in the structuring of their lives. For single people work is particularly important (Stein, 1981). Single women are more likely to be employed in full-time jobs, to be in high-status occupations and to be in male-dominated jobs than married women (Sokoloff, 1981), but the majority of them are in occupations dominated by female employees. Single women, compared to married women, work more like men, but get paid as women (Simon, 1987). Research into women and work does not pay a great deal of attention to the significance of singleness. For example, in Finland, where the differences between women in relation to marital status can be expected to have narrowed because the majority of women work full-time, combining work and family has been researched, but it is difficult to obtain information on single women. The heterogeneity of single women is particularly important in relation to employment; there are differences between unmarried and divorced women, women with or without children, and women of different ages, for example. The significance of singleness is thus difficult to isolate.

Women with small children, regardless of marital status, experience difficulties in combining work outside the home and their domestic responsibilities (see Sharpe, 1984). Single women who do not have children are not, however, necessarily in an advantageous position compared to married women who are childless or have older children. Research into the position of women in universities indicates that the career progress of single women is problematic; this has been attributed partly to the importance of mentoring and of participation in information networks (Davies and Astin, 1990; Stiver Lie, 1990; Luukkonen-Gronow, 1987). An academic man acting as mentor to a single woman is potentially ambivalent. The sample of women in this study is heterogeneous, but there is a definite bias in it. A large proportion of the women have received university education and the majority of them have had some kind of further education or vocational training. Only 11 had no education or training after school. Though single women tend to be better educated than married women, the sample is not representative. Nevertheless the information on work provided in the interviews is illuminating about singleness, despite not being definitive.

The jobs of the women interviewed are listed in the appendix. Twenty women worked in semi-professions (teaching, social work, nursing); 11 were employed in administrative work at different levels; 11 were artists, freelancers and craftswomen; seven were managers, consultants or entrepreneurs; seven worked in a range of unskilled, semi-skilled or skilled occupations; five worked in clerical jobs; five in professions; one was a student, one was unemployed and four were retired. Several women had two jobs. Few women worked in predominantly male jobs.

The importance of work

The 'initial' citizen was a man and his household. Single women were without a firm footing in the public sphere; in the private sphere they did not enjoy the same advantages as married women. Increasing entry to the public sphere through paid labour has given single women more opportunities to strive towards individuality and autonomy than women in the nineteenth century had.

Work was important for three-quarters of the women in this study. It structures the lives of single women with no small children. For married, cohabiting and single mothers childcare and domestic responsibilities structure their paid work, and pose limits to it, which differ in Britain, the USA and Finland. Finnish single mothers are most likely, and British single mothers least likely, to work. The limits are also differentially negotiated by different women. For childless single women the edges between public and private spheres were more blurred than for married women. This was illuminated by women talking about how hard they work.

Working hard

Over three-fifths of the women interviewed said they worked hard. Many said they worked harder than their married colleagues, but only a few thought that that was expected of them; it was their choice. Only one woman in this study said that her willingness to work hard was exploited; she was a disabled woman suffering from arthritis:

> I felt that I was somehow bad, so I did a tremendous amount of overtime. I mean I worked really hard. I somehow tried to sublimate my weakness by at least being a good worker. ... And the more I did, the more work they gave me to do ... I agreed to be exploited in a way (*Hanna*, Fin)

In other studies (see Simon, 1987) single women were more likely to refer to pressures from employers. It may be that single status has become less visible at work in metropolitan areas and among younger singles. The range of jobs of women in this study is also significant; many were self-employed or worked (with commitment) in semi-professions, though women in administration and clerical work typically did not note the relevance of their single status either. If is of course possible that they have, like *Hanna*, 'agreed to be exploited'.

Reasons for working hard varied. Women from middle-class backgrounds who had enjoyed success in their work were more likely to emphasise job satisfaction and personal high standards they wished to meet: 'I set my own goals and my own targets and I'm the one that's putting the pressure on me to meet them' (*Peggy*, Cal). Women from a working-class background and from ethnic minorities were more likely to give different reasons. In particular women with children stressed financial compulsion to work harder than they would have liked to, in jobs that they did not like; many had tried to improve their financial position:

> I decided, well, I'm not going to work in the slums practically all my life – the rest of my life, so I went to a vocational training school to learn how to type and do shorthand, to become a secretary. (*Bridget*, Cal)

Broadly defined political goals motivated some women:

> I've had a hard road in getting there ... and I [try] to make my contribution towards bettering this society, towards bettering the conditions for people of colour ... and that means health, education, opening doors for people who are disenfranchised etc. (*Carlotta*, Cal)

For women with education or training, social mobility through work was possible.

Being able to work hard and long hours was also experienced as a positive possibility: not having to leave work before tasks were completed or taking work home. Artists, freelancers and craftswomen were able to concentrate intensively. Only about a fifth of the women referred to stress at work. This may be because as single women they are able to work in a flexible manner. Such flexibility is not relevant in all jobs, such as factory work, which is not represented in this sample.

Some of the reasons for working hard can be connected to what is thought of as 'working like a man': prioritising work over other areas of life. An example is given by a successful freelance graphic artist:

> Because work is a priority for me, when I have a tough workperiod, there is no room for anything else in my life, so that border areas like friendships are taken care of in a way that maintains work. And when it's less busy it works out so that life experiences, friendships and so on, they feed work. I mean they offer my work a chance to grow, because creative work has to be done through yourself, so that you can't externalize it. So that life is necessary in order to work [laughs], because you can't get something from nothing. (*Reija*, Fin)

But attributing importance to work, and working hard and long hours, with work spilling into other areas of life, is more complex than 'working like a man'. Establishing a clear borderline between their time at work and outside work can be difficult for single women.

> If ... they really need me to work, then I really feel like this obligation to do it. So I have to really remind myself that I shouldn't do it ... I don't think it's because I'm single. I think it's because I'm pleasant to work with and – – – I'm available. And perhaps they know I can't say no. But I'm willing to help out. I'm not a stingy, selfish person. ... And I have this thing where I have to be a good girl, so I do it for that. (*Sue*, Cal)

Regular evening classes helped *Sue* to protect her non-work time; unstructured activities were not sufficient. *Sue* continues: 'I'm fully aware that if I had a family to get home to, I'd get out. I would just like [snaps fingers] do it so that I was out of there. But because I don't have anything to go to I don't.' Work spills into other areas of life, because time outside work is not shaped by family responsibilities; trying to meet one's *own* needs can be considered selfish by others. Working hard means also 'working like a woman'.

Content of work

Many women work in semi-professions which involve contact with people, where the need for their input is obvious, and feedback can be visible. Heavy demands may be integral to the work, The welfare state has provided opportunities for women regardless of their marital status, but is also dependent on their hard and committed work. For example, nurses and nurses' assistants are engaged in physically and mentally exhausting labour whether they want to be or not. Women were critical of the hierarchies at work, the institutional settings of their jobs and organisational aspects of work processes, but this did not strongly reduce their *commitment* to work.

The majority of women liked their jobs because they offered contact with people, expressive and creative possibilities and/or intellectual, emotional and political satisfaction. About a fifth did not indicate clear intrinsic job satisfaction. Work for them was a financial necessity or crucial in establishing and maintaining independence. Many of them said they liked their jobs, but their descriptions were brief: 'no complaints', 'I wouldn't do it if I didn't like it'.These can be compared to the most positive descriptions of work: 'magic', 'brilliant', 'loving work', 'great fun', 'luxury', 'key to my life', 'primary' and so on.

Ambitions

Paid work was significant to feminist mothers (Gordon, 1990) in establishing a sense of self not wholly defined by motherhood. They emphasised the importance of work, but boundaries between paid work and other areas of life tended to be distinct for them. In this study a small number of women with young children[1] were in a comparable situation. They were less likely to work long hours, but more likely to be busy at work because the 'spilling over' was not a viable solution to them. They were more likely to refer to stress and related it more to overall sets of responsibilities rather than the demands of work itself.

Though work was considered important by feminist mothers, many of them indicated a lack of interest in careers and criticised the processes involved in construction of careers or the hierarchical organisation of careers. Single women I interviewed did not express as much criticism of the concept of 'career'. They criticised hierarchies for functioning in a way that discriminated against women, but the existence of

Excursion into the public sphere 71

a career structure was more likely to be accepted. Feminist mothers often referred to themselves as ambitious, but most of them did not define ambition in terms of career progress. They connected it with personal development, development of work practices or social and political aims. About a fifth of single women talked about ambition,[2] or about goal-related planning in a way that can be defined as ambition. But about a fifth said they lacked ambition: they had 'backed into things', 'stumbled along' or 'followed a path'. Satisfaction with their jobs for some women is due to their having pursued their ambitions, and for others it is due to their *lack* of ambition: they considered their jobs 'fine', because they did not have future goals against which to measure the present job or because they had been more successful than they had expected.

A few women who had been ambitious and had been setting goals for themselves got to a point where they found it hard to plan their future direction. Though work was central for *Reija*, she thought that she had achieved her goals (at the age of 42) and her work could only go 'downhill'; the most she could hope for was that the 'downhill' would not be steep. *Irene* (Cal), a Chicana whose jobs have usually been connected with Mexican and Mexican–American women is unhappy in her present job and is planning to leave, but cannot think what to do next: 'I know what I *don't* want to do, but I'll be damned if I know what the hell I want to do.' Irene's difficulties are connected to the broadly political content of her work and the narrow job market for such work. *Norma* (Cal) was in a relatively high position in administration, but reached a 'glass ceiling' because she had no academic qualifications. Women are faced with institutional barriers; also social connotations of 'success' are such that women have less desire (as well as less possibility) to compete than men (see Marcus, 1987; Coward, 1992).

The development of work orientation

A sample of 72 men with similar educational qualifications to this group of women would have jobs with higher status and better pay regardless of their marital status. The location of single women is connected to the overall position of women in the gender-segregated labour market in more low-status, less paid jobs than men.[3] I shall explore information in the interviews which illustrates the construction of their work orientation.

Childhood hopes and messages

The majority of women did not orientate themselves exclusively towards marriage and motherhood (Chapter 3). Mostly they emphasised that they were interested in getting a good education and a job. They wanted to 'do better', 'be independent', 'maintain themselves'. Most women had no specific orientation or goals. This has differential effect for women from a middle-class background whose parents have high educational qualifications and working class women and women from ethnic minorities whose parents have not received much education. *Judy* is a British Afro-Caribbean woman from a working-class background who lived most of her childhood in an orphanage. She did not plan her future. She became a painter and decorator, enjoyed her work and felt positive about it. *Shirley* is a white American from an upper middle-class background, living in Britain. She did not plan her future either; she was highly educated and became an artist. These examples provide a reminder about the complexity of the formation of lifecourses. *Judy* was a craftswoman and a single parent living in a council flat, having to worry about getting her next job; *Shirley* was an artist living in her own flat, with an independent income. The 'career' of neither was predictable, but differences still reflect their structural and cultural positions.

The majority (nearly two-thirds) of parents had emphasised the importance of work and education to their daughters; marriage was often assumed as well, but not strongly emphasised (Chapter 3). Nearly a third of the women were not aware of steering in any specific direction. Less than half of these thought they were encouraged to make up their own mind, but over a half felt they got no clear guidelines because of family problems.[4] An example of no parental pressure is given by *Eeva* (Fin): 'My mother was really smart ... she didn't push her advice ... but said wise things that are still relevant today. ... Her guideline was that you should not take responsibility away from children, you should give it to them.' An example of no parental guidance is provided by *Christine* (Cal), who felt that her parents did not particularly care for their children, and were especially unconcerned about the future of their daughters: 'Nobody suggested I should do anything. It was never suggested that I should even go to college.' The influence of parents' expectations is mediated through a structural and cultural context. Both *Eeva* and *Christine* were ambitious. *Eeva*, from a working-class single-parent family (her father died), and with minimum education eventually owned a small store. The emphasis on responsibility in her upbringing facilitated her adoption of this particular avenue of social mobility. *Christine*, from an upper-class family, is, despite the lack of encouragement, a university professor.

In the development of work orientation mothers are important. Daughters of highly educated mothers are more likely to be highly educated; the educational level of the father is less significant (see Sokoloff, 1981). The employment of the mother is also significant; a very small proportion of women in this study described their mothers as housewives. It would have been useful to ask specifically whether their mothers were employed while their daughters were children. This information is not available, but it is significant that the majority of women mentioned work when describing their mothers. Although a number of women said they had become like their fathers, mothers are important role models.

Many women emphasised that they make choices; they do so in the context of understandings about femininity around them. Sometimes these are communicated very strongly. *Michelle* (Cal) remembers that as a child she wanted to do something 'exciting': 'I was going to be a fireman for a while and people laughed at that. And then I was going to be a lawyer and people laughed at that and told me girls weren't lawyers.' The context of femininity influences adult women as well as young girls; *Lorna* (Bri) feels 'abnormal' as a carpenter, but hopes that the choices women in trades have made broaden the opportunities for others.

Work as a 'rite of passage'

Marriage is a route through which the transition from childhood to adulthood is traditionally realised by women (Chandler, 1991; Allen, 1989). They leave daughterhood by becoming wives. Many women with married sisters noted that parents treated unmarried women differently; parents interfered in their lives, gave them advice and commented on their lifestyles. Parents found it easier to receive advice and comments on their lives from their married children. Unmarried daughters might be told, for example, that they could not understand the relationship between their mother and father. Divorced women, however, had accomplished the rite of passage into adulthood, even though they had become single again.

Striving towards autonomy and independence in relation to parents has to be accomplished by single women in ways other than marriage. Education and work are important in this process. Many women said that wanting to leave home was one of the considerations when making decisions about how to organise their lives. For some, working was seen as the option which gave them greater independence; many started work and decided to train or study later. For others, training and further or higher education provided an opportunity to leave home. Where to study was chosen partly in order to facilitate detachment from the influence of parents.

There is no direct connection between leaving home and establishing one's 'rite of passage' through education or work and remaining unmarried. Many women who do marry leave their homes initially to study or work. We can only speculate whether striving for independence and adult status through work is particularly important for those who remain single. For some, work *becomes* important in constructing their lives because they are not married. Other women do not marry because work is *already* important in constructing their lives.

The significance of work as 'a rite of passage' is evident in single women being less likely to care for elderly parents than previously (see Simon, 1987; Allen, 1989). The development of the welfare state has been important in at least partially releasing women from the duty of caring for the elderly. Geographical mobility has increased the number of women unable to provide daily assistance. Geographic mobility itself can partly be explained as a 'rite of passage'. Increasing participation in the labour market has posed obstacles to looking after parents. On the basis of the information from this sample of women, many single women are involved in caring work in the public sphere through their jobs, but less in the private sphere. This does not mean that the break has been complete. I shall discuss these issues further in Chapter 5.

Career/partner choices

Though work was central for some women in structuring their lives because they were single, others were single because of the centrality of work. In the past, many women opted to concentrate on work instead of their partners. *Norma* (Cal) describes her earlier lifestyle as unconventional; she drifted around the country, planning to be an artist. This did not free her from a traditional role assigned to women in her common-law marriage, where she was playing a supportive role. When she was offered her first full-time position she considered it an opportunity to break out of that pattern:

I felt like this was an opportunity for me to be more on my own and do something that was just mine, make my own circle of friends with these interesting people I'd just met. And he was out of it. So it was something just for me. ... I developed a whole circle of friends ... and a feeling of self-esteem for being successful and getting these promotions.

Norma did not make a conscious, clearcut career/partner choice, but her job was instrumental in the break-up of her relationship.

Other women had made more definite choices:

[with partners] very often I felt either trapped ... I think mainly because I felt that I would have to change, make too many compromises ... I wasn't willing to do that, both emotional and career-wise. (*Ella*, Bri)

I realised that work was the key to my life. That if I didn't have work ... but meaningful work, I would become what women are supposed to be but which I didn't want to be. ... And so from then on what became my sort of major goal in life was to find work that was meaningful and relationships were always sort of secondary to that goal, and I let them go as soon as there was any conflict. (*Christine*, Cal)

[In] many marriages ... women ... have wanted to get ahead in different fields, but it has ground to a halt ... especially if they have children. (*Rosa*, Fin)

These women had not prioritised work over relationships as such; it is more accurate to say that when compromises seemed necessary they decided not to make them. Many conflicts in relationships were connected to a traditional, secondary role that was required of them.

There were also women who had not made partner/career choices, but worked in a way which in practice reduced the likelihood of forming and maintaining relationships. This was a source of regret for some of them; for example, *Maxine* (Cal) refers to herself as a 'a relationship person' for whom work nevertheless takes precedence. Relationships are thought to require time, energy and commitment both by heterosexual and lesbian women; *Maxine* and *Christine* (above) are lesbians. Heterosexual women are likely to need to deal with a greater share of domestic responsibilities and housework. *Ulla* (Fin) had cohabited with a fellow student. The flexibility of studying meant that organising the household had not caused particular problems. When both started working, *Ulla* found that she was expected to conform to a traditional role at home. Her career took off when conflicts led to the break-up of the relationship:

It all really got started after my separation, it was quite quick then. Up to that time it was sort of muddling and in some way I didn't really know what I should do and what I should concentrate on. And if there was something interesting going on I had to stop and go home. But when I got the opportunity to start organising my time and energy, and started getting going, my superiors also noticed it, and my career took off. (*Ulla*, Fin)

Ulla had not consciously decided to attach more importance to her work than to her relationship. But if she had remained with her cohabitee without a decisive shift in their relationship she would not have been able to concentrate her energies in the way she did subsequently.

Particularly successful career women or artists, whose work gave them expressive, emotional or intellectual satisfaction, referred to career/partner choices. Singleness had a particular attraction for them, on the one hand, and on the other hand other options seemed more difficult to pursue. Work provides content and meaning in their lives in diverse ways which are not visible in stereotypes of 'selfish' career women. *Ella* is a psychotherapist. She works privately part of her time in order to be financially in a position to work in the public sector with less pay, and to do voluntary work among ethnic minorities; *Christine* explains that her work is politically as well as intellectually motivated; *Maxine*'s 'workaholism' is connected to her general commitment to music; *Rosa* works to convey messages through her art. *Ulla* is most typically a career woman; she does not refer to reasons extrinsic to her work when discussing its centrality. She has a great deal of scope in organising her work, participates in high-level decision making, and results achieved are financially rewarded; she had the highest income among women interviewed. Her job challenges and satisfies her and requires commitment which cannot be explained by reference to others. In men such an orientation to work would be less likely to be considered 'selfish'.

Significance of singleness at work

Though singleness was significant in the way single women worked and in the way that work constructed their lives, they thought that in their workplaces their singleness was not relevant, but being a woman, regardless of marital status was (though not all women thought their sex was relevant). Having stated this, women typically gave some examples about the relevance of singleness. These related to patterns of work, as already discussed, and to social relationships at work.

The significance of singleness was mentioned several times in connection with one issue: the choice of holiday times. Married women were given the opportunity to choose their holidays before single women. This belies the perception of women that in general their singleness was relevant to themselves, not to others and, if work/outside work boundaries were less easy to draw, this was because of their own inability to draw them. The choice of holidays indicates that others also considered their commitments outside work to be secondary and flexible, whilst commitments shaped by husbands and children were viewed as primary. If women typically organise their time with reference to others in general, and family members in particular, then those who have no such reference points find that they have to defend their 'space'.

Social relations at work

Women often mentioned informal discussions at work which concentrated on domestic issues and children, and placed them at the margins of social interaction. They did develop ways of dealing with this, and did not necessarily remain at the margins. For example, they interacted with married women with children by talking about children of friends and relatives. They did not tend to perceive such social interaction as a process of exclusion; their interests were different and thus less likely to appear as topics of conversation.

More clearly felt exclusion was experienced in connection with particular people or incidents which could stay in the minds of women a long time; if there were other single women in the workplace, they possibly used the opportunity to discuss the incident to see whether their sentiments were shared. *Mari* (Fin) explains that several divorced women in her workplace were present during a conversation where others referred to divorced people as 'rabble'. As joking and laughter spiced the talk it did not seem possible to take offence. But, *Mari* explains, 'it stuck in our minds'.

Social relationships at work were important to single women. There were several references to work being like 'family'. This had mainly positive connotations relating to closeness and support, but there were some references to negative aspects: control, interference and tensions. Single women were often interested in formulating closer relationships at work, discussing with colleagues in the context of work, or making suggestions about outings and so on: 'I sometimes suggest that we should go out to eat. And it ends up being quite a small group. You see the differences between single and married women in that' (*Ursula*, Fin). Married women more typically have to leave work promptly: 'They rush to the shops and go home to cook. I don't usually say that I might make a cup of coffee before I go home ... because in these sorts of things there can be a bit of envy ... sort of "it's all right for you"' (*Helena*, Fin). Many single women seemed adept at negotiating possible tensions.

Relationships with patients, students, pupils and so on were important to many women. For women who had wanted to have children but did not, working with children was important. Women in health care in particular referred to meeting their own needs while caring for others; work afforded possibilities for getting close to people in a way that was not possible for all of them outside work.

Freelancers, artists and craftswomen had to tackle potential isolation at work. Particularly during intense work periods there was little time or inclination for interaction with friends. Being single and living alone could be lonely. Many had contacts with people in their field, perhaps shared a workspace, participated in organisations and concentrated on social relationships in quiet work periods.

Discrimination at work

One woman felt discriminated against at work as a single woman: 'I was just ostracised for being a single academic woman – – – it sort of drove me to marriage' (*Christine*, Cal). Some thought there was no discrimination at work at all. If they were of low status, they explained this by referring to lack of ability and ambition or personal difficulties, or emphasised aspects they liked in their jobs. Many, however, felt discriminated against as *women*:

> I decided I really wanted a college education when I found myself surrounded by younger men who were getting promotions and appointments because, I felt, because they did have a college education. I was not sensitive to male/female discrimination for a very long time, and I felt that the college education made the difference. ... I don't really feel discriminated against because I'm a single woman. I feel that women in general are discriminated against, and I think women discriminate against women. (*Martha*, Cal)

In promotion, women were said to be bypassed and men 'were put on a pedestal'. Discrimination is hard to prove; many references to it were tentative. Women with a feminist orientation found it easier to claim discrimination without having to question their own abilities. Women whose work took them beyond their job descriptions were more likely to think that men were getting easy promotions: 'I was being managed by men that quite honestly I didn't have any respect for, and was doing their job' (*Liz*, Bri); 'Half the stuff I've done for companies were things that two people higher up would do ... and I was paid twopence-ha'penny for it. ... I applied to the industrial tribunal for unfair dismissal' (*Miriam*, Bri).

Of the lesbian women some had 'come out' in their workplaces; some had not, but were not intent on hiding their being a lesbian; two women wanted to keep their sexual orientation a secret. One woman had come out at work (and elsewhere) because of earlier problems caused by the discovery of her lesbianism; she felt that it was necessary to bring lesbianism out in the open and that coming out was also a more secure option. *Sanna* (Fin) was a social worker who, when called to discuss a complaint a client had lodged about her (not related to her lesbianism) was asked if she had difficulties in dealing with men. She talked of this incident with irony, but it was disconcerting. Lesbian women are especially likely to be faced with social interaction at work where their experiences and interests are not represented whether they are single or cohabit.

The indirect or direct discrimination experienced by ambitious, educated women of colour contributes to their singleness. Their progress has required a struggle which has involved compromises. *Inez* (Cal) had to make a partner/career choice. She is a Chicana interested in relationships with men who shared her cultural background. She had a Mexican boyfriend, but when considering moving to Mexico, she decided against it for reasons which she explained as being connected with work. *Carlotta* (Cal) and *Irene* (Cal) felt that, in order to achieve their aim of independence and autonomy, and, in *Carlotta*'s case, supporting her family of origin, they had to be single-minded. They were not simply concerned with building careers. Their own experiences of discouragement and discrimination, starting in schools, motivated them to connect work with their communities. Single women outside their own countries can be particularly influenced by discrimination, because they are completely dependent on their own resources; examples were recounted by *Galina* (Fin) and *Clara* (Bri).

Financial position

Financial difficulties were not greatly stressed by women. They complained about salaries being lower than they should be, but most women did not experience difficulties with money. They repeatedly emphasised that they had got used to managing with what they had.

> I sort of come from the lower echelons of the working class and ... I've struggled financially all my life but I've never ... felt deprived of anything. ... It's probably my working class world view. I don't have holidays, I don't have a colour television, I don't have a washing machine. (*Molly*, Bri)

> I can always convince myself – I can always decide I don't need that – and that's fine. (*Judy*, Cal)

> I get by, I don't need so much, I've never dreamt of a lot of money. (*Taina*, Fin)

It would be a misinterpretation to say that women are content with low wages. Women in this study are reasonably well educated and very poorly paid women are not represented; some women were well paid, some had had assistance from their families of origin in buying houses. Some referred to having had grave financial difficulties in the past, particularly single mothers when their children were small. Many felt their work was not adequately rewarded, and complained about the low pay of women generally. Many women had been through greater hardships before, and as the prospect of retirement and old age loomed, they considered themselves to be relatively secure *at present*. Those women who did not own their own houses complained about the difficulty in buying a house. Women often noted high taxation; whilst some considered that to be discriminatory, others considered it to be justified. Overall the extent of women's resources seemed less important than being in control of their money and financially independent (Chapter 8).

Politics and feminism

Coping with instabilities framing their lives can make politics and feminism appear irrelevant or threatening for women (Stacey, 1990). Many women were reluctant to place themselves in the political spectrum, but when asked about the right–left continuum placed themselves on the left. About half of the women were 'leftish'; often they referred to a general political orientation, though Britons included Labour Party supporters and Finns supporters of the Social Democratic Party. Understanding 'left' is complicated and involves different meanings in different countries. Only six women identified themselves as conservative. Eight were liberals, mainly in general terms, one British woman was a member of the Liberal Party. Six American women referred to voting for Democrats. Four Finnish women had voted for Greens.

As the USA had Republicans, Britain Conservatives and Finland a Centre Party/Conservative coalition in power, the majority of women were critics of the political system and processes in their countries, though the radicalism of their approach varied a great deal. I do not know studies of the political orientation of single women, so it is not possible to say whether single women are less conservative than women on average. Few women were politically active and fewer still involved in party politics; activists dealt with issues connected with black women, disability, anti-imperialism, community issues, sexual politics and the Women's Liberation Movement (WLM). There were no clear differences between women in the three countries, though in general liberalism was strongest in the USA. British and Finnish women were more likely to mention environmental issues and green politics. When asked about the future, many women were concerned about the environment, war and recession. Women working in semi-professions were worried about their own job security and working conditions, as well as about the effects of public spending cuts and deterioration of services on people they dealt with through their work. These women were not active citizens in terms of participation in formal political processes. In that sense they did not adopt public roles. There were no differences between American, British and Finnish women, though in Finland the proportion of women in parliament (38 per cent) is relatively high.

The women were, for the most part, post-feminists in the sense that Stacey (1990) uses the term to refer to those who have been influenced by feminism and its achievements, whilst holding their distance from feminist identity and politics. About a quarter identified themselves as feminists. A fifth were positive about feminism or the WLM, without any personal identification. About a fifth mentioned positive and negative aspects. Ten women were clearly negative about feminism, and of 12 who were 'not interested' or 'did not understand' feminism or the WLM many were clearly critical, though some simply said they had no information.

More American women than British or Finnish women identified themselves as feminists. More Finnish women than American or British women were negative about feminism. This can be related to the position of women and feminism in these societies. American WLM has been more strident and is fairly visible in the San Francisco Bay Area. In the USA the culture of femininity is strongest and overall women still occupy more traditional roles there; the proportion of single women has risen recently to levels similar to those in Britain and Finland. In Finland equality of opportunity ideology is more clearly integrated into the welfare state, and the welfare state has been significant in releasing women from their homes by providing care for children and the elderly and jobs for women. Traditional notions of femininity are less prevalent, and the feminist movement has been the least strident. Finnish women are more likely than American women to believe that achievements for women should and can be promoted through the political system.

Feminists were criticised for being too militant, anti-men, extreme, middle-class, white, educated and frustrated. Those who gave both positive and negative answers expressed criticism, but thought that feminism and WLM had made significant achievements which were important for women in general and/or single women in particular. Women who were feminists, or positive about feminism, mentioned achievements of the movement, such as increased alternatives and options for women and solidarity and commonality among women.

Public activities

This excursion into the public sphere is completed by reconsidering the blurring between the public and the private. Focusing on work and politics is not sufficient. Most of the women are not 'activists' in a traditional political sense or feminists, but they operate in the public sphere in other ways, outside work. This information was obtained by asking women to list what they did outside work. Many were involved in public activities not directly connected with their work duties or politics. The line is difficult to draw sometimes. But activities in professional organisations, for example, are voluntary. Membership of organisations such as the Anglo-Soviet friendship group, Sami Association or Chicana Foundation is not strictly political. Over half the women were involved in such broadly defined public activities and hence their location to the public sphere was mediated in diverse ways. A few women involved in organised religion engaged in philanthrophic activities such as visiting hospitals, but overall the nature of public activities was less philanthrophic than in the past. Women were more involved with groups campaigning for rights of minorities, self-help groups and so on. Focusing on politics and feminism masks the many ways in which women connect their private lives and public issues.

Conclusion

Work structures the lives of single women by providing reference points, possibilities, and constraints and limitations. Singleness is more relevant at work than women's first responses in the interviews indicated. Some processes of marginalisation and exclusion take place at work, but single women are often active in building positive relationships. Generally these women had a critical perspective but they were not vociferous, vocal rebels concerned to draw attention to wrongs. They criticised the operation of hierarchies which were advantageous to men, but they also criticised women for discriminating against other women, for being too passive and too lightly accepting the place assigned to them, on the one hand, and feminists for being too militant and anti-men, on the other.

There are continuities and changes in the position of single women. The job opportunities are broader than in the nineteenth century or in the 1950s. Education and training are more readily available. Single women are better placed to strive for autonomy and independence. But low pay and fewer prospects for promotion for all women as compared to men form a framework of restrictions on the establishment of autonomy. Although pay differentials have improved since the last century, over recent years changes have been slow or non-existent.

Single women in this study are not greatly concerned about their political or legal status as citizens; many, however, were concerned about social aspects of citizenship, with reference to themselves *and others*. Single women are active in constructing their own lives. Predominant perceptions of 'femininity' and 'women's roles' were only partially applicable to them. Tensions between the public and the private sphere are not solved by them through 'dual roles'.[5] Single women seem to have the energy and willingness to zigzag between different spheres and spaces.

5

Excursion into the private sphere

'Blurring' of the public and private is more typical for single than for married women. In the private sphere single women have more of a task in structuring their lives, which are less defined by needs of others than lives of women who live with their families. I shall first deal with the most private area for single women: their homes.

Home alone

The typical pattern is, on the basis of the interviews, that single women are out a great deal[1] and that home is a private retreat: not many visitors, not much eating, less cooking, and housework is kept to a minimum.

Three-quarters of the women interviewed lived alone and a quarter with their children, their mother or other relatives, other adults and lodgers. In Finland women lived alone, unless they lived with their children. This is consistent with the highest proportion of one-person households there. Some 60 per cent of women lived in owner-occupied flats or houses; the greatest number of owner-occupiers were in Finland, which is also consistent with levels of owner-occupation in the country. It reinforces the conception of homes as private places, which was typical overall, but most typical in Finland.

When women are away from home they go to work or 'public' activities, evening classes, homes of friends, restaurants and pubs, concerts, theatre, cinema and opera, sports, walking and rambling, they play music, travel, go to stay in the country and so on. Returning home usually means arriving at a welcoming place where, as a contrast to a busy life, they can relax, be at peace, engage in 'private' activities such as reading, listening to music, sewing and knitting, renovating and decorating, watching television, gardening, thinking, sleeping, computing, flower arranging, research, painting, writing, meditating, stamp collecting, yoga, cooking, seeing friends, smoking, playing music, writing letters, telephoning, drinking wine, 'philosophising', daydreaming and spending time with children, other people living in the house and pets.[2] Single women can shed demands of work and public activities at home, and be in control.

> This is my house, I can do what I want in it. (*Bridget*, Cal)

> You throw out everything away, you know, from the outside world – I mean you disconnect whatever angry dissatisfactions and come home and relax and be yourself. (*Amy*, Cal)

> It's my independence, it's mine, I can shut the door and no one else is gonna walk in. (*Tina*, Bri)

> I need to have a place where I can be at peace, considering what my work is like. (*Harriet*, Fin)

> I definitely need time alone. When I say I'm going home I don't need to solve anybody's problems and I don't need to take other people into consideration, and there are no demands all the time addressed to me, and I can just be and laze around. (*Ulla*, Fin)

Home as a private, personal area is important in establishing the independence of single women, when in the public sphere this is a more contentious and contradictory process (Chapter 8). Being a head of household is more accessible to women today than in the nineteenth century.

Not many people are invited into this private space. A majority of women said that they had visitors sometimes or rarely. Reasons vary. Many women do not like to cook, so it is difficult to invite people round; their flats may be fairly small, or too untidy. Having visitors would disrupt the privacy of the home by making extra demands. Gullestad (1984) studied family life and friendships of young working class mothers in Norway; homes were expected to be tidy (though some leeway existed) and visitors expected to be looked after. By not inviting many people into their homes single women evade these normative restrictions.

The majority of women live alone. Many have lived with other people but, even when experiences had been positive, living alone was now preferable. Those who lived with other people generally found the situation satisfactory. Sharing arrangements were relatively loose, and not much time was spent with other people in the household, unless they were their own children. Those who had lived and still lived with children generally were positive about that; they enjoyed their children. There were negative experiences with children too; in one case these were connected with living arrangements.

Several women had bought their homes with help from parents or other relatives. For many, buying had involved financial sacrifices, and women who were not satisfied with their homes thought it would be difficult for them to move.[3] Owning a home provided a sense of security as well as a responsibility. *Norma* has 'settled down quite a bit' since her youth. Owning a house has contributed to that.

> When I was 20 I would just go off at the drop of a hat and pursue an adventure, and now, as a home-owner and a cat-owner, I have these obligations that I have to take care of things. I think every once in a while about just saying, 'I'm going to dump my job, I'm disgusted with it, give my house to my parents, and my cats to my neighbours, and go hitch-hiking off into the Canadian wilderness or something.' But I don't really believe I would ever do that any more. When I was younger I would, but now I would modify that and maybe daydream about these things to entertain myself, but I'd never do that any more.
>
> [*TG*: And why not?]
>
> I don't know. I value the comfort and security of having my own home. After years of being dependent on others in various ways, that to me is something that is very rewarding. I've managed to own my own home and have it as a place I can always go to ... it really is a strong base that I have. I wouldn't let go of that. I have that much together finally. I realise this is valuable to me and I don't want to blow it. (*Norma*, Cal)

Creating a home out of a physical living space was an important activity. Many women had decorated their houses, often learning new skills while doing so. But there were also women for whom the importance of home was more symbolic and the physical aspects of space were not significant. The more women tended to be away from home, the more likely they were to consider its appearance as secondary.

Taking care of oneself

As the majority of women live alone, and do not often invite people into their homes, domestic maintenance is mainly related to caring for oneself, and standards are set by women themselves, rather than by external norms.

Housework

As home is a place to retreat to and to relax in, the majority of women disliked housework,[4] though for some it was an important aspect of 'nest-making.' If cleanliness was considered important, women tried to allocate a concentrated time for housework periodically. Some women said they had a high standard of cleanliness and spent quite a lot of time cleaning. Women who disliked housework were prepared to lower the standards they wished to maintain.

Single women spend less time doing housework than married women, as was indicated by comments such as 'washing dishes once a week', 'I leave my clothes lying around', 'I never do housework' and 'my place is upside down'. Divorced or separated women made comparisons with the amounts of housework they used to do when living with their husbands or partners, and referred to reductions. Women with children still living at home did more housework than those without children, but they were also more likely to take domestic tasks for granted. Without a husband to cater for there were no tensions about sharing the housework; it was a necessity to get through, though with older children women have had disputes about their contribution.

Single women were able to make decisions about how much housework to do, what standard to set and when to do it. This was an important aspect of being in control of their lives; being relatively free from household chores can be considered liberating. But housework can also be considered as maintenance of self in everyday life. Is it easier for women to look after other people rather than themselves? This question has particular relevance in relation to eating.

Food

About a quarter of women interviewed said they tended to cook often. The majority of women said that they did very little or hardly any cooking.[5] They eat at work, at friends' homes or in restaurants, have takeaways or eat salads and sandwiches. Some thought they were neglectful in their eating: 'sometimes I even forget to eat', 'I slip lots of meals', 'I eat convenience foods', 'sometimes I have to eat rubbish food'. Others tried to eat well, if simply, and were concerned about the quality of their diet. Women who did a little food preparation might cook a large quantities for several days, or stock up the freezer. Cooking was typically done during the week-end.

The reasons given for not cooking were several. First, tiredness after work was referred to. A second reason was dislike of or not being skilled in cooking. A third reason was most significant in terms of the question of looking after oneself: women said they did not like cooking for themselves.

> I hardly ever cook meals for myself. ... I think that last year I must have cooked around ... five times. ... I don't cook full meals unless I have some people over. ... I just, I can't [cook for myself]. Maybe it's just growing up in a large family ... Who wants to cook for one? (*Carlotta*, Cal)

> When it's just me it's just a chore and I do the minimum. (*Lorna*, Bri)

> If I cook, there has to be somebody coming round to eat. I rarely cook for myself. ... When I have visitors coming I do everything myself – not just heat up convenience food. (*Minna*, Fin)

Cooking for oneself was uninspiring work. Eating is a social activity, where enjoyment is connected with sharing food with others. Without such a shared social context, eating becomes feeding oneself. Dislike of cooking for one was also shared by women who spent more time in food preparation.

Many women explained that they did not generally care much about eating. Pleasurable meanings are often connected with consumption of food; for these single women such meanings are not particularly significant. Maintaining life through day-to-day activities is considered less pleasurable and meaningful when it is done for one person, particularly oneself. Eating is also connected with social and cultural distinctions. Many women who did not want to cook for themselves did not invite visitors either, because cooking then required too much work or because people who invited them to eat cooked better. *Saara* (Fin) spelled out what underlies this:

When people get more established and so on then something like food begins to acquire tremendous significance. And I'm not a particularly good cook. ... I think expectations are now higher, and I don't have the gumption to offer my sausages.

It is more difficult for single women to produce food for larger numbers of people[6] and to meet standards they consider are required.

Exploring the experience of single women at work indicated a blending of the public and the private in particular ways. Exploring eating habits indicates similar blending. Single women use public facilities, such as dining at work[7] or in restaurants, and less food preparation is done in their homes than in larger households.

Irene gave an example of using food and eating to look after herself. She talked about her habit of having a 'party for one': a good meal, music and wine. There were women who did cook, women who cooked fairly often and women who enjoyed cooking, but because in discussions dealing with 'home', housework and food there was a 'typical' majority pattern, I have spent more time illustrating that pattern, than variations upon it. That homes are private is not particular to single women, but how privacy is constructed, what activities are involved and what meanings are attached to it contain tendencies typical of them.

If looking after themselves is an unwelcome necessity for single women, it would be interesting to study how they relate to their bodies. Perhaps there is a tendency for embodiment to be experienced in particular ways by single women. Not cooking and looking after bodily needs in a sense that women living with other people tend to do, that is, not being 'domesticated', can release single women to look after themselves and pursue bodily pleasures in other ways. A fairly large number of women included walking, hiking, rambling, swimming, racket ball and so on in their out-of-work activities. Sexuality was not typically connected with bodily pleasures, but with intimacy (Chapter 6).

Being alone/loneliness

Although women welcome going home to get away from tensions in their more public roles, about half said they did get lonely. For some these were moments that passed; for others loneliness was a more persistent experience. About half did not consider loneliness a problem. Many emphasised that being alone is not the same as feeling lonely.

> I don't feel lonely generally speaking. I have a sense of being on my own. (*Liz*, Bri)

> 'Alone' in itself is a neutral word and sometimes it's wonderful. (*Rachel*, Cal)

> My life requires loneliness. (*Reija*, Fin)

As many single women lead active lives, work hard and do not spend a great deal of time at home, being alone is welcomed. For some aloneness is so important that moments of loneliness do not seem a great drawback. But others do get lonely. This sense of loneliness is not simply a matter of being with people or not. Involuntary singles may connect it to not having a partner: 'I afraid of loneliness, I hate to be alone, I feel like being less without a partner' (*Amy*, Cal). More often loneliness is an ambivalent feeling without a clear explanation and is not connected with the presence or absence of other people:

> There's times I feel lonely when no one can reach me. (*Carlotta*, Cal)

> I don't feel terribly lonely, I'm not feeling cut up. ... I can have a – a gap feeling, an empty – not – I'm not lonely for company because I have a great many friends who I can tap if I need to just simply be with somebody. (*Betsy*, Bri)

> Of course [I get lonely]. Everybody does. ... I get that feeling when I'm overtired and filled to the brim with other people's problems. (*Nina*, Fin)

Loneliness can be defined in different ways. Weiss concludes that a person, when lonely, 'maintains an organization of emotions, self-definitions, and definitions of his or her relations to others which is quite different from the one he maintains when not lonely' (Weiss, 1981, p. 153). The type of loneliness described by women here does not meet Weiss' definition of an unpleasant, gnawing feeling.

They refer to being alone and perceiving both one's separateness from others and connectedness with them. This type of 'aloneness' *eases the process of individuation*: seeing where self begins and ends. If women move between the public and the private in a way which blends these oppositionally represented spheres more than is the case for married women, as I have argued, their loneliness is particularly likely to be structured by tensions between connnectedness and separateness in the construction of individuality and independence. I shall turn to this question when I deal with 'existential angst' in Chapter 7.

Ways in which women cope with loneliness also indicate tensions between connectedness and separateness. Many turned to friends, their own children and other relatives: they sought the support of others. But more typical ways of coping involved self-sufficiency. The first was to engage in activities at home (shifting furniture, sewing, reading, watching television, sleeping and so on) or outside the home (hiking, walking, activities in public places such as going to meetings, going to restaurants etc.). The second way was to turn inwards to the self.

> I think, generally, loneliness comes from within oneself and it's the kind of – for me it's the kind of spiritual hungering that needs to be filled. (*Maxine*, Cal)

> I've got quite a lot of self-control; I tell it to go away. ... I think I am quite good at dealing with myself. (*Betsy*, Bri)

> I just had to learn [to deal with it]. I think it's kind of accepting yourself; that's our right. It's just there, the inner strength. (*Else*, Fin)

Single women have had to learn to rely on their own resources, on the one hand; on the other hand, those capable of relying on their own resources are perhaps more likely to be single.

But there were also women who found it difficult to deal with loneliness.

> I don't like people to feel sorry for me so I don't tell them about it, you know, that I'm lonely or I'm depressed, you know. ... I just don't talk about it, I keep it to myself. ... I figure it's my problem ... nobody can do anything about it, right? Yes, I tell my cousin that I'm tired of this life, you know, it's so lonely, and then she goes: 'Oh, you're lucky!' (*Shoshana*, Cal)

> I feel desperately lonely. ... I do worry about being on my own. (*Emily*, Bri)

> I have been a bit of an onlooker so that I have not really wanted to join in. Now that I'm retired you get used to being with yourself so much that you don't even want to. You sometimes get a bit torn, should I do this, do I do enough – I don't know. (*Helka*, Fin)

It is not easy to distinguish between loneliness and depression; responses on these were often mixed. For a few women loneliness/depression had caused great problems; they had considered suicide. One went to therapy; one (a retired woman) got housed in a building for the elderly, where social contacts were readily available, and two had got divorced and decided that their children should live with their fathers.

About a third had sought professional help (this includes marriage guidance). Therapy was not necessarily sought because of loneliness, and some women did not connect it with a particular crisis either: they wanted to understand themselves better, for example. Turning to therapy has different meanings; it is more common in the United States (Bellah *et al.*, 1988). Similar numbers of British and American, and fewer Finnish women had used therapy. Finnish women with something to be dealt with were most likely to rely on themselves in coping with loneliness.

Many women referred to having been lonely in the past. These feelings were related to singleness, but there were differences between unmarried and divorced women. Unmarried women were more likely to report a crisis when they first started living alone, but had developed ways of coping and had got used to or learned to enjoy being alone. A crisis often occurred when women were in their early thirties and had become aware of their singleness as a 'fact of life' and had to establish how they related to that; the majority became voluntary singles (Chapter 3). Meanings attached to loneliness by divorced women were explained by reference to their marriage: for example, they had been lonely within the marriage: 'It seemed from the outside that I had somebody. But I didn't. I didn't have anything' (*Minna*, Fin). There were references to loneliness after divorce, or fears about such loneliness, and also processes of learning to deal with it. Divorced women have to construct a new identity and to learn to balance independence against loneliness (see Chandler, 1991). They experience insecurity in this process, as there are few conceptual models for the benefits of life without marriage.

Though there were women with boy- or girlfriends, there were few references to turning to them when lonely. Twenty-six women had ongoing relationships, but the intensity, regularity and closeness of these varied a great deal. About half of those who had boy- or girlfriends did not refer to loneliness, though they did not specify that the relationships were significant in this. The very existence of the relationship may keep loneliness at bay by altering the sense of connectedness and separateness. Similarly, for women who had close networks of friends and relatives, the existence of these was comforting when lonely, even if they were not turned to. Single mothers were less likely to experience loneliness because of their relationships to their children, but perhaps experienced loneliness as a unit *with* their children.

Alone in public places

If single women living alone decide that they wish to go somewhere without having made previous arrangements it may be difficult to do so if they do not wish to go unaccompanied. Those with live-in partners or children may find a readier companion. The distinction between public and private spheres as spaces is useful when we consider how accessible and safe public places are for women alone.

There were women who did go out alone, to wherever they wanted to go, without much concern for their physical safety. Others went alone to particular activities, and as the cinema, theatre, restaurant, concerts and so on. Most women did not go to restaurants, pubs or dances alone. If they did, they experienced varying levels of social discomfort. For example, *Lynne* talks about going for a drink alone:

> I always take a book, I mean I always have an alibi – – – I mean it does feel as though you're looking as though you're wanting a pick-up or something. (*Lynne*, Bri)

Women who went out alone often referred to having had to 'learn' to do so. *Caroline* got depressed because of the dependency that needing others to go out with entailed; she now goes out alone a great deal:

> I've fought really hard for that. ... I got myself into the situation where I wasn't afraid to walk into a place, where I could go into a club, stand there the whole evening without anybody. (*Caroline*, Bri)

The issue of having to negotiate social aspects as well as the physical safety of public places is important for single women.

Social discomfort is not only a personal experience of women, though some say they *feel* uncomfortable whether others contribute to that or not, or that during their learning process they have realised that the reactions of others are less significant than they thought. But there were many experiences of being propositioned by men.

> I'll be listening to music with my eyes closed and I'll open my eyes and there'll be some guys there: 'Can I buy you a drink?' And ... it really puts me off, you know. Cause I know, I mean I'm a fairly attractive woman and if you come into a place like that alone, the guys just can't accept it. ... It's open for you to go and offer [a single woman] a glass, I mean, they think they're being very nice. ... I consider it very annoying. It's not why I came there. If I came to a singles bar or some place where people do that, that would be different. (*Kate*, Cal)

Many women had had similar experiences, or expected that they would have such experiences if they did go out alone. Women nowadays can go to restaurants and pubs alone, but the break with the past is not complete; they are not likely to be comfortable in that situation.

Though there were women who gave physical safety as the strongest reason for not going out alone, overall women did not express a great deal of concern about it. This was often qualified by their saying they used their own cars or taxis, were careful about where they walked and at what time, how they were dressed ('I wear dull clothes') and so on. Women, though apparently not concerned, had developed ways of coping which they took for granted (see Stanko, 1985). Women are so used to potential physical threats that, unless they actually feel fear, they are likely to say that they feel safe. But there were also those who felt they had a general demeanour which was a protection.

> I think ninety per cent of that is because I'm as big as I am. I just cannot see that anybody in their right mind is gonna attack me when there's somebody five foot two down the street who's an obvious victim in their stilettos. ... I just don't see myself as a victim. (*Tina*, Bri)

Several women referred to having passed through places which are considered dangerous; as they had not had bad experiences, they felt safe.

> I've been all over London at all hours, drunk and sober ... and I've never come to any harm. I've never felt threatened outside. (*Molly*, Bri)

There was at least a mild sense of adventure in some of the comments. *Jill* (Bri) explained that she was 'wreckless really'. It is possible, that if single women do not feel directly responsible to anybody, risk-taking seems easier. Women with dependent children tended to be more concerned about safety: 'If I drop dead, who's going to mind the children?' (*Valerie*, Bri). Going out alone at night was avoided by retired women. Disabled women were unable to move in public places without assistance.

A few women said they were not interested in going out alone: 'Why would I want to go out by myself?' Solitary outings were not considered fun if there was nobody to share the experience with. Some could find company most of the time when they wanted it. Going out alone sometimes intensified a sense of loneliness.

There were no significant differences between women in London, the San Francisco Bay Area and Helsinki, though Finnish women used public transport more, and less cars and taxis. That women in the two larger and less safe cities did not express more caution then women in a smaller city indicates that women adapt to their surroundings and try to keep fear at bay wherever they are.

The perceived threat of sexist propositioning, harassment, rape and male violence generally have a controlling effect on women and their freedom of movement; public places involve a great deal of negotiation. It is characteristic of single women that many of them engage in that negotiation. Some of them, by considering themselves not to be 'victims', seem to imply that other women may be. As single women tend to rely on their own resources, other women can appear more feeble to them. Their sense of safety was, to an extent, dependent on not being like a woman: 'I think I'm pretty off-putting', 'I don't look like a woman in the dark.' I do not suggest this more than tendentially: overall single women share with other women problems of being in public places, but, in their concern not to be dependent on others and not to curtail their own movements too much, single women have undergone a learning process in the negotiation of what public places mean for a woman.

Inside/outside – social relationships

I shall now turn to processes of inclusion/exclusion in the terrain of social interaction. Women completed a 'Top Ten' list; they were asked to include people whom they considered 'important' – no criteria were given. The lists were not directly indicative of their social networks, but women were asked further questions about people they listed: how they had met them, what their marital status was, whether they had children and how often they met. These data give an impression of their social networks, and of the type of people they considered important, not whom they met regularly. Thus, for example, women who did not live in their countries or areas of origin could include people living there; women could include parents, relatives, friends and other important people (mentors, teachers, public figures) who were dead. Women made their own interpretations of the list: this was indicated by entries of more than one person (a couple, family, comrades and so on) or of pets. Many included ten entries, but some more, some less: there were 667 entries altogether.

Several analyses were carried out on the lists.[8] The entries have been categorised in Table 5.1. The total numbers of entries are not counted here; thus 'friends: women' indicates how many women had at least one entry in this category in their list. Some of the categories overlap (for example, father/dead person).

Table 5.1

Category	In how many lists?
Mother	31
Father	23
Parents	7
Family of origin	3
Sister/stepsister	28
Brother/stepbrother	26
Grandparent(s)	7
Other relatives	14
Own children/grandchildren	10
Other children	24
Friends: women	54
Friends: men	32
Couples	10
Current boy/girlfriend	27
Ex-husband, partner, boy/girlfriend	17
Neighbours	18
Dead persons	20
Mentors, etc.	14
Therapist/therapy group	8
Pets	5
Colleagues/co-workers	36
Ex-colleagues/co-workers	20

It is interesting to note that though women talked more about fathers (Chapter 3) mothers were more often included in the list of important people. Three-quarters of women mentioned at least one female friend to whom they were not related; nearly a half mentioned a male friend. A third mentioned children who were not their own or their grandchildren (12 were children of siblings, 12 children of friends).

Social networks of single women typically consist of relatives and friends (Simon, 1987; Chandler, 1991). Middle-class women are likely to include more friends than relatives; working-class women are likely to include more relatives than friends (Chandler, 1991). Simon (1987) did not find such differences. Here no significant differences were found, except that American working-class women were less likely to include relatives than middle class women. No significant differences were found between ethnic groups, although in Britain women of colour were more likely to include a considerable number of relatives in their lists. Finnish and American women in older age groups were more likely to mention relatives than younger women. Divorced and separated women, and women with children, were likely to include more relatives in their lists than unmarried women. Caution is necessary in relation to this information: a larger sample might alter the tendencies.

Families of origin

Only a few women did not mention *any* members of their families of origin or families of procreation in their lists. Nearly a third composed lists where half of the people were relatives from their families of origin or procreation; nearly a third composed lists where about a third of the people were relatives. Single women, even if they do not have children, are not 'outside' families, even though they may not have a family of procreation. Members of the family (especially sisters) were an important source of practical and emotional support; they provided financial assistance, helped with children, were available to talk to in times of difficulties and were turned to when in need of intimacy.

> I think ... the family people [on that list] are the ones that I feel are going to be there for my entire life, or their lives. The other kinds of friends, the friendship just depends on availability and circumstances. It's not a solid rock, the way these others are. (*Norma*, Cal)

> I know I can ... be spiteful, hurtful to my mother, my father, and they will carry on bad for a week or so, but at the end of it they ring me up and say 'Well, I don't like the way you behaved the other day, but, you know, come good the next time.' I mean, you go on again. (*Valerie*, Bri)

There were women who were at the receiving end in relation to their relatives. Others considered relationships with relatives reciprocal and mutually supportive. Some women felt ambivalent about family relationships; they were valued, but the relationships also included tensions. Women might harbour resentments about their childhood and some felt that they were still controlled: 'The day my mother dies I will be free' (*Anni*, Fin). Other women did not feel that the attachment was imposed on them: 'I shall be devastated when [my parents die] ... I can't imagine life without them' (*Tina*, Bri). They found it difficult to detach themselves from their families and to accomplish 'a rite of passage' from daughterhood to adulthood if this was not mediated through wifehood or was disrupted by divorce.

> [my parents] *still* wish that I had a proper job and a family ... they have made quite upsetting comments, and have said things that have been unpleasant. ... They seem to think that if you have a man and you get married then you are somehow a proper member of society, so that the man would look after some things, sort of. (*Laura*, Fin)

Being a 'daughter' tended to be one salient role for single women; this had both positive and negative implications, ranging from support to control.

Women I interviewed were much less likely to have looked after aging parents, or thought that they were likely to do so in the future, than single women in Simon's (1987) or Allen's (1989) study. Some had looked after their parents, usually for short periods; none had done so full-time. Responsibilities that a few women had taken on had a great impact on their lives. They had moved closer to their parent(s) or had organised their parent(s) to move near them and spent a considerable amount of time outside work travelling to visit their parents in their homes or in hospitals. Some women reported a strong expectation by parents or siblings that they, as single women (if without children), would asssume the main responsibility. At times women agreed; they felt that their lives had more flexibility and it was easier for them to take on new tasks than for sisters or brothers with spouses and children. But women also had siblings who were, or expected to become, responsible for caring for parents. Some women positively wanted to help their parents. Others said that they would not do so. Several women also said that their parents had emphasised that they did not want support.

> [My mum] is always saying, 'We don't want to be a burden on any of you.' ... They really don't want me to be the one who, if anyone, is to look after them. ... It wouldn't surprise me if one of my married brothers or sisters took them in. [But] I'm the one in the family who's most concerned about their health. ... And I suppose I've got more time to be concerned about them because the others are married or whatever. (*Lorna*, Bri)

The welfare state has been significant in relaxing the need (or expectations) for single daughters to look after aging parents. Because of full-time employment and geographical mobility many are not in a position to provide assistance. Parents are keen to rely on their own resources when organising for old age. Daughters are more likely to refuse weighty responsibilities. A process of individuation makes them draw their own boundaries more clearly and question what is expected of them.

But there are continuities as well as changes. Many women had helped to look after parents or expected that they would do so. But there is more diversity around the social construction of what is 'responsibility' now than there was in the 1950s. I do not suggest that not assisting elderly parents is merely a positive development and that all such assistance should be located in the public sphere. The crucial question is whether help that takes place in the private sphere should be the *duty* of women in general and single daughters in particular. Welfare provisions in the United States are less significant than in Britain or Finland, but because of public spending cuts in Britain (and more recently in Finland) more publicly provided services may be shifted back to the private sector.

Friends

The friendships of single women are mainly with other single women.[9] A total of 129 single women were included in the lists; of these 106 were unmarried and 23 divorced. Several reasons were given for interacting mainly with other single women. Single women reinforce each other's lifestyles. They have time:

> I have a lot of single women friends, I guess, because we have the time to do things with each other. (*Sue*, Cal)

They are available:

> It's easier to organise things with people who are free [laughter]. (*Lea*, Fin)

They are in a similar position:

> One of the reasons you're together is because you haven't got a man to go out with. It sounds awful to say. (*Lorna*, Bri)

They have shared interests:

> We [single women] are with square ends with one another, we have all sorts of hobbies, we travel and do all sorts of things together. (*Helena*, Fin)

In a less tangible way what they share is being 'different'.

> [Other single women] become important because we're similar. You know, you sort of seek refuge with people who are like yourself. (*Lorna*, Bri)

> If you're single you seek out single friends. Or you seek others kinds of misfits, I guess. ... I guess I see myself as a misfit ... because the culture is so heavily into, you know, monogamous relationships. (*Sue*, Cal)

There were many positive reasons for friendships between single women; being able to share lifestyles and interests pulled them together. But there were also pushes which strengthened interaction among single women; they experienced a sense of being different (or even deviant). Single women were able to shift from 'outside' to 'inside' in friendships with other single women.

Women tended to socialise with people (and particularly single women) within their own ethnic grouping. Lesbians tended to socialise with other (particularly single) lesbians. Many women emphasised the 'alternative' nature of their networks: for example, *Molly* (Bri) describes her social life as being 'around therapists or ex-drunks, and they're not the most ... ordinary bunch of people'. Women who constructed networks outside the mainstream did so for both positive and negative reasons: either they did not find themselves comfortable or accepted and included among other types of people, or they themselves were not interested in moving beyond the type of social relationships they had.

There were also women who had less access to alternative networks and who found that the number of single women around them was diminishing. Divorced women who had not maintained many friendships outside the context of their partnership had to spend a great deal of time, energy and effort in rebuilding their networks after separation or divorce.

Networks of friends are protective and in that sense have assumed functions normally associated with families. *Betsy* (Bri) refers to her single friends who share her outlook and political orienation: 'You make your own bubble of friends and you create it to make life easier.' If, *Betsy* continues, many of her friends were in couples, she would feel 'much more peculiar'. To further understand the prominence of other single women in social networks, I shall explore social relationships single women have with couples or families other than their own.

Friendships and interaction with couples and families

A great deal of diversification of the 'family' has taken place; have 'old maids' at the margins become more integrated single women, 'inside' rather than 'outside'? Many single women do have women friends who are married or cohabit. Some also interact with families of these friends. Cultivating friendships requires time and energy. Some single women preferred their friends to have other demands on their time; *Anni*'s psoriasis and treatments for it limit the time she has available and therefore she is pleased that most of her friends are married: 'They don't make demands on me, and I don't want to be tied down.' Those with both married and single women friends find differences in patterns of interaction. Single women are more 'free'; interaction with married women was shaped by their timetables. A sense of difference was therefore strong also among single women who did have married friends. *Ursula* (Fin) did not think of herself as single and did not consider singleness relevant in the construction of her life. As the interview progressed, and social interaction at work and friendships in general were discussed, she made several references to differences between married and single women. She talked about different things with married women, found it difficult to organise joint activities with them and concluded that the lives of single and married women 'revolved round different tracks'. Lesbian women also felt that single women were differentially positioned in networks: lesbian couples interacted more with other lesbian couples.

> Lesbians quite often imitate the institutions ... in terms of 'coupledness' and excluding – you know, putting all the focus on couples and not on friends and not on politics and not on other experiences in life. (*Christine*, Cal)

Socialising with families was thought to be even more difficult. There were women who did so, some a great deal. Many of them referred to having 'to work at being included' when visiting family homes, talking about different things and taking children into consideration. Single women with children of their own did not necessarily find it easier to socialise with families; for example, *Soili* (Fin) referred to 'different starting-points' and 'different worlds' – families, she thought, were like 'a clump'. Married women and their families were seen to be less individuated than single women.

If single women are more individuated and autonomous (because they have to be in charge of their own lives), it is not easy to carry this experience into interaction with families. This was often not clearly spelled out.

> I've found that, strangely enough, when I was going to the opera last week ... Louise and her husband would pick me up and take me and bring me back, and sometimes, I don't like sitting in a back seat. I felt sort of single, and so one day I decided I'd go on my own and do something different. And I felt sort of better. There was something I wasn't liking. I didn't feel that comfortable with being picked up and dropped off. Something about sitting in the back seat. I just felt sort of odd. Or maybe I was just reminded that I'm single. There was something. (*Susan*, Cal)

Alone, a sense of autonomy was easier to maintain; with a couple individuation was more likely to acquire shades of vulnerability than strength. *Martha* (Cal)'s comment that she had been 'adopted' by some families exemplifies strains in individuation. That children are usually adopted indicates tensions in constructing equal relationships.

A sense of vulnerability or a sense of 'lacking something' is associated with interaction with families. Tendentially this excludes single women. Single women also felt uncomfortable in interaction with families or in social situations with many couples because of the place occupied by, or allocated to, married women. In so far as married women spent a great deal of time in the kitchen, were responsible for care of the children and talked about 'recipes' and 'kids', their lack of individuation irritated single women.

Generally single women observed that there were tensions when people with different lifestyles interacted. Families had shared interests and similar patterns of life; it was easier for them to socialise with each other and for single women to socialise with each other. Therefore there was not always a sense that families operated to *exclude* others, or that single women *wanted* to dissociate themselves from families. The difficulties in balancing different expectations were evident in comments about visiting the homes of married women; some single women were irritated if the husband was present and interpreted this as the wife not being given space to organise her friendships autonomously, but others felt that, if the husband removed himself from the interaction, this was a slight on the single woman.

Processes of social interaction are complex and include voluntary withdrawal as well as exclusion of single women. Thus there was no clear-cut way in which single women were pushed to the edges of a family-centred society. That many women did interact with married women or families indicates that social changes since the 1950s have altered the social position of single women; they are less pitied outsiders. But there are also continuities. These were evident when single women talked about interaction with married women and families, and especially when they talked about interaction with married men and families, and men in general.

There were many men in the Top Ten lists; these included fathers, brothers, grandfathers, uncles, colleagues, ex- husbands, ex-partners, ex-boyfriends, current boyfriends, husbands of women friends, and married and single friends. There was a great deal of variation in the ease with which women socialised with men, particularly those they were not related to; women with (several) brothers were most at ease. Interaction with men was difficult because few interests were shared. Men were generally thought to be more detached than women. Further difficulties related to sexual tensions in relationships. Particularly in friendships with married men single women are often still considered a threat.

> I have noticed that some married women can't take it and they become jealous, if their husband pays too much attention, so you have to be fairly careful. (*Helka*, Fin)

> It's tough when you get into circles where there's couples and then the single woman becomes seen as a threat. That has happened to me. (*Carlotta*, Cal)

> There are women who are married and whose marriages are a bit difficult, and I've noticed a sort of hostility in their attitudes sometimes. They think for example that I'm trying to get their husband ... Other women fear a woman who's sort of free. (*Rosa*, Fin)

Single women are potential rivals, but the threat they pose to families may also be less tangible. Families cannot take their own lifestyles for granted when confronted by a single woman. The taken-for-granted familism is shown as not all-encompassing.

> Maybe couples are threatened by single people, 'cause it represents certain aspects of their lives that they think they can't do ... it reminds you of something you're scared of. (*Frances*, Cal)

The social location and identity of a married woman is reinforced in her interaction with others – she 'has the "constant conversation" with her husband to stabilize her identity, as well as the daily exchanges with friends, relatives, associates and tradespeople ... that validate her membership of a socially accepted couple' (Richardson, 1988, p. 214) – whereas a married woman receives positive reinforcement of the normality of her marital status, a single woman is more likely to receive *reminders* of her marital status as a difference. Usually single women past their thirties have learned to ignore such reminders.

Support persons?

Single women find their niche in the public sphere through work and a range of public activities. In the private sphere single women find their niche in networks typically combining friends and relatives. Though the social integration of single women is still somewhat tenuous, there have been changes in their 'outsider' situation. But there are also continuities. Single women in the nineteenth century justified their existence by relying on notions of moral superiority and were engaged in supportive activities in public and private spheres. Many women in this study are 'support persons' in their relationships.

Information on support was obtained from questions such as 'what do you do if you are lonely?', 'who would you turn to in difficulties?'. There were also questions about intimacy and physical comforting, and questions about assistance when ill and so on.

> I am ... the backbone of the family. Everybody leans on me and sometimes I get tired of it. (*Bridget*, Cal)

> [People lean on me.] They do automatically and always have done, and I'm used to it. Sometimes ... I feel a bit drained by it ... that's why it's really nice to go holiday where no one can tough on you. (*Betsy*, Bri)

> I've been too flexible ... I am too accommodating by nature. ... I am a good listener. I listen very fluently [!laughs]. (*Ursula*, Fin)

Women who were support persons often made some effort to redraw boundaries between themselves and other people, and to redress the balance. *Hanna* used to 'exist through being needed by others', but tried to alter that:

I don't spend too long in a relationship which is not balanced. It's very important for me in my friendships, now, that there is both give and take. (*Hanna*, Fin)

There are tensions in learning to 'take'. Codes of traditional femininity still encourage women to consider others rather than themselves. Women found it difficult to dissociate themselves from these codes even when they challenged them. Biographical aspects made it difficult for some women to turn to others for support, though they were able to give it. Single women have less duties towards others today; some are 'support persons', some equivocally so, and some not at all. But there is a strong tendency towards other-directedness in their activities in the public and private spheres. It is partly for this reason that homes of single women were such important personal retreats.

Conclusion

Couples and families, like single women, reinforce each other's lifestyles through social interaction with people in similar situations. Single women are not likely to take their singleness for granted; they have had to reflect on their single status at some point in their lives, or in some situations. Married women are less likely to be confronted with a need to consider their coupled status, which is reinforced in a myriad of social and cultural patterns. Families are crucial units structurally, culturally and ideologically. Single women have to negotiate their inside/outside spaces and engage in a learning process while doing so. Their social relationships, as well as sources of pleasure, are props in this process.

6

Partnerships and sexuality

Madonnas/whores

Are single women interested in forming close partnerships; if so, why, and if not, why not? What tensions and contradictions are experienced in the area of relationships? By being single, what have these women gained and what have they missed? How do they deal with sexuality? In the nineteenth century women were thought to have greater moral purity than men, and spinsters were supposed to exist in a realm above or beyond sexuality. After the sexualisation of women, single women seemed to have no legitimate relationship to sexuality. Celibacy came to be seen as abnormal and deviant, but sexuality was to be expressed in the context of marriage. With growing permissiveness and tolerance in social and moral attitudes the opportunities for single women to define their sexuality increased. But stereotypical views of single women as a sexual threat have not disappeared; women still walk the tightrope strung between a continuum of representations from madonnas to whores. A sexually active woman, who does not express her sexuality in the context of romantic attachments institutionalised in companionate marriage, is still judged and feared.

Intimacy

Family is a privileged societal institution which defines lives of those outside it, too, argue Barrett and McIntosh (1982). Overvaluation of family life leads to a devaluation of lives arranged in different ways. Family has monopolised caring, security, sharing, trust and intimacy; if this was not so, human relationships and interaction outside the context of familial relationships would contain more of these aspects. Now family has 'claimed them for its own' (Barrett and McIntosh, 1982, p. 80). Single women, then, appear to be in a difficult position.

There was great variation in the extent of intimacy women in this study thought they wanted or needed, and in how much intimacy women experienced in their social relationships. But there was a prevalent sense of intimacy not being taken for granted. There were frequent expressions of having to 'work at' obtaining intimacy, and having to *learn* both to give and to receive intimacy. Many women thought that loving intimacy was easier in the context of monogamous partnerships, marriages and families. *Greta* talks about people in her Top Ten list:

> Let's say, whenever I see these people we have a hug and a kiss. ... I wouldn't have a particularly close physical relationship with a woman. ... Intimacy for me is ... very much about opening up your emotions, I think, and I can do that with all these friends, to have really intimate talks and cry with them and all that. ... If I'm in a crisis ... I can always tell people, you know, 'I'm really very depressed now' or whatever ... so there is a very very strong emotional support system going on. (*Greta*, Bri)

Greta emphasises a close network she has built with determination, and which is supportive and offers intimacy. She has also developed ways of ensuring physical touching through massage given by a female friend. But all this does not match up to intimacy in relationships:

> There are times when you feel it would be lovely to – well, cuddle up to somebody or, you know, have this sort of intimacy which you probably only have with a loving partner.

Other women express similar sentiments:

> Good relationships offer a degree of intimacy that you can't always accomplish with friends. (*Jody*, Cal)

If women had boy- or girlfriends, these were a likely source of intimacy, but not necessarily so; the intensity and quality of the relationships vary a great deal.

Single women have differing 'access' to intimacy, organised in a variety of ways. Though friends were an important source of intimacy, many women found it easier to turn to relatives.

> If I'm miserable and need holding, the person who does that for me is my brother. I find it more difficult to completely tell my friends that I'm miserable. (*Lorna*, Bri)

For single mothers their children (including adult children) provided opportunities for intimate interaction. In many aspects of the lives of single women, friends and social interaction with them were crucial; in relation to intimacy, familial relations were of equivalent significance.

Some women ask for intimacy when they need it: 'otherwise I get a little bit prickly and then nobody can touch me' (*Gwen*, Bri). But those women especially who were supportive to others in relationships found it difficult to obtain intimacy. They were weary of making demands on people, though they were willing to *offer* support and comfort to others. Tending to the needs of others was easier for them than expressing their own needs. Many women, when lonely, were not likely to turn to other people; in their need for intimacy they were more likely to do so, though there were those who tried to rely on themselves ('I can provide everything I need for myself, by myself') or on the companionship and closeness offered by pets ('It really makes a difference having the cat around. It sort of takes the edge off. I talk to her and it's nice to have another warm body') and a range of other ways of coping ('Sometimes just holding [my] little old teddybear will do it').

Intimacy was connected to a *learning process*: women had to learn to handle their need for intimacy if it was not available; or they had to learn to give intimacy, and/or learn to receive it. References to learning indicate that voluntary singleness and ease and comfort with single status were not given but *constructed* with energy and determination, whether women had wanted to be single or not. They had to learn to cope with social relationships at work, learn to draw boundaries between work and non-work, learn to engage in activities alone, and to go out alone in particular, and learn to deal with fears and vulnerability connected with physical safety. When the prevalent pattern for women is to marry, doing that is less likely to demand decisions on how to organise one's life. Being outside this prevalent pattern means having to confront one's sense of self: 'Until you really gain hold of your conscious mind you are following a path' (*Kate*, Cal).

Marriage and partnerships: scepticism and idealism

In the word association lists about a quarter of references to *marriage* were negative, and about a fifth positive. Almost a half of the responses contained both negative and positive aspects, and the rest were neutral. Almost a half of the responses to *family* were positive and less than a sixth were negative. Women were thus a great deal more critical of 'marriage' than of 'family'. Their observations and experiences of the 'family' were more positive because many felt that their families of origin were or had been supportive, and because they often connected families with children, references to whom were predominantly positive.

A total of 33 women had been married or had cohabited in marriage-type relationships. An additional 15 had at some point lived with a partner, while 24 had not had any experiences of 'live-in' partnerships. When women talked about marriage and partnerships, many had experiences of their own as well as observations on others. Though the majority of women were voluntary singles, many were actively interested in forming partnerships, or open to the possibility of them, though not necessarily interested in, and open to, marriage.

Positive aspects associated with partnerships were intimacy, strength of feeling, companionship, sexuality, social status, protection, financial and emotional support, and the possibility of having and bringing up children. For example:

> I really miss – – – sex too, but also I miss a safe shoulder. You know, so that I wouldn't need to do everything myself. (*Hanna*, Fin)

> Although you're a unit by yourself, you're not fully developed if you can't get on with others ... Because you can't live yourself. ... I don't care how strong you think you are, you need someone to be watching your back for you; and if you think you can watch your back, you'd better have it against a wall. And you've got to make sure that wall is impenetrable. (*Valerie*, Bri)

Having a partner would mean having someone to talk to, to cuddle, to go out with, to sleep with, to have sex with, to share the joy and pain of day-to-day life, and someone to have children with.

Many women who emphasised positive aspects of partnerships gave very idealised descriptions of them:

> It must be wonderful if you've got a lovely relationship with a man and that you're both doing it together, that must be the best thing in the world. (*Emily*, Bri)

But many of them thought that their ideal fantasies and dreams did not match up to reality:

> I go round with this idea that I want to be married and have children. But it's an idealised thing. I'm beginning to realise that. (*Lorna*, Bri)

The fantasies were connected with increasingly dominant perceptions of marriage and partnerships as companionate, supportive enclaves in a harsh world, where two equal people form a unit stronger than either of them, but with similar inputs.

> I really wish that I had someone that I saw every day and could develop a relationship with him. Someone to sleep with every night and someone that I was real comfortable with and was just really part of sharing things. (*Sue*, Cal)

Some women have a desperate yearning for a close partnership; some are actively looking for it; some would like it as 'an icing on the cake' (*Gina*, Bri); some are open to, but not too concerned about, partnerships; some are not interested.

The perceptions of positive aspects of partnerships are congruent with prevailing cultural representations and with familism. But when talking about negative aspects of marriage and relationships single women diverge from popular conceptions: marriages restrict and confine; women lose their independence in marriages; women make many compromises; they are oppressed; concentrate on meeting the needs of others; have little space for themselves; they become dependent; they cannot pursue their dreams.

> The danger in marriage is always that the woman has to deny herself an awful lot. She might get something but she has to deny certain needs as well. She has to deny a certain amount of her personality. She does become a secondary object, I think. A woman who is married has to struggle very hard to develop an individual self. Otherwise it's just immersed and lost. (*Ella*, Bri)

> I think ... there are lots of women ... who believe that their sole purpose in life is, you know, to – to make men happy. (*Molly*, Bri)

> I would like to be in a relationship very badly but I think also it would be very hard because I would feel somehow confined. (*Frances*, Cal)

> I see relationships like the opiate of women, I mean, love is the opiate, I mean that's where most women put their energy. (*Christine*, Cal)

> Women who are alone, they have to be able to do things which women who are married necessarily don't have to. You see helplessness is part of femininity in a way, so women alone, they don't have that helplessness in a way that married women do. (*Rosa*, Fin)

> There are women who need to be oppressed before they feel they are anything. (*Kaisa*, Fin)

Women made references to having observed good marriages which were companionate, with both partners having maintained their own space. But overall marriages and partnerships meant, for these single women, loss of space, of autonomy, of individuality, of independence and of a sense of separateness. I shall return to this discussion in Chapter 8.

The construction of sexual difference is based on binary oppositions: women and men are different, but complement each other. Cockburn argues that a new woman envisioned by feminists is 'complete without a complement'. Many single women emphasise that, as they can rely on themselves, and are *not prepared to make compromises*, they are not likely to be able to establish and maintain partnerships.

> I would greatly resist being anybody's servant, if you like. ... I don't want to be anybody's little skivvy bit, you know, and ... I don't expect to be either. It really annoys me when men expect you to sort of serve them. So I suppose there's that aspect which makes me more abrasive than some women. (*Lynne*, Bri)

> I don't think I'm supposed to be like this, confident and ready to go out and take what I want in a way, but I am. (*Caroline*, Bri)

> I've never had that thing about accepting a man's authority. ... I'm not the sort of woman who gets controlled by men. Nobody tells me what to do. (*Miriam*, Bri)

> I ain't willing to sit back and cater to no man. You know, usually you got to like me for what I am or how I am or how I don't like to do this and I don't like to do that, and if I don't like to do it I ain't gonna do it. (*Bridget*, Cal)

> The idea of having to, now, suddenly split decisions with somebody else that I make for myself all the time, every day, quickly and my way, and very much to my liking, to suddenly have to give away part of that is giving away something that I don't really want to give away. (*Rita*, Cal)

> I've never felt any need to please men. (*Minna*, Fin)

In comments like these a contrast made between abrasive single women and accommodating married women is evident. That modern women are accommodating in relationships is borne out by research (for example, Hochschild, 1989; Coward, 1992).

Women who have a sense of self-confidence and self-worth have undergone a learning process in being single, and are still open to relationships, repeatedly emphasising that they have great expectations of the kind of partnership they would accept.

> If I ever find somebody that I really think that I could share everything, yeah, that I share political opinions, that I share the same goals in life, that is prepared really to put others before himself, that he's prepared to give of himself to what he believes, perhaps then I could say I might consider this person. But I haven't. (*Clara*, Bri)

> I would have wanted to be married to somebody that considered me an equal partner. (*Peggy*, Cal)

> I have become quite demanding. (*Laura*, Fin)

The strength of the above comments indicates why the majority of single women are voluntary, even though they raise negative aspects of singleness, experience insecurity, depression and loneliness at times, long for partnerships and dream about soul-mates. They consider the price to be paid in compromises necessary in maintaining partnerships too high. Having been through a lengthy learning process in relying on themselves, being their own protection, being responsible for themselves and making their own decisions makes them reluctant to unlearn what they have achieved. There were also economic factors in the inclination to remain single. The average income of women is lower than that of men, and marriage has been one avenue of social mobility for women. Single women in this study made references to positive aspects of controlling their own income, however small; this gave them a sense of security and self-reliance. Several divorced women recounted drastic experiences of impoverishment after divorce, because of unequal sharing of resources.

The stereotype of an old maid who could not 'get' a man is not applicable to these single women. The majority of them had been in a position where they opted not to pursue marriages and partnerships. Only a few said that they had been rejected by a lover; they could not have a man they loved and were not interested in men who were available. The modern stereotype of a single woman who does not want a man is not entirely applicable either. Though women were critical of men and marriages, and emphasised high standards they would apply to a partner, many were sad that the kind of equal relationships they wanted were not available to them. Some women regret not having partnerships; for others a boy- or girlfriend is necessary, though not a close, intense live-in relationship. The majority of women have not consciously chosen to be single.

But the picture is more complex still. Many women refer to not being *able* either to form or to maintain relationships. In some cases it is evident that this is due to their unwillingness to make compromises and to fulfil a role expected of them by men. Other cases are less clear. *Lynne* (Bri) referred to herself as 'abrasive' and said she was able to live without men. She continues: 'Most people feel better if they're attached. And I suppose I feel acutely uncomfortable if I'm attached and slightly better if I'm on my own.' Her difficulties in attachment may well be connected with her criticism of prevalent patterns of relationships, where 'women will tolerate all kinds of things' because they are unable to remain on their own. *Rebecca* (Cal) considers herself to have been unable to form relationships: 'I get very upset whenever any man becomes very interested. I feel that I have to defend myself.' Though *Rebecca* refers to her psychic constitution and connects this with her family background, she adds: 'Also in those days you were supposed to let a man pay for you and I felt bought.' Again *Rebecca*'s reactions can be connected to a rebellion against codes of traditional femininity. *Laura* (Fin) talks about a series of difficult relationships, where there have been tremendous power struggles, and concludes that 'there may be something in me that makes men want to put me down' and considers herself unable to form lasting relationships. But her independent lifestyle (a freelance reporter who travelled a great deal) went against prevailing notions of femininity. *Martha* (Cal) assumes that there 'is something in her' which makes it difficult to make commitments. She has no assumptions about what that might be, and I was unable to find any clues. *Reija* (Fin) tells of a good relationship she had, which she had to break up, because she was unable to adjust emotionally: 'I accepted my own original self.' *Betsy* (Bri) says she is very keen to establish a partnership, especially in order to have children. At the same time she feels ambivalent, because then 'you have no other option'. This worries her because 'I have a very strong thing about always wanting an easy exit. It's not just psychological, it's physical as well. I like to sit in the front of the car so I can get out easily.'

I am unable to analyse psychological aspects of women – it is possible that the personal biographies of women discussed above have produced a weaker ability to form relationships – but connections between their psychic structures and the social structures they inhabit can be made. These women are not necessarily engaged in explicit, articulate rebellion, but they may be rebels in their everyday lives, even though this is not consciously expressed, and even though they have doubts about themselves and their actions.

The learning processes single women frequently referred to were indicated in an interesting way in the context of relationships. Some women talked about 'holding back' their emotions; they had experienced strong feelings of love in the past, and now tried to avoid them.

> I keep myself more to myself, you know, whereas before I went a hundred per cent with all my feelings ... now I think I've learned to sort of be a bit more in control of my emotions. ... I think I'm probably holding back a bit more and concentrating on myself. (*Greta*, Bri)

> It's not a relaxing thing, to be in love with someone at all, I don't think. ... I have an easy life now, no heart-strings and not wishing anyone to phone. ... I absolutely loved with all of me. (*Betsy*, Bri)

> I just went into this thing and I just gave myself up. (*Sue*, Cal)

Women have learned to 'hold back' either because they find the intensity of their emotions disruptive in their own lives, because they fear becoming dependent, or because men are frightened of women showing strong feelings. Lesbian single women also shared worries about partnerships, the energy required to maintain them, and patterns of dependence and fusion among lesbian couples. Women with disabilities hold back in relationships; in particular, attachments between able-bodied and disabled require strong barriers to be crossed.

There was a group of women (about a quarter) who had had extremely bad experiences with men. It is difficult to make clear judgements about these; I counted, for example, those women who said they had been raped, who had been physically beaten or threatened by partners or other men, who had been seriously cheated in marriage or divorce proceedings, and whose boyfriends or husbands had been alcoholics or drug addicts.

> I married a maniac ... a psychopath. And this was a man that was living in a small college town for about nine years. You know, he owed money all over ... he was teaching but he'd never finished university. ... He was very attractive ... people liked to have him around ... And no one enquired too closely into his personal life. ... [We had] a sort of whirlwind romance and we were married ... And, you know, one thing after another – creditors started calling up ... And when I confronted him with all this stuff, he tried to kill me. So I left. (Bri)

> We separated behind him gambling and not working and I was battered and he used to beat my ass. And – – – I just decided it was time for me to go. And he didn't believe I would go until the day I left. (Cal)

When we were going out together I did not see that this guy had problems with alcohol. I didn't understand how serious it was. ... I had lived in a relatively stable family, and there weren't really people around who had alcohol problems. [We got married] and it just got worse. The drinking periods got longer and he got more aggressive and started knocking me about. ... Then I reached a turning point ... [I had been away from home on a course for a week] ... I came home and started organising the divorce the next day. (Fin)

These women were relieved to be by themselves and did not have idealised notions of male–female relationships. They were unlikely to trust men and most of them thought they were likely to remain single.

Over a third of the women had boy- or girlfriends. For some these relationships were important and satisfactory, and made a great difference in how they viewed being single. They had the 'fun' side of partnerships without needing to cope with everyday realities. Some of the relationships were very loose because one party or the other was unwilling to make an increased commitment, because they lived in different towns or countries, or because, in some cases, the boy- or girlfriend was married or cohabited. Some women preferred the relationships to remain loose because of dissatisfactions and problems in the relationship, and they were happy to maintain the relationships on a non-committal basis. Others would have wanted greater commitment from their partners, and found it painful when they did not obtain it; these women were often involuntary singles, or voluntary temporary singles, who were interested in marriage (or cohabitation) in the future. Those who were happy to maintain a loose relationship felt that closer relationships would invade their space and would entail more compromises; they were voluntary stable singles, not interested in marriage.

Sexuality and the modern tightrope of normality

Around the biological sex of females and males a whole edifice of cultural, historical, economic and sexual power relations of gender are constructed. Representations supporting the gender division include concepts of difference and complementarity which assume sexual content. That is, sexualities of women and men are considered to be differentially constructed and complementary. It seems impossible to consider single women without considering sexuality. The conception of women as asexual was turned over by sexologists whose work contained assumptions about the necessity of sexual experiences for 'normal', 'healthy' adults (Jeffreys, 1985; Räisänen, 1991). Yet traditional familial ideology contains a moral code whereby women are supposed to engage in sexual relations inside marriage, whilst assumptions about 'the nature' of male sexuality contain a double morality: male sexuality is characterised by impulses and drives which are not easily contained (Wilson, 1983; Jeffreys, 1985; Hollway, 1987). Therefore difference and complementarity does not mean the meeting of equal, autonomous participants in sexual relations.

In the context of assumptions about female sexuality women are represented as 'good' or 'bad'. Alongside representations of women as asexual mothers there is a picture of untamed female sexuality which must be controlled. Theorists have referred to the 'dread of women' (Theweleit, 1987; Cockburn, 1988). The possibility of the autonomous sexuality of women is threatening to men; hence single women can be considered a challenge. Women are controlled through sexuality; Lees (1986), in her study of adolescent girls, notes the importance of girls safeguarding their sexual morality when constructing their sexual identities. She analyses the tightrope girls walk when establishing themselves within the continuum of 'slags' and 'drags'; they should appear to be neither sexually available nor unfeminine. Willis (1977) and Wood (1984), for example, have studied how boys make these categorisations.[1]

How do single women construct, negotiate and express their sexuality? Contradictory trends provide the context for this negotiation: on the one hand, women as autonomous sexual beings are considered a threat; on the other hand, there is considerable diversity in actual sexual practices – radical approaches to sexuality have emphasised politics of lifestyle and difference, and large numbers of people live outside the institution of marriage. Hence there may be increasing scope for single women in their construction of sexuality, though the New Right has included conservatism on sex/gender in a renewed onslaught on liberalisation of attitudes on sexuality. AIDS and moral panic connected to it have also influenced sexual attitudes and practices recently. Single women are faced with control *of* their sexuality and control *through* sexuality.

Sexuality is an intimate and personal area. Simon (1987) found that many women in her interviews were reluctant to discuss it. The majority of single women here were willing to discuss sexuality,[2] though there were variations in how much they wanted to discuss it. Overall their responses were somewhat surprising; they did not talk a great deal about moral attitudes and cultural representations constraining their sexuality, but concentrated more on connections between sexuality and intimacy. About half the women were active sexually at the time of the interview; the rest were celibate. The general picture on the basis of information on sexuality is that single women connect sexuality with intimacy and relationships; they are not interested in casual sex; many of them are or have been celibate at least periodically; and they consider their views on sexual morality to be personal rather than a consequence of prevailing attitudes.

Sexuality and intimacy

That intimacy is an important and difficult area for single women is evident in their discussion of sexuality. Though there was variation in the importance attached to sexuality, there were repeated assertions that sex as such was not what they missed most.

> There have been times when I have felt just crushingly lonely and what I felt lonely for is an intimacy of mind, more than anything else. I don't think in pure sexual terms. I'm a very sexual woman, but I don't – I have women friends who talk about being quite horny as though – – – sex is a thing ... sort of compartmentalised and self-contained. I don't work that, I don't think that way, my mind doesn't work that way. (*Rita*, Cal)
>
> I do like sex and I miss that ... but ... it's not about sex per se, it's about intimacy. (*Lynne*, Bri)
>
> Sex on its own, I'd rather go without it. It's all the things that go with it that I'm after. (*Emily*, Bri)
>
> I have a tremendous need for closeness. It's more that than sex. A need for closeness and gentleness. (*Laura*, Fin)

There are some exceptions.

> I've got a little ... ongoing dalliance; he's married ... He and I sort of meet in a hotel occasionally ... We can do it illicitly and we can creep about the hotel – – – We both enjoy it. ... I don't have any emotional connection with him ... It's just sort of frolicking about that's fun, and the wickedness. (*Tina*, Bri)

Miriam has two lovers, whom she meets regularly, if not frequently; she views these relationships in functional terms – they satisfy her sexual

needs. *Miriam* has, she says, 'a masculine attitude to sex'.
If women missed sex, most of them thought it was freely available.

> There are many men out there who'd love to have sex, right, I mean, no problem. But you know, to me ... it has to be right ... the emotional, the romance, you know, the passion. And those things don't happen every day. (*Shoshana*, Cal)

> I think some men see themselves as doing women a favour by going to bed with them. They think, 'Oh, she must be lonely, must be hard up.' (*Martha*, Cal)

It is generally not difficult for women in metropolitan areas to find sexual partners, except for retired or disabled women. Yet most women do not engage in casual sex.

Casual sex

It is clear that if sexual needs are connected with intimacy and companionship, casual sex is not a satisfactory solution. Many women had had 'one-night stands' and short affairs in the past, but were no longer interested in them.

> I had one night stands ... but it sometimes highlights the lack of a satisfying relationship so, I mean, it would be kind of ironic. (*Frances*, Cal)

> I used to have one-night stands; I went anywhere, and nothing mattered to me. At some point it became boring – because there were no emotions involved, it just happened. Nowadays ... there has to be some emotional content to it. (*Ursula*, Fin)

> [Casual affairs] don't satisfy me, I mean I might miss it, but in the end they don't satisfy. I mean I have so many experiences, but now I think of the next day too. (*Reija*, Fin)

> I used to go round with this girl – we tried it [casual affairs with men] and thought, hell, this is stupid ... it lost its shine. (*Soili*, Fin)

Experimentation with sexual practices was a possibility framed by liberalisation of attitudes to sexuality. Many women said they were never interested in casual sex; for those who were, the appeal palled after some time. There were several reasons for this. Casual sex did not offer the kind of intimacy that most women hoped for. Experiences of exploitation led some women to discontinue casual sex. For example, *Lorna* does not engage in short affairs anymore:

> That was actually a decision I made eight years ago because I – I had a couple of very peculiar relationships with men, one of whom I ended up having to take to a mental hospital and the other who ended up in prison for rape. (*Lorna*, Bri)

Some discontinued because they had themselves been the ones who were being exploitative:

> I was acting out of – – – an aggressive independence. And so in some ways I was trying to act like a man, so I was using men and I would sleep with them briefly and throw them over. (*Frances*, Cal)

Women who have experienced difficulties when displaying the intensity of their feelings want to be able to control their emotions. In relation to sexuality, throwing oneself into an experience with someone not well known makes women vulnerable.

> I think my heart gets broken too easily. (*Rachel*, Cal)

> I think there's a lot of pain involved, for me anyway ... I can't really dissociate sex from feelings. ... And therefore if it is just going to be a one-night stand there's bound to be some kind of emotional turmoil going on. (*Lorna*, Bri)

Thirdly, women emphasised connections between mind and body; casual sex was connected to the body. The social contract was based on an assumption that women are located in the natural sphere (Chapter 2); their embodiment assumes different meanings. Conceptions of embodiment are so heavily culturally inscribed that such judgements are difficult to make. Research indicates that women are more likely to connect emotional closeness with sexuality than men, who are more likely to connect having sex with pleasure, conquest and relief of sexual tensions (Leigh, 1989). This was evident here too, in the emphasis on intimacy, companionship and emotional closeness. Intense sexual experiences involve a range of feelings and sensations:

> I never find [casual relationships] satisfying and I never really went for them. ... I never sort of use sex just as an outlet ... I could never use my body just as my body, I couldn't split myself into these bits. (*Ella*, Bri)

> It's better if you have an emotional relationship with it ... it's like a meeting of the mind and the body together, and it makes it zap. (*Valerie*, Bri)

> I need [sex] but my need is not physical. Unfortunately I can't separate the two, mental and physical. I have both of them together, and if they are not in step, separately they don't get by. (*Galina*, Fin)

In Chapter 8 I shall explore the possibilities and limitations of individualism for women, and ask whether single women are engaged in a process of constructing a particular sort of individuality.

Consideration of why single women (of this age group) are not interested in casual sex raises questions of power and sexuality (protecting oneself from exploitation), control (submission in unequal relationships leaves one open to being controlled) and dependence (caring in a situation lacking emotional closeness leads to vulnerability). If women and men are not equal structurally and culturally, permissiveness in sexuality does not constitute freedom of expression. Freedom means not only saying 'yes', but also saying 'no'. *Shirley* (Bri) went through a 'promiscuous' period: 'for a long time I thought I had no option ... but over the years I've realised that I have had a choice.' Growing assertiveness for women is a question of having sex only if they want to, but also of having sex which is satisfying; 'I didn't think very much of myself or I didn't really know what my own pleasure was ... I've learned that and ... now I feel I can really sort of get what I want' (*Greta*, Bri).

Short affairs were not always thought of as casual. Women recounted experiences that were brief, but intense, intimate and pleasurable. I have described the general pattern in relation to casual sex above. There were exceptions to this. There were women who did engage in casual sex and had enjoyable experiences. Most of these women had not had casual sex before; moral pressures relating to sexuality had stopped them.

Sexual morality

Many women felt either that other people were not concerned about their sexual behaviour or, if they were, that this did not constitute a problem.

> I feel free, if I want to, to pursue a relationship. I don't have a problem with that anymore ... I'm free to do what I want. (*Violet*, Cal)

I don't trip on what other people think. I do what I want to do. (*Bridget*, Cal)

I don't do one-night stands. That's not moral, it's 'cos I don't want to. (*Betsy*, Bri)

I think it's most important that people judge themselves. ... If you think about the reactions of others, I mean they are in a sense always negative towards people who are not 'in' the system. (*Rosa*, Fin)

I couldn't care less about what other people think. Anyway, it was the opposite at some point, you know that people thought [not having casual affairs] was strange – that sort of casual attitude was favoured. (*Ulla*, Fin)

Traditional sexual morality did not seem relevant to many women; nor did they think it was relevant if other people upheld such morality.

Though women claimed that they were not influenced by traditional morality in the way they felt about sexuality, many were concerned about the *consequences* of it: they wanted to guard their reputation.

my reputation which ... I guard, because ... the men's feedback systems are so much more efficient than women's. ... I mean I go dancing every weekend, and I go to a place that has a reputation as being a place where women go to pick up men of a certain type or category; and I've gone in there, I know I'm stereotyped. (*Caroline*, Bri)

I don't like casual affairs ... I don't care about them anymore. Also the circles are so small ... in Helsinki. Everybody knows everybody in some way. (*Harriet*, Fin)

There were more comments about the guarding of one's reputation in Finland. This was connected with the size of the city rather than stricter sexual morality; compared to the San Francisco Bay Area and London, women have less anonymity in Helsinki.

There were also women who connected their disinclination to engage in casual sex, or sex outside marriage, with moral issues. Most of these women were either from religious backgrounds or were religious themselves, and perhaps active in the church. They expressed contentment with their religious conviction and did not experience great contradictions and tensions; if religious women experienced a strong desire to have a sexual relationship, they did so. Though *Naomi* (Cal) thought that sex outside marriage was a sin, she referred to a god who was loving and forgiving, so she was able to have a relationship that included sexuality. Further, being involved in the church, and in social networks connected to it, offered protection from sex; men respected the attitudes of women. A few women who had had strong religious convictions criticised this protection as a denial of sexuality. They, and a small number of other women who had experienced moral pressures, talked about 'giving themselves permission', 'stopping to say "no" to themselves' and 'shoving away the view that sex belongs to marriage'.

Many women had, at some point in their lives, wrestled with questions of morality. In the context of sexuality some women made references to a learning process: freeing themselves from conventional morality in order to set their own standards.

> I'm finally able to do that, not judge myself. I don't try to be a good girl all the time. (*Amy*, Cal).

Amy had one casual affair after her marriage. Thereafter casual sex did not interest her, though one reason for valuing the relationship with her boyfriend was access to a sexual partner. The affair was a stepping stone which helped her to determine her own morality, but in connection with sexuality references to learning were not prevalent.

As very few women were opposed to sex outside marriage on moral grounds, those in relationships did not experience the sexual aspect of the relationship as a problem. For women who did not have boy- or girlfriends, access to sexuality was more difficult. Some of them missed sex, though a greater number said they missed sex combined with intimacy. Sexual tensions were dealt with through masturbation, engagement in physical activities or were channelled into creative pursuits such as music. Of course we do not need to concur with women's own perceptions about sexual morality and its influence on them. When they say they do not engage in casual sex in the absence of a regular sexual partner because sex is only satisfying when connected with intimacy, one may ask whether this is a product of female socialisation, which prevents them from taking what they want. This is an impossible question to answer; sexuality is socially and culturally constructed and cannot be contrasted to a notion of 'natural' sexuality. However interesting insights can be gained from the discussion of celibacy. Although women who are sexually active outside a romantic relationship are generally considered 'bad', women who do not engage in sex are considered 'odd'. Pressures on women are thus contradictory: to engage in sex and not to engage in sex.

Celibacy

Six women has always been celibate; 44 women had been celibate for varying periods.[3] In the past being unmarried was associated with celibacy. With the relaxation of restrictions in sexual attitudes celibacy became deviant and unmarried women came to be seen as 'unnatural', not just because they did not reproduce, but also because they were not sexually active. Though recently a renewed interest in celibacy can be detected as a response to AIDS and the spread of sexually transmitted diseases, single women are still likely to be perceived as deviant if they are sexually active, and deviant if they are not.

Of those who had always been celibate, one was disabled, two had religious convictions, one referred to her upbringing and two considered themselves asexual. Sexuality and celibacy was an uncomfortable issue for some of these women and they did not want to discuss it a great deal. For the severely disabled, sexual relationships with other disabled pose practical obstacles; with the able-bodied the obstacles are social and cultural. Women who were involved in the church had built up protective networks; one of the 'asexual' women had also managed to do so. Two women talked at greater length about pressures connected with celibacy.

> Most people would say, your sex life isn't normal. ... Men argue with me. ... You're supposed to want sex, so what's the matter with you? (*Rebecca*, Cal)

> It seems to be such an important part of so many people's lives and so much hype by the culture that you can't help being aware of the fact that you don't do that. (*Peggy*, Cal)

Only one (Californian) referred to possible shifts in attitudes to celibacy; in the context of the diversification of sexual practices it has become 'kinky but safe'.

Difficulties and possibilities connected with celibacy were highlighted further by women who had been celibate for long periods but not always. Some felt regretful about their celibacy:

> I don't see anything inherently uplifting in celibacy. (*Laura*, Fin)

Some felt ambivalent:

> I will soon become identified with a sort of shrivelled up old spinster, I think. You know, I'm sure I shall start to be less and less likely to have a sexual

> relationship. ... I do like sex and I do miss that ... I have missed having a full sexual life in a broader sort of sense, and I – I regret that. ... I do feel quite grumpy actually [laughs] (*Lynne*, Bri)

> [If] you don't have sex and you don't have physical affection except in a very limited way ... that's a huge deprivation, one which, however, I don't feel. But I know because it's like when you're cold you often can't remember what it was like when you were hot, so I've sort of forgotten what it's like to have it and I don't miss it. But I know about myself and I'm a very affectionate and passionate person, sexual person, when I have somebody that I love and I really enjoy it a lot, it's very important to me ... I've made several attempts in the past to try and rectify that by sleeping with somebody that I don't really like – – – particularly or don't have strong feelings about or I'm not in love with and it's, it's usually a fiasco. I mean, I don't mean sexually, necessarily, but emotionally – – – that person sometimes – – – gets very attached very quickly, women are apt to. And then you have to deal with feeling like a man, guilty that you're not interested ... So I haven't had casual sex [that] worked and – – – as I say, I don't – I'm not falling in love with anyone so I don't really have much choice. I mean, it's not a decision in the sense that if I – – – felt attracted to somebody I would pursue it. (*Christine*, Cal)

On the personal level celibacy was considered, by these women, a contradictory experience. They connected their celibacy with not having met anyone they were sufficiently attracted to in order to pursue a relationship, and with their reluctance to have casual affairs.

But there were also a few women who felt positive about celibacy and considered it a conscious choice they had made.

> I'm celibate because I truly choose to and not because I don't have an opportunity. It's a lifestyle that I wish upon myself. I consider it healthy. I don't want to sleep with a lot of partners. I don't want that. I want to feel good about myself. (*Carlotta*, Cal)

> I don't need relationships, I don't need sex. ... I feel absolutely great about [celibacy]. ... I feel as if it's a choice. ... The more I talk about myself being celibate, the more, strangely enough, I find that ... there are celibate people ... who are happy to – to lead a life which is uncluttered, uncomplicated in some ways by ... using sexuality. (*Molly*, Bri)

Channelling sexual energy into other interests and activities did not seem like negative compensation, but positive sublimation, as alternatives these women pursued were of great interest to them.

There were references to social pressures to be sexually active.

Partnerships and sexuality 125

> I think in the last ten years when I've not been having a sexual relationship, I've had a very keen awareness that the vast majority of guys see this as a waste. As though I'm some kind of receptacle, you know, a commodity that isn't being used. (*Caroline*, Bri)

> We're constantly told that coupledom and sexual relationships are important – you know, you got to have love, ecstacy and, and – passion, so that that makes our expectations a bit peculiar. So that people are not ready to take it easy, but there's ... unnecessary tug and pull among young people who have to acquire experiences, and among middle-aged who still have to try. You know there are pressures to make accomplishments, so that a person who has not got a sexual partner or a partner is seen by others as incomplete. (*Reija*, Fin)

In this context of emphasis on sexuality, celibacy could be seen not only as a problem but also as an achievement.

> I've got a great blast out of not ... having a sexual relationship, and I've actually got a thrill out of turning guys down when they've approached me sexually. (*Caroline*, Bri)

If sexual relations incorporate unequal power between women and men (Holland *et al.*, 1990) then withdrawing from them can give one a sense of being in a powerful position. If women have had negative experiences when they have approached their sexual partners as equal, and have found themselves to have been used and/or abused, then the illusion of equality is shattered. Single women did not necessarily express a general critique of conceptions of male sexuality and power connected with masculinity; lesbian women also made references to being used or abused in sexual relations among women. Women were more likely to withdraw gradually from sexual activity and drift into celibacy without having made a decision, and felt ambivalent about it. Several women said their sexual interests had declined as they were getting older. There is contradictory evidence for reduced levels of sexual interest. It is difficult to dissociate effects of social and cultural understandings, the effect of individual biographies and physical, biological changes. It is difficult to discern when we give messages to our bodies and when our bodies give messages to us. It is interesting that a few women talked about gaining weight as they stopped having sexual relationships; they thought that this was a protective layer that signalled to themselves and to others that they were not available.

Sexuality is seen as an important aspect of human experiences, as well as a fundamental psychological drive and a physical need. Though such conceptions can be oppressive to women (see Jeffreys, 1985) and ensure their availability to men, feminists have also emphasised the importance of women being able to pursue their sexual preferences free from moral censure. That women lack access to positive sexual practices is a deprivation imposed by male defined sexuality, and the use/abuse of male power in sexual relations. It is difficult, from many angles, to consider celibacy positive. Definitions of 'normality' are complicated and social, cultural, moral and psychic aspects combine for some women in such a way that celibacy is a viable, if at times ambivalent, sexual stance for them. If such a stance is labelled as deviant, this can be connected with the sexual contract preceding the social contract, where women are seen to be located in the natural sphere, and connected to their bodies differently from men (Chapter 2). Not being sexually active in heterosexual relationships means, in this context, not being like a 'woman'.

Conclusion

Both a sexually active and a celibate single woman are seen, in a sense, as aberrations in the context of the establishment of sexual difference. Greater tolerance apart, we can still discern vestiges of the attribution of 'a third sex' to single women. Classification and framing of categories (Bernstein, 1975) have shifted from strong to weak, but have not disappeared. Though single women today are in a different position from spinsters of the nineteenth century and old maids of the 1950s, marital status has not disappeared as a crucial category in establishing normality and deviation from it.

When asked whether they felt they were viewed as sexually available, women's responses were both affirmative and negative – those who said no thought they were feared. Either way it seems that single women are widely considered a threat to men and to marriages. Richardson (1988) has researched single women who had sexual liaisons with married men. On the basis of her analysis it seems difficult to view single women as a threat: their relationships with married men were characterised by a power imbalance where 'the male has greater structural and social psychological resources because of his marital status' (p. 219).

Lives of women are judged against a popular construction of the happy, companionate marriage (Chandler, 1991). Though single women, to some extent, also judge their lives in relation to partnerships, in practice most of them have few illusions about the ease of constructing or maintaining partnerships which are equal. Involuntary singles nevertheless yearn for marriage or partnerships. But the majority, voluntary singles, either are not interested or are only interested if any compromises required are balanced by positive gains. Though women frequently refer to their personal characteristics and psychic make-up, these are connected with social structures. Sexuality is also socially constructed. Changes in sexual practices have provided women with greater freedom, but have also made them more available to men (Chandler, 1991). Temporary or long-term celibacy is a response adopted by many single women vis-à-vis the latter trend. I have so far talked about their experiences of singleness mainly in the context of particular themes. I shall now consider 'singleness' itself more directly.

7
On being single

I shall now focus on the ways in which women experience being single, how they perceive pleasures and gains, difficulties and tensions in singlehood, and how they react to views and perceptions of others around them. Both positive and negative aspects ar discussed. I shall not try to conclude as to which aspects are predominant; such a judgement would belie the complexity of women's experiences. It is useful to bear in mind, nevertheless, the context set in Chapter 3: the majority of these women are voluntary, if not voluntary stable, singles.

Old maids

There are both continuities and changes in the way single women are viewed, how they perceive themselves and in the framework of possibilities and limitations that contextualise these. This is evident in the co-existence of 'negative' and 'positive' stereotypes of 'fictive' single women. Are they seen as old maids who could not get a man, or as modern career women who have not wanted one?

There was a sense of ambivalence about the old maid stereotype in the interviews. Some women brought it up themselves, but others were less certain of its existence. The perception of single women as old maids still has some prevalence, though.

> I think they're still lurking there: 'Why are you on your own?', 'Why haven't you any children?'; you can sort of hear it [laugh] you know, ticking away there (*Liz*, Bri)

> After a certain age, if you're not married it's because you're not desirable. (*Norma*, Cal)

> It is dependent a bit, of course, on how old you are. But maybe at my age not being married is a bit – there's easily this idea that she didn't *get* (a man) [laughs]. (*Laura*, Fin)

The old maid stereotype is related to a perception of single women as lacking something, being incomplete, deviating from the norm and the normal.

Single women move typically in networks consisting of a number of other single women. Therefore many did not personally come across old maid stereotypes, though these still existed.

> The people I'm together with are a bit similar like me – – – but I suppose if you go into other areas of society I think it would be negative. (*Greta*, Bri)

Networks consisting of important people are crucial in protecting single women from negative perceptions that exist; such perceptions do not touch them in their day-to-day lives. Women did not usually refer to negative stereotypes in popular culture.

Not all women thought that single women are seen through the old maid stereotype:

> I think that people ... are becoming much more aware of the importance of treating people as individuals and regarding them for their own worth rather than stereotyping them ... you're a 'this' or you're a 'that'. (*Peggy*, Cal)

Single women connected changes in people's attitudes with the increase of singleness. The incidence of singleness and single parenthood is particularly prevalent among black women; this is reflected in *Naomi*'s comments:

> Nowadays that's not a stigma on single women because ... everybody's doing it ... because most families now is raised by single parents ... so there's really no stigma on it. (*Naomi*, Cal)

The structural, cultural and ethnic backgrounds, and the present social locations of *Naomi* and *Peggy*, are different. I did not find any particular features which connected women who thought negative stereotypes still existed and women who did not.

For a few women an 'old maid' was not simply a stereotype. They thought it described some single women, who were bitter, who were sexually frustrated or asexual, who desperately would want to get married, and who cling to men seeking available partners.

> There are surprisingly many women who are bitter about life, and according to my classification they are somehow typical old maids. They have not found their own sexuality and womanhood and these sort of wonderful things. Somehow one would wish them at least a night [laughter] with some good man. I do see that sort of old maid phenomenon in existence. (*Hanna*, Fin)

There were also women who related the old maid stereotype to themselves, in different ways. *Lynne* was worried about becoming like a stereotypical old maid:

> Probably I shall become more like that stereotype. I'm sure. Get more cranky as I get older [laugh], gather more cats around me and – you know, all the usual cranky stuff. (*Lynne*, Bri)

Hanna was determined not to associate herself with the stereotype:

> At my age I could be an inveterate old maid, but I don't want to be. I don't know how much others experience me as having that sort of old-maid bitterness and catcare and that sort of stuff. I don't want that role, but I sort of play with that idea, and in a sense hold it as a point of honour not to be like that. (*Hanna*, Fin)

Anni used the term 'old maid' in referring to herself, in order to *confront* other people's unspoken assumptions before they were expressed:

> At work they readily use the word old maid. And I use it myself to make things easier for others. So that they don't need to think that now they're going to say 'hey, old maids' ... or something. (*Anni*, Fin)

A sense of caring and a willingness to put others at ease coexist with a sense of defiance in *Anni*'s comments. *Tina* expresses this defiance a more clearly:

> It just frustrates me that there's this sort of image that you're supposed to be eventually part of a couple, and I can imagine, once you get older, you've either got to be eccentric, you know, or you're a spinster. And I can see I'm gonna be eccentric [laughs], cultivate the eccentric image [laughs]. (*Tina*, Bri)

Other women were also explicitly or implicitly engaged in challenging the stereotype.

If single women were seen as 'old maids', this was not explained by reference to cultural and social pressures, and negative effects of the marginalisation of singles. The onus was placed on women who conformed to the stereotype because of their personal emotional problems or shortcomings. Such comments were not numerous, but were significant in the context of a more general strand of thinking among women interviewed – *putting a great deal of responsibility on individual people*. Most single women over 35 have had to confront their singleness, negotiate their stance in relation to it and construct as positive a life as possible on the basis of such a negotiation: therefore they see themselves as strong and determined. Women who have been less effective in challenging stereotypes may seem weak-willed and woolly-minded to them.

Many single women felt that the stereotype of an old maid was increasingly becoming a thing of the past. Older women referred to strong prejudices against single women having existed in their youth. Today a new and, on the surface, positive stereotype is applied to single women.

City singles

The stereotype of a modern single women cannot easily be conveyed by one phrase, like 'old maid'; the stereotype is a relatively recent phenomenon. A modern single woman is seen as urban, highly educated, relatively young, ambitious, single-minded, determined, active and a career woman. By rejecting marriage and children she has made a conscious choice to be single; she did not and does not want a man. She is unattached and free.

> I think [people] would see [my lifestyle] as very independent, and this was a choice and because she's a feminist ... It's not the total truth ... I don't know that it is that positive stereotype really. (*Liz*, Bri)

> I was thinking sort of about my family. They sort of – I'm trying to think of what sort of image they had of me. I'm sure that on some level they think I have this sort of carefree life, that I'm earning stacks of money, and can go visit them whenever I want, and have this sort of gay, frivolous lifestyle. And it's not like that. So I think it's rather a myth about the single lifestyle. It's not all it's cracked up to be, I don't think. It can be for some. (*Susan*, Cal)

> I think [my friends] think that I am so choosy that nobody is acceptable to me. (*Lea*, Fin)

On the surface seeing women as carefree city singles is more positive than seeing them as old maids. But negative aspects lurk behind the positive surface, as the above comments indicate.

The negative aspects are increasingly emphasised by the New Right (see Faludi, 1992, pp. 119–30): a modern single woman can be selfish, choosy, intent on an easy life, unwilling to make sacrifices or compromises, workaholic, carefree and so on. Whilst the old maid stereotype is something to live down, the modern stereotype is something to live down *and* to live up to. When confronted with this stereotype, single women relate themselves both to negative and positive aspects of it. Being considered a modern city single contributes to a process of exclusion. If you are considered selfish and your life is seen to lack emotional content, then you are to be pitied, no matter what compensations your lifestyle offers. If you are seen as glamorous and free, leading an active, exciting life, you are defined as something 'other than me'. Differences between single and married women are underlined and contribute to the process of exclusion.

> It's glamorous to your friends, to your married friends especially, because they think that they're the ones going to go home and cook for their husband and, you know, feed the kids and then it's like 'You're gonna have all these excitements [over] the weekend.' And it's – you don't, right? And then you think I should because they're expecting that from me, right? So, you know, it gets to be a problem. ... Lot of my friends say, 'Oh, I envy you, you know.' You know, 'I envy you.' 'You're single and happy and you don't have nothing to do, you don't have any children.' ... I mean, you know, what do you want to do with us, we're boring, you know, married couple. They all say that and I did spend the weekend with a married friend of mine, last weekend. And she keeps saying, 'I'm sorry, you're so bored', you know, and 'there's nothing here for you to do'. And I said 'I came to visit you guys and besides I don't have that exciting life.' 'Oh come on! I bet you do!'. Figure [that out]. They don't believe you, they really don't. (*Shoshana*, Cal)

Single women in metropolitan areas have to balance contradictory conceptions of what they are and how they live. Interaction with other single women in a similar position facilitates the evasion of stereotypical perceptions moving beyond them: 'I'm more concerned with how I feel about myself and my life than I am concerned about what other people think about myself and my life' (*Liz*, Bri).

Reactions from others

When women talked about reactions of other people, there were traces of themes contained in traditional and modern stereotypes. Being single often still has to be explained; in particular, never marrying is considered atypical.

Rite of passage

Accomplishing a transition from childhood to adulthood is more complex for women who do not marry than for those who do (Chapter 4). Historically 'citizens' and 'individuals' were male constructions (Chapter 2) and though women have been pushing the boundaries of citizenship and individuality, these concepts have undergone only a partial transformation. Single women still have a somewhat problematic status which is constructed in the shadow of the 'family', in the context of familism.

> It's as if, you know, you are your parents' responsibility until that responsibility is transferred to a partner. (*Lorna*, Bri)

> Every time I see [my mother] I slip into being a child ... what's always there is that I'm still her family, but my sister's got this other little family; 'cos like when we all go round there – my sister usually goes with her husband and her children and then when it's time for them to go to take the children home, my mother's still being hostess. But then when they go, you know, she's relaxed, she takes her shoes off, because, you know, I'm still counted as her family. (*Gwen*, Bri)

> At one point my sisters were not real accepting of [me being single] ... at one point I did feel real isolated ... I mean, the impression she gave me was ... that I wasn't a real adult. (*Inez*, Cal)

> I still keep getting advice [from my mother] ... But she never talks – she says herself that it's a point of honour that she has never interfered in the lives of my sisters ... and has not guided them, as they are married and have families. She has never said to them do this or do that. So it has all been channelled so that – yes, I think I have had to struggle and I still struggle all the time. (*Anni*, Fin)

> [My parents] sort of clearly thought that when you have a man and you have got married you are somehow a fit member of society and that the man looks after some things. Then when I got divorced, they started to interfere in my life again. (*Laura*, Fin)

These comments indicate that the 'otherness' of women who are not attached to a family of procreation can assume very concrete substance.

A woman's social and societal position is ambivalent if it is not mediated through some reference point besides herself. Mothers in particular seem to be active in the process of differentiating between their married and single daughters. Perhaps this is based on their *implicit* recognition that the construction of their own social position has been dependent on family connections. For some mothers this recognition was *explicit*: a few daughters had been advised never to get married.

'What's wrong with you?'

The relevance of the old maid stereotype has declined in metropolitan areas, but descriptions by women of some of the attitudes they encounter still contained themes connected to that stereotype.

> If I come back to my parents' place, I think people do look upon me a little bit as somebody who needs to be pitied because she doesn't have a family and she *still* hasn't got a husband. (*Greta*, Bri)

> The person who is just dreadful is my mother. ... She defines me first of all as single, and she defines me first of all as 'This is Celia, the one that never got married.' (*Celia*, Bri)

> My mother in the old people's home always asks, 'Have you not got a man yet?' She somehow thinks that a woman needs a man to keep her. (*Eila*, Fin)

Reactions of members of the family were often referred to. But references to more general attitudes were also made by women.

> I think people think that, you know, if you're not married there must be something wrong with you. (*Shirley*, Bri)

> I think, unless you're still in a position to attract people, people will assume that you're single because you couldn't attract one rather than because you didn't like what you attracted. (*Caroline*, Bri)

> Well, maybe there is this idea, straight away, that yes, she did not get anybody and there must be something wrong with her. (*Helena*, Fin)

Women in the San Francisco Bay Area were least likely to have encountered assumptions that questioned their personal characteristics in relation to singlehood, but references to subtler formulations were made: 'I've gotten the message, whether it's spoken or implied, that "you weren't good enough".'

'I feel sorry for you'

Some women explained that members of their families of origin felt sorry for them. This was often a source of irritation, except for women who were *involuntary* singles.

> [My parents] are not happy because they know that I'd rather be in a relationship. (*Liz*, Bri)

> Oh, they're just longing for me to have a man. Because they know that I want one. (*Betsy*, Bri)

> My mother is sad about me being lonely ... and [some relatives] I think somehow feel sorry for me for being unhappy, that I have been left out in the cold. (*Helena*, Fin)

Less commonly some women said that their friends felt sorry for them.

> People just will not believe that you actually are perfectly happy as you are. I think most of my friends are unconvinced by my protestations that I'm happy single. (*Tina*, Bri)

> [A friend] said to me something like, well, what, she's lonely, she really would like to be in a relationship. I said, 'Oh, I've given up on all that' and she sort of looked at me and said: 'I feel sorry for you.' I couldn't believe it! You know, the patronizing thing. She feels so sorry for me! She's miserable cause she's lonely – I feel fine. (*Christine*, Cal)

Other people feeling sorry for you is more easily accepted by involuntary singles; to them it can indicate concern and caring. For *voluntary* singles it is infuriating.

'You're so lucky'

Reactions of others also indicate themes contained in the modern stereotype of a city single.

> People I know who are married, I mean they complain, you know. I mean sometimes they say to me that I'm lucky, I don't have a man around me all the time, you know. (*Judy*, Bri)

> [A married friend] goes, 'God, you're really lucky because look at all the things that you do and everything.' (*Shoshana*, Cal)

> I know that many people – women that is – are envious of my freedom – freedom in quotation marks. Precisely these people who are tied with their families because of small children or mortgages or something like that, whose present situation is that they would go around more if they could – many of these people have, over the years, let me know that they envy me because of my freedom and independence. (*Reija*, Fin)

'You're so lucky' attributions have negative as well as positive connotations, and place pressure on women who are on the receiving end. Many single women emphasised that their lifestyles had offered them pleasures and gains compared to married women with family responsibilities which required compromises (Chapter 6). But difficulties and losses, which particularly centred around intimacy or children, were also emphasised – one-dimensional attributions ignore these.

'What are you?'

In the nineteenth century single women confused categories; references were made to 'surplus' spinsters and 'the third sex' (Chapter 1). In the interviews there were no direct comments about the sex/gender of single women. But there were references indicating that single women were seen as 'incomplete' or to assumptions that they were not 'real' women because they did not live as women 'normally' do; that is, they did not have husbands and children. But there were numerous comments about people finding it *difficult to categorise* single women. They were often asked why they were not married.

> [On holiday] this woman suddenly in the middle of this great sort of huge drinking group or whatever, said, "And why are you not married?", she said [laugh]. I always remember this ... And it was just like the whole, you know, group kind of waited for the answer, you know: 'Why are you not married?' – – – I said 'well, 'cos I don't want to be' ... It's just this sort of assumption that it's odd, you know, 'Why aren't you?', 'Why aren't you with somebody, why are you like this?'. And – it's as if there's something wrong with you ... and perhaps there is, I mean I don't, you know, but I suppose – the normal thing to do or the average thing to do is to marry, isn't it? (*Lynne*, Bri)

Questioning about reasons for not being married implies that single women are seen as a problem. Being called to account for oneself can produce uncertainty, though some single women shrugged it off by laughing at such comments, or reacted defiantly.

Questions are particularly asked if a single woman *cannot* be categorised as an 'old maid': there is *not* anything obviously 'wrong' with her, she does not elicit pity and she appears to be comfortable with her life.

> They wonder, why on earth have you not got married, such a beautiful person, why has she not got married (laughter). So it is a sort of – a sort of inconceivable thing. (*Lea*, Fin)

> You know, it's not that I'm a horrible person, cause I'm very nice [laughs], so yeah, I think in general people do have a hard time accepting that. (*Kate*, Cal)

Old maid or city single stereotypes make people feel more comfortable with single women.

Single women are difficult to categorise, and the potential sexual threat that they are seen to pose (Chapter 6) becomes a broader threat to people's conceptions of themselves; they are forced to question their own lives, and they are confronted with the taken-for-granted familism.

> The question that has been asked of me very often is ... 'What do you want?'. As if, you know, the choice I made not to get married was because I am so difficult, or people will say, 'You're probably only interested in intellectual things', as if I'm ... truly sort of somebody which is just a mind and no emotions. I think peple find me very uncomfortable. ... The majority don't know what to make with me. I am not usually aggressive, so they can't make me out into this dragon that nobody really wants. I'm not ugly, therefore ... that I'm really selfish ... Sometimes it's an attack. ... very often I do make people uncomfortable. Because they can't put me in a category. (*Ella*, Bri)

> People don't really know what pigeon-hole a single women should be put in. Is it somehow enticing or interesting that she's unmarried, or is it a threat, and can a single woman somehow live her life to the full more than married people, and also – – – is her life somehow dreadfully miserable? There isn't sort of – it isn't sort of free and easy ... it's either idolising or commiserating. (*Saara*, Fin)

Numbers of single women have increased, particularly when they are defined as women who have no husbands. There was a process of liberalisation of attitudes in relation to family formation during the 1960s, 1970s and 1980s. But neo-conservative populism has gained ground. More negative connotations have been incorporated in modern stereotypical representations of single women. A notable example is provided by the film *Fatal Attraction*, where Alex, an attractive, independent single woman longs for a man and a child. She becomes deranged in her desperation and poses a symbolic and actual threat to the man she has picked, and her rage encompasses his whole family: 'Alex is a symbol of femininity, unpoliced by men, a femininity linked with neurosis, psychosis and madness' (Chapman, 1988, p. 246). Recent depictions of single women in popular culture have been part of a process of defining a modern single woman, placing her in a category – a search for an answer to the question: 'What are you?'[1]

Dealing with the reactions

Reactions of other people have no automatic, simple impact on the lives of single women. There is typically no *one* general reaction. For example, parents and relatives are more likely to make an issue of singleness than friends, older people are more likely to feel sorry for single women than younger people. Stereotypical labelling is particularly attached to single women by casual acquaintances and strangers. Singleness seems, if not a deviation, at least a parting from general norms. Ambivalent, negative reactions of others that single women report are only part of the story. Negative attributions do not necessarily concern them. Single women have their own social networks and are largely *protected* from negative attributions in their daily lives.

> Most of my friends accept me as I am. (*Lynne*, Bri)

> In the groups that I associate with, the alternative people, I don't feel that judgement so much. (*Rachel*, Cal)

> I move in those type of places where these sort of things are not emphasised. (*Lea*, Fin)

Single women above 30 have typically confronted their single status and most of them have dealt with it by becoming voluntary singles. They have also learned to ignore comments of others:

> Largely I don't pay any attention to it. And what I find is that people do accept me, you know, for myself. (*Shirley*, Bri)

> I've got a very good do-it-yourself system against it, but ... it does get through (occasionally). (*Celia*, Bri)

> Since I feel so strongly in myself that I'm not missing anything, that I have an extremely full life, and I've engineered the whole thing to my liking, [it] doesn't bother me. (*Kate*, Cal)

> I used to think of myself as unmarried, sort of, someone who was a surplus woman. And then also people's reactions were somehow ... they felt different than now that I get along with my own singleness. (*Saara*, Fin)

Women's responses to reactions of others were shaped by their networks, how they viewed themselves and by their local area. The majority of women in this study have been geographically mobile and many of them can make comparisons with other places. Many women have also been socially and/or culturally mobile and therefore have a range of reference points. Generally women said it had been more difficult to be single in the countryside or in small towns than in metropolitan areas. Thus it is easier to be single in Helsinki, in London or in the San Francisco Bay Area.

> There's a lot of single people in the city, but I've also chosen to be in places where it's acceptable. Bay Area, it's much more comfortable to be single than Seattle. ... Everything was done in couples. I mean everything. ... But here, as soon as I moved down here ... I felt much more comfortable being single. (*Sue*, Cal)

> This man was once very unpleasant to me – 'Don't you regret not having children and a family?' He was from the countryside, from [North of Finland]. You still get that there. (*Eila*, Fin)

> It's easier being a single woman in London. (*Ella*, Bri)

More specific references were also made; for example, it was easy to be single in specific parts of North London.

Women from ethnic minorities were less likely to be culturally isolated in metropolitan areas. In particular, highly educated single women of colour who might have experienced some differentiation in relation to their cultural origins, but also in relation to their current peers and colleagues, found it easier to construct supportive networks with other women like them. There were some examples of women having to seek distance from their own communities. *Amy* (Cal) felt left out from the Chinese community after her separation. *Rosa* (Fin) had decided not to be enmeshed in the Romany 'system', but to be an individualist who steers her course between the minority and majority cultures, drawing from both of them. Though women may feel that singleness is untypical in their cultures of origin, these cultures are important sources of strength, acceptance and solidarity; therefore they are willing to make an effort to be accepted despite their single status.

The incidence of singleness is high among African–Americans and among Afro-Caribbeans in Britain. For them networks of relatives and friends among their ethnic groups are crucially important when several overlapping processes of exclusion operate in mainstream cultures. Many women emphasised how significant the support they obtained was; Afro-Caribbean women who had children alone found a ready source of practical, financial and emotional help among their extended families. The resilience and flexibility of these extended families are highlighted by the fact that in the process of geographical mobility the families may have been split, but they have come together again. There are those for whom the pressures are too great and estrangement too advanced, so that reconstructing the kinship networks is difficult. In this study one woman was in that position.

Considering the reactions of others as experienced and perceived by single women indicates changes and continuities in their social status. I conclude this discussion by citing two contrasting remarks.

> The culture is so heavily into, you know, monogamous relationships. ... The world is made for couples, I think. And not for people who are single. (*Sue*, Cal)

> I don't think single women are a group that should be related to in any way. ... There are all sorts among them, all ages, all social groups, all sorts of educational levels, those who have children and those who don't, it's such a heterogeneous group; what shared characteristics could there be? We might as well say blue-eyed people. Or brown-eyed. That's how I see it. We live in such a plural society, that you can find all sorts of trends side by side. (*Ulla*, Fin)

Pleasures and gains

Western notions of absolute individualism imply that people are unitary entities. Analyses focusing on the construction of subjectivities emphasise the fragmentary, contradictory aspects of consciousness instead. Absolute individualism is connected particularly with the way men are represented; representations of women are more relative. When talking about the realities of their lives, single women are likely to express many facets. Often comments about positive aspects of singlehood were qualified by negative aspects. Such reflections are more congruent with conceptions of individual subjectivities as multiple and fragmented, rather than unitary (Chapter 2). *Being alone* was an important positive aspect of singleness.

> I love my own company. (*Molly*, Bri)

> I think it builds self-confidence because you have to, everything that you're doing in the world, your work and your play, you're doing it by yourself ... I love my solitude. (*Kate*, Cal)

> Being by yourself is quite a valuable thing. (*Helka*, Fin)

Being single enables women to be *in control:*

> I get to be creative and decide what I'm doing ... I feel very much in control of my life. (*Gwen*, Bri)

> I love being single, I like being able to do what I want to do when I want to do it, without having to answer to anyone. (*Bridget*, Cal)

> I couldn't feel any better. ... I made it clear to myself when I got the divorce ... that when I am alone I know what I've got. And if I have something in this hand, I have something also in the other hand, but if someone came along I might end up with two empty hands. (*Eeva*, Fin)

Being single allows women to engage in a great number of *activities* and to strive for many *achievements*:

> I don't want a man to have money; I wanna have some money myself. I don't wanna know someone who drives a Porsche, I want to drive the bloody Porsche myself. (*Miriam*, Bri)

> There's so many things I can do and I have done by being single that I could never have done if I weren't single. (*Frances*, Cal)

> We have opportunities in so many directions, I mean in principle you really can live – in men's world or in women's world, in world of families and children – you can take a pick and choose. (*Reija*, Fin)

Freedom was an important aspect of being single.

> There's a bit of me kind of quite likes to sort of just throw myself at the wind ... I mean the good bit about not having a house, not having a husband, not having children, not having a career, is – sometimes an absolutely elating feeling of travelling very very light in every sense, and occasionally I get hit by that, and there's nothing like it. ... I love it. But you can't hang onto it very often, you know, it doesn't come very often. But when it does come it's ... absolutely lyrical and wonderful, and I adore it. (*Celia*, Bri)

> I have a lot of freedom and things to do, I set my own schedule. (*Jody*, Cal)

> I am a free woman. I am free to act. (*Galina*, Fin)

> You got your own freedom. Of course there are two sides, but I think it's quite positive that you are a single woman and can do what you want. (*Harriet*, Fin)

Meanings attached to freedom are complex. Several single women talked about being free, and in the association lists (p. 40) 'single women' were often described with the words 'free' and 'freedom'. Many women refer to being free in the context of being able to decide what they do and when they do it, and the contrast they have in mind appears to be a woman who is married and tied down with more responsibilities.

When women talked about positive aspects of singleness, there were many references to having *learned* to enjoy being single.

> I'm just beginning to feel that ... I just am myself and I am a woman, so I'm just one of the many – – – women around. You know, I don't have to feel ashamed or bad or whatever. (*Lorna*, Bri)

> You get used to it. It is a frightening experience at first actually ... But then you ... make up your mind and settle down. (*Sylvia*, Bri)

> I had no positive role models for being single. So, you know, I could only think of myself as being married with a family. And now, if I look at my life, it's, you know, it's quite full. (*Norma*, Cal)

Learning to be single was referred to in many contexts. Singleness was connected with many positive aspects and being single afforded many pleasures and gains. Significantly, such pleasures were also mentioned by women who were involuntary singles.

Problems, contradictions and tensions

Many negative aspects of singleness have already been discussed. Here I shall summarise issues mentioned in the interviews and then concentrate on what I call 'existential angst'. Problems with being single centre around *constructing daily lives*. Several women referred to having to organise and plan in order to ensure sufficient social contact. The second problem relates to being alone and to loneliness; having to worry alone and make judgements alone. For women who have children without another supportive parent, lone parenting is hard work. The third problem relates to practical matters; for example, it is expensive living alone without sharing expenses with others, and it is difficult to organise holidays if one is reluctant to go alone. Fourth, socialising with couples or families can be difficult. In some social situations single women are excluded or, if included, they are pushed to the edges. Fifth, the social stigma attached to single women makes their lives more difficult. Sixth, if they have spent a lot of time alone, women worry about becoming 'peculiar'. Seventh, single women may feel personally inadequate because they have not formed partnerships.

If women have expected to marry and have children, they have to adjust these expectations and learn new ones. Women *internalise* many aspects of prevalent assumptions and cultural understandings; altering them is not a question of making a decision, but a lengthy process of coming to terms with oneself and one's lifestyle. Single women frequently refer to having more space, more control, more opportunities for making choices and more freedom. Learning to use all these is not necessarily a simple matter.

Existential angst

By 'existential angst' I refer to ontological questioning of the meaning of life and the purpose of one's existence. I was struck, in the interviews, by a sense of single women needing to *construct* their lives. As a majority of people still expect to marry and have children, and also do so, those who remain outside this institution are more likely to be confronted by a need to *make sense* of their lives. Those who pursue the same path as the majority of others are less likely to be placed in a position of having to explain their lives to themselves or to others. As the majority of single women do not choose singlehood but 'float' into it, often as a result of a cumulation of particular decisions at specific junctures, they are likely to go through a process of assessing their lives and their current and future expectations and hopes in order to come to terms with their singleness. On a more day-to-day level, if there are no clear, pressing demands made by others, construction of the pattern of living can be a considerable task.

Difficulties in having to adjust one's expectations were referred to frequently in the interviews:

> I grew up with, thinking that you got married, you stayed married and you made the best of it, and I had to readjust, I had to change, you know, the reality, that wasn't the reality for me. So I think that those of us who grew up with these, with these entrenched notions that didn't work, that are no longer reality, have had a hard time readjusting to it. (*Michelle*, Cal)

Some women had fairly idealised views on marriage and family, and assumed that, if they were not single, their lives would be much easier. Those with a less rosy picture thought that, even though marriage and family do not necessarily offer emotional support, the practical aspects of family life would nevertheless be protective. *Susan* (Cal) explained that, when stressed at work, 'unwinding' at home is difficult: 'I find myself thinking about things, weekends, and thinking if I was married or had a family I think a lot of that would probably recede.' Being single can mean being particularly dependent on one's inner resources: 'I think one of the penalties of actually living on your own [is] that there's no one there demanding that you do something different' (*Lynne*, Bri).

Existential angst is an abstract concept and evades categorisation. *Peggy* (a voluntary single) talks about issues which I have termed existential angst; I shall quote her at length to illustrate the phenomenon to which I refer:

> I remember lying in bed one morning with the sheet pulled over my head and thinking, 'What is the reason to even get up?' I mean, at least if you have children ... somebody's going to want breakfast or, you know, you have to get out for some reason and it's not, I feel that all of us are both totally expendable as well as very important. So sometimes it's really hard to figure out why to get up. And why to keep going. And what's the point. ... I think that's the biggest thing, I would say about being single and not having children, is just finding a certain level of meaning and purpose to get up and to keep going because whether you're single or you're married or whatever, it's hard lots of times. And ... you know you come home and you're tired and – – – or you've had a bad day and basically there's nobody there to say, 'Oh, don't worry,' or 'It's OK.' ... There's none of that, you just have to do it yourself and it's very exhausting. I find that probably the worst thing of it all is just that you have to do everything ... How I feel is I have to do it all myself. I mean, I think that is the truth for everybody and anybody. But at least sometimes you can be deluded if you have a relationship and there's a little bit of respite. ... I think, as a result of being single and not having children, ... I've looked towards – – – other purposes to be here or to be connected or for meaning in my life ... Now, the biggest thing I feel is that

not having children is – there's no personal connection for me into the future. And – – – I think I've felt bad about that. ... there's no way that I'm personally plugged into the future other than through my work, which will be fine, but it's different. (*Peggy*, Cal)

Being a childless single woman raises issues of separateness and connectedness. Women refer to potential detachment from others, which has to be countered by actively seeking contact. But they also refer to a less tangible potential detachment from time and space. They talk about having to deal with greyness of everyday life, with a future which stretches ahead of them, with empty spaces in their lives and with uncertainty. They are faced with the necessity of making decisions big or small, worrying about having a narrow view of life and 'having to endlessly construct things' (*Celia*, Bri).

It is difficult for single women to avoid asking questions about the purpose and meaning of life. During such questioning it is arduous to sift through what is essential and what is not. Lorna (an involuntary single) talks at length about this process.

> [I think being married and having children] would in a way free me. ... I don't think I'm particularly typical, I think I'm a bit peculiar, but I feel sort of stuck sometimes. Not free. Not free to just do. To sort of pick out the – the essential things in life and just go and do them, I get all tied up with all sorts of other silly things that aren't really essential. ... [In a relationship] I felt free in some way. Sort of – to see clearly. Not to be hung up about things. ... I think I felt more free because the – because I can get obsessed and worried about being single, and just that sort of worry ties me up in knots, do you know what I mean? And stops me doing things. Because you live alone and you work alone there's sort of space in your head to sort of think about things. I mean on the occasions when I'm with other people for days on end I would never think about myself or my problems or whatever. You know, you're just busy with the day-to-day things like cooking meals for people, you know, talking to people; you know, the space is filled up. But when there's all that space you – I tend to fill it with sort of 'Oh my God', you know, 'What am I doing with my life?' and, you know, this sort of – these are the crucial questions, the meaning of the universe and sort of religion and politics and what's happening to the country and, oh my god, what's happening to Europe – you know, all these sort of huge questions – – – all this space and I just sort of get tied up in knots really. ... If I was a very busy mother of four my time would be so precious that I would only do the most essential things and have very clear aims. ... I'm completely free in a way, to do anything I want. ... So in a sense one should feel completely free, but you don't. (*Lorna*, Bri)

Large existential issues are connected with daily living. When talking about what she is free *to* rather than free *from*, the comparisons Lorna makes with a period when she was in a relationship are illuminating. Focusing on small issues can lead to a contemplation of big issues if no *external demands* interrupt chains of thought.

Many women had developed ways of coping with existential angst. Some had made a clear decision not to seek for a purpose in life:

> A lot of people really dedicate themselves to figuring out what life is all about, and finding one answer that they can accept and say, 'Well now I can see what my purpose is.' I have never felt that life is like that. I've always thought it was just a series of adventures. You can kind of steer it one way or another and I've learned more recently to pursue those things that I want to pursue and avoid those things I don't, and just sort of steer my way through it. But I don't feel the need to have a strong central purpose. (*Norma,* Cal)

Religious women, particularly those active in the church, found both purpose of life and practical preoccupations. There were women who were interested in spiritual development, meditation, Buddhism and so on. For some, creative pursuits either at work or outside work were important. Thus existential angst was not something that single women necessarily had to *live with*, even though they are *confronted by it*.

It is difficult to substantiate my claim that single women are more likely to experience existential angst. A few points can be made, though. In my interviews with feminist mothers, issues related to existential angst did not appear, except in the form of feeling guilt about the state of the world that they brought their children into. During the interview process with single women, when themes to do with purpose and meaning of life had come up, I was sensitised to the issue and was hence more likely to pursue it at least implicitly in later interviews. But questions about meaning and purpose of life were not in my original interview scheme. Overall discussions that I have analysed in relation to this area did not take place as a result of direct questioning. Secondly, the so-called 'empty nest' syndrome attached to married women, particularly housewives, whose children move away from home, and who are faced with a void which for some is difficult to fill, seems to indicate that many of them have not found time or reason to consider the purpose of their lives previously. Though modern women are less likely to be so other-directed that a sharp contrast between a 'full' and an 'empty' life is applicable, nevertheless there is a qualitative shift, though the sharpness of it varies. Thirdly, I myself was confronted by questions of meaning and purpose of life whilst conducting the interviews. The issues raised by women made me face these too, in a way that I was not typically accustomed to, and often lengthy travelling to and from interviews in large urban areas gave me the time to do so. Fourthly, existential angst particularly affects childless single women. Though the social situation of single mothers is in many ways dissimilar to that of married mothers, having children places them in particular relationships vis-à-vis their children as significant others. On a practical level, single mothers are faced with daily tasks and responsibilities. On a more abstract level, they have a 'foothold in the future'.

If singleness was considered and experienced as more normal, existential angst would be less likely to arise. But I do not suggest that existential angst is merely a problem. Questioning the meaning and purpose of life cannot be negatively evaluated, even though it may cause pain. Nor am I suggesting that only single women are faced with existential questions, but I do suggest that such issues have a particular pertinence and specificity to them.

Familism and single motherhood

The number of single parents has increased in all three countries in this study. Most of them are women, unmarried or divorced. Single motherhood has become increasingly acceptable in attitude surveys. But in public debates great worries are expressed about children in single mother families. In public daycare and schools these children are often perceived as coming from 'incomplete' or 'broken' homes. The rise of neo-conservatism, with its emphasis on traditional family values, indicates that the liberalisation of attitudes has reached its peak. Debates on boys and masculinity in Finland and the USA, and to a lesser extent in Britain, have emphasised that young boys who are too close to their mothers find it hard to establish a positive adult psychosexual identity (Gordon, 1992). Biological sex differences have been the focus of renewed scientific interest and it is claimed that results indicate that women and men are not as culturally constructed as feminists have argued.[2]

As single motherhood has increased and reached a greater level of social acceptability than, for example, in the 1950s, debates focusing on rights of fathers have gained momentum (see Rutherford, 1988). Whether artificial insemination by a donor should be available to single women has caused some furore recently in Britain. Positive portrayal of a single mother in an American television series also generated discussion and criticism at the time of writing this book.

Voluntary childlessness

Married (or cohabiting) women are assumed to want and to have children. All women are seen as potential mothers; though single women are not likely to be under pressure to have children as they are single, the corollary to the question 'Why are you not married?' is 'And why do you not have children?' The term 'voluntary childlessness' is typically used to refer to women in stable partnerships; I use it here to acknowledge the modern disjuncture between marriage and maternity, whilst noting that the disjuncture is not absolute.

In this study, 22 have not wanted children. Typically their voluntary childlessness has been uncomplicated. Though some are very fond of children generally, they have not felt the need to have children of their own. Divorced and separated women were more likely to have experienced difficulties in relation to childlessness. Some reported relationships which had broken down because of their disinclination to have children. For *Christine* the pressures had been very strong: her husband gave her an ultimatum that if she did not have children he would divorce her:

> He'd pushed me into psychoanalysis, going four times a week to some stupid psychoanalyst who thought I was sick because I didn't want to have children. I hate children. I hate family scenes. (*Christine*, Cal)

Those who had not experienced personal pressures thought that the general assumption is that women want to and do have children. They referred to not having 'a maternal instinct' and some added that they did not consider themselves 'less of a woman' because of it.

Women who were fond of children looked for ways of being in touch with them. A few worked with children and thus satisfied their need to be in contact with children and care for them; two women referred to 'mothering' grown-ups. Others had close contact with children of friends and relatives. The two disabled women said they could not cope with children because of their disability, but both of them had close contacts with children of friends and relatives. A few women were not in contact with children and some did not want to be either. For these women, expressing themselves through their work was important.

Several women emphasised that their childlessness was precisely *voluntary;* that if they had wanted children, they would have been prepared to do so alone.

Frankly, I think that I'm the type that, if I wished I could have children, I would go out and have one. ... I think I can provide a loving, wonderful environment for a child, but then that child becomes number one in my life. I'm career-oriented right now in the sense that I've established myself, ... not materialistically but my personal objectives are growth and development, professional development. (*Carlotta*, Cal)

The prospect of having a child alone seemed potentially more of a problem for women who had wanted, or still wanted, to have children.

Involuntary childlessness

Women who wanted children but did not have any had decided that they did not want children alone (except two women who were not able to conceive). For some women it was self-evident that they did not want to be single mothers. Others had carefully considered the possibility of having children alone and decided against single motherhood. Though some felt that their decision was a personal one, others experienced external pressures against having children, either in a general sense or specifically applied to them through relatives.

About half the women were very sad about not having children; for some this issue was very painful. Many of them referred to not having children as a loss; for example, *Ella* considered it a 'loss that one has to acknowledge, and come to terms with *more than anything else*' (author's emphasis); *Lynne* wonders 'whether you ever stop feeling clear of that'. The rest were no longer sad about not having children; they had dealt with the issue and had overcome their pain: 'I'm ready to accept what life gives me.' Many of them were in contact with children and had formulated close relationships with them, or worked with children. Women who provided practical support such as baby-sitting, to friends and relatives with children, all emphasised that they did so willingly, not because it was expected of them or they felt under pressure to do so. These women had moved beyond some tenets of familism; contact and time with children had become more important than having their own children.

Women who still might have children

Seven women still wanted to have children. Only one considered having a child alone, the rest wanted to have children only in the context of a close partnership; several reasons were given. A partner was important for financial reasons. Though women had learned to manage with the financial resources available, and though most women were not poorly paid, economic considerations were important when making decisions about children. Second, partners would be a source of practical support. Dealing with children alone was considered too hard work, often through observation of single friends. Third, partners would provide emotional support: someone with whom to discuss and share joys and pains of parenthood. Fourth, there were social reasons: many women thought it was important for a child to have a father. They often referred to their own relationships with their fathers. Those who had not been brought up with a father, or whose fathers were relatively distant, had experienced a sense of loss which they would not want their children to experience.

As women in this study were at least 35, those who wanted children did not have many childbearing years left. This was stressful for women who thought that not having children would be a source of great pain to them: 'One might find oneself charging into a relationship just in order to have children, which I think would be awful.' Others felt it was something they could cope with: 'There would be a certain sense of regret of not having a child, but ... I think I could accept it.'

Lesbians and motherhood

Lesbian women are least likely to be under pressure to become mothers; lesbian motherhood is generally disapproved of. None of the lesbian women I interviewed had children; two had tried to become pregnant but did not. One was relieved – the decision to have a child had been made primarily by her partner. One was very regretful: 'It's just something I'm sad about. It's something that I didn't do that I'm sad about. Most things that I didn't do I'm not sad about.' Being a lesbian mother was considered increasingly acceptable. A few lesbian women thought that children need two parents, and some thought that children should have fathers. Therefore they did not consider having children either with or without a partner: 'I know lesbians who have families and they live together and a lot of them are coparenting, but – I guess I don't think of them as a family. Which is a bit disgraceful really' (*Gwen*, Bri).

Lesbian motherhood is still comparatively rare; I interviewed lesbian mothers in my study of feminist mothers. Most of them had been in heterosexual relationships when they had children, and had come out as lesbians subsequently. None had experienced grave difficulties, but for them, as for mothers in that study generally, feminism was a great source of strength and also provided the possibility of forming alternative, supportive networks.

Single mothers

The issue of single motherhood illustrates the influence of familism. There is, still, a strong ideology that children should be brought up in nuclear families; this was reflected in the views of women when they discussed their disinclination to be single mothers. But familism is more than an ideology; it assumes material effectivity and is reflected in the structuring of the context of childrearing. There are differences between societies. In the USA and Britain lone mothers are less likely to do paid work, and social and welfare services available to them do not encourage or enable them to do so (see Chandler, 1991); some differences between the USA and Britain exist (Maclean, 1991). In the Nordic countries lone mothers are encouraged to engage in paid work, and services are constructed in such a way that this is facilitated (Arber and Lahelma, 1992); hence Finnish single mothers are less likely to be impoverished than their British and (especially) American counterparts. But nowhere have hardships connected with single parenting been removed; as long as familism is prevalent, legislation for provision of services alone could not remove such hardships. Familism is also integral in assumptions about the best environment for children; there is a strong sense that single mother families are incomplete and problematic. They are compared to the yardstick of normality provided by the nuclear family as an ideal; 'mother-only family has become a touchstone for a much broader set of struggles around changes in women's roles, the relationship between the state and the family, and class and racial inequality' (McLanahan and Booth, 1989, p. 557).

Single motherhood in the context of familism contains difficulties and hardships, but also joys and pleasures. The diversification of family formations indicates social and ideological changes. Familism is prevalent but not all-encompassing. Particularly in metropolitan areas, single parenthood has increased and become more commonplace and more accepted. Those women in this study who wanted children and went ahead and had them (not having planned their pregnancies) had not experienced a great deal of external pressure. A large proportion of people in attitude surveys have indicated that single parenthood is acceptable.[3] Making a decision to embark on single parenthood is not easy, however. Most people would want to have children in the context of marriage and a family. But because of the increase of single motherhood, and because of the liberalisation of attitudes vis-à-vis other people's family formations, women who do become single parents in large cities have not been faced with a great deal of personal criticism.

Single mothers are a heterogeneous group (see Morris, 1992) and the pleasures and difficulties they experience depend on their economic and social circumstances, but generally, *children filled the lives of the single mothers*. There was a great deal of variation in the extent and type of 'filling' depending on financial resources, the availability of support from fathers (of the children), friends and relatives, and the number of children women had (this ranged from one to four). Women with children did not make references to 'existential angst'. In practical terms they had been busy and their lives, at least partly, centred on their children. They also had something that several women without children remarked they lacked: a foothold in the future.

Women with children were less likely to be lonely, they had a source of intimacy and many of those who had adult children felt that they had a ready source of support; they could turn to their children in difficulties.

> It's been a hard life in terms of trying to provide for my family. ... I said that we have to be like the three musketeers, but instead of three we are five. ... We have to support each other ... and the world outside is not going to come between us. We have to be together. And that's what we are. These are my four children, they are part of me, but I am really glad of having them because there's so much love coming from them. (*Clara*, Bri)

> It's just the fun that kids will change the way you feel yourself. And play with the child and see them learn and just to watch what they do ... my kid is just incredible, he's so full of energy ... it's fun, it's wonderful. (*Frances*, Cal)

> I think the thing that makes me happiest is my relationship with [each of my children]. (*Dorothy*, Cal)

> I consider myself privileged compared to those who do not have [children]. (*Soili*, Fin)

Children provided, for these women, enriching experiences. Many positive aspects of having children they referred to were the same that childless women thought they were missing out on.

Bringing up children alone, often with little or no support from the children's fathers, was hard work, though, particularly for those who received little help. Financial hardships had been considerable. Women who had older children were very brief in their descriptions of the difficulties:

I just coped with it, you know. (*Judy*, Bri)

There are all the hard times and the good times as well. (*Violet*, Cal).

Well, I managed. Sometimes well, sometimes not. (*Mari*, Fin)

There was a sense that these women had survived despite the problems they had experienced, and were now reluctant to dwell on the negative aspects.

Whilst not having children was a source of pain for some women, problems with their children were a source of pain for some of those who had them. As well as pleasure, children bring worries. When a mother feels that her resources for coping with difficulties are limited, this causes a great deal of anguish.

I've tried to do my best to have kids who would think, who would question everything, who wouldn't be gullible ... not accept everything. And I have one who is born again [Christian] and does nothing without consulting God! (*Simone*, Cal)

For *Simone*, observing her daughter's lifestyle is painful. She and other women referred to their children having had difficult periods, or to conflicts with them. Five women had a child who had fairly serious problems. One woman's son was a crack addict, another's son had been in trouble with the police. Three women had asked their young adult daughters to move away from home, and one of them was, temporarily she assumed, not in contact with her daughter. These women and others who reported more minor conflicts and difficulties in relation to their children said that they had been blamed by their children, in some cases specifically for being single mothers; they all resisted these accusations. These individual family relationships must be seen in the context of social factors, rather than as illustrations of internal dynamics of single mother families. Two women were black Americans, one was British Afro-Caribbean, two were British and had mixed race children. The problems they or their children experienced cannot be understood simply in terms of difficulties of single families, or children brought up without fathers; racism is significant in shaping the context.

Some women had children who had been away for differing periods. *Sylvia*, an Afro-Caribbean British woman, had fostered out her first child. Some women in my study of feminist mothers had also solved their childcare problems by fostering their children. This was partly because British society is selective in its encouragement of familism; black families have experienced difficulties in sustaining the British (or American) ideal of a nuclear family. Additionally, in African and Afro-Caribbean cultures, responsibility for children is viewed more collectively, and the practice of fostering can be understood in this context. This practice has now diminished; fostering in the British framework was not comparable to the kind of collective care women were used to in their communities (Gordon, 1990, p. 81). Women whose children had lived with relatives (especially grandmothers) had experienced fewer difficulties.

Two women had children who lived with their fathers after separation. Both found it difficult to cope as single mothers. They were closely involved with their children and felt that their decisions were generally accepted.

> I was very worried about how people would react to the woman giving up her children, because it seems to be OK for a man to do that in people's eyes, but there's some kind of stigma about a woman doing it. And I was very worried that people would assume I don't love my children. But it wasn't that at all. ... [But] they've been really positive. Nobody's been negative at all. (*Emily*, Bri)

Amy (Cal)'s situation was more of a problem; she found it difficult to interact with members of the Chinese community, among whom getting a divorce, children living with their father and singleness generally are more unusual than among many other ethnic groups.

Single motherhood brings many positive experiences. Nevertheless only six women had their children as lone mothers; three of these had unplanned pregnancies and one has a longstanding boyfriend closely involved in the care of the children. Although single motherhood is more acceptable than it used to be, there are also continuities: having a child alone is still a major decision, one beset by financial, practical, emotional and social difficulties. Changes are most clearly crystallised in the case of *Frances* (Cal), who decided to adopt a child as a single woman and was able to do so through an open adoption in California.

For her having a child is a wonderful experience, despite problems of single motherhood; but she is socially and financially in a comfortable position.

Overall it is easier to decide to have children in the context of marriage or a close partnership. Familism, despite changes, provides some continuities. One of the more startling aspects of the Amazonian lore was that Amazons brought up and controlled their own offspring (see Introduction). That children need fathers is a widely accepted precept – although this is explained in terms of the needs of the children (and their mothers), there are nevertheless patriarchal rights and control at issue as well. As women have increasingly chosen to become single mothers, side by side with this development there has been increasing concern about the rights of fathers and particularly about the needs of male children in establishing their masculine identity.

Unmarried women/divorced women

Divorced single women have accomplished an initial rite of passage by getting married, though there were indications that renewed attempts to integrate divorced women in their families of origin were made. Nevertheless there is a crucial difference between them and never-married women for whom the accomplishment of transition from childhood to adult status is more problematic.

> Some of my friends or people say that, if you have been married, even though you are divorced, you are somehow accepted in society, as a fit member of it, as you have been able to get a man, and have managed to get married. (*Lea*, Fin)

> The woman that is single but divorced, they ... see her in a different way. She has been married, it doesn't matter. She has fulfilled her part in society and she's not an unhappy woman, somebody has cared for her. So there is more value on the woman who has been divorced. (*Isabella*, Bri)

Women who have been married have confirmed social expectations and have acquired their rightful place in society, but there is also a sense that they have not fulfilled those expectations successfully.

Many divorced women felt a sense of failure because they had not been able to maintain their marriages. In particular, those who had children had worried about a divorce. Women were worried about loneliness, about reactions of others and, if they had children, how they would cope with them. The decision to separate is not lightly made. Despite the sense of failure, divorce was often a *relief* for women, because their situation had been intolerable. Many had had bitter experiences in their marriages, some of these very drastic. For them the romantic coating of an idealised institution had gone sour: 'My marriage did not give me anything, it just took something away.' Many women had worked hard to keep their marriages together; they tried to please their men, they tried to change: 'He liked some of my qualities but at the same time he tried to temper them. I decided if I kept changing, eventually who was I going to wind up being? I certainly wasn't going to be myself. So I left' (*Irene*, Cal). Women often referred to compromises they had had to make in relationships. They had experienced the need to adjust and to be flexible, which unmarried voluntary single women viewed as an ingredient of marriages (Chapter 6). *Minna* (Fin) explains that she has lived three lives: one as a child, the second in a marriage which she entered into very young, and a third after her divorce – '*and the third life is my own*'.

Divorced women experienced difficulties as a result of the break-up in reconstructing their lives: 'Everybody thought I was spoiled, and I couldn't cope with the rigours of marriage' (*Shirley*, Bri). They had often not been able to maintain their own personal friendships in a committed manner and after the divorce they had to spend time developing the kind of supportive social networks of important people that many unmarried women have already managed to establish. They have to learn to be in control and to make their own decisions. The learning process single women have been undergoing for a longer period confronts divorced women much more suddenly and acutely, and the social stigma applied to single women is also a new aspect to be handled. The difficulty of learning to live alone after having followed the path of normality can be exasperated by difficult divorce proceedings. Single women, though financially in a moderate position, consider themselves safe in knowing what their resources are. Marriage typically improves the economic position of a woman, but after divorce this deteriorates (see Maclean, 1991). A few women had experienced considerable financial hardships after their divorce and felt that the legal system had not protected them from vindictive husbands.

Divorced women are less likely to remarry than divorced men. For them establishing themselves as voluntary singles can be difficult. They are most likely to experience ill-health (married women are least likely to do so) and least likely to report life satisfaction (married women are most likely to do so). A plethora of studies[4] on life satisfaction counter the claim that marriage is beneficial for men but not for women. Such studies pose problems of interpretation. Married women have pursued a path that is still the most accepted; this might give them a sense of normality, despite difficulties they may experience in their marriages. Association between health and marital status is also complex. For women it is mediated by other factors, notably employment; Arber and Lahelma (1992) found, in a comparative study of Finnish and British women, that women's family roles affect their health more in Britain than in Finland, where the majority of women participate in the labour market. Women who have health problems are more likely to remain single (Pearlin and Johnson, 1981). Able-bodiedness is valued and any deviation from it is likely to make women less 'marriageable'.

Conclusion

Single women are a heterogeneous group; women in this study reflect a great deal of this heterogeneity. Therefore simple categorisations are not possible when discussing their experiences of being single. There is a great deal of variety in the way in which singleness is experienced. Many of the positive and negative features were referred to by large numbers of women. But how negative and positive aspects balanced out in the lives of individual single women differed greatly. I have referred to continuities and changes in the experiences of single women. There is no doubt that in the areas of this study singleness is easier than it was in the 1950s. But because of the strengthening of neo-conservatism and the weakening of the welfare state, continuous improvement in the position of single women is not likely. In a context of diminished choices for women in general, singleness may become a less likely option for them, but one that is nevertheless forced upon them. The rapid increase of singleness in the USA is not only due to modern women opting for autonomy and independence; it is also a result of structural changes which disrupt women's lives so that marriage and 'family' become increasingly less attainable as the secure havens that familism purports them to be.

Many single women I have interviewed would not, I am sure, wholeheartedly agree with the significance I attach to marital status. Many have struggled long and hard to establish their voluntary single position, but talk a great deal about their present experiences of singleness as a fact accepted by them and others. Nevertheless there was a repeated sense that independence comes at a price. Women in this study live in areas likely to offer most possibilities for positive experiences of singleness. Further, they are relatively well educated and do not suffer from grave poverty. For many groups of women singleness is likely to be a more difficult experience.

8

Independence

Individuality and independence

The analytical themes of this book centre on individuality and marginality. The development of Western citizenship required a concept of the modern, abstract individual (Chapter 2). Such an individual is not neutral in terms of gender, social class or 'race'. As formal citizenship has extended to women, single women are less likely to evoke conceptions of 'a third sex'. But have they reached absolute individuality? Are they no longer constructed as the other? Such questions are difficult to explore empirically, but I was nevertheless interested in pursuing the possibilities. This could have been done by exploring how single women are affected by legislation, social policies and so on, but, as I was interested in the experience of singleness in the context of the diversification of family formations, I wanted to conduct my exploration through perceptions and experiences of single women. It is difficult to ask questions about citizenship and individuality, but as I approached the interviews in a way which gave the interviewees an opportunity to reflect on the theoretical and analytical themes of the research directly, I had to consider what level of discussion would enable me to do so.

My tentative method of doing so crystallised in the first interviews. After gathering the background information in the interviews, my first question usually was 'Do you think of yourself as a single woman?'. *Greta* (Bri), the first interviewee, answered 'yes', and then clarified her reply:

> I see myself as an independent person which is – is a woman, but I see myself as a pretty strong individual – – – And I think I've always been pretty independent – – – I've always done my own thing, and that has often led to conflicts.

160 Single Women

In the association lists three out of the first five interviewees added the word 'independent' next to 'single women'. 'Independence' was brought up by many women in interviews without initial probing. I decided to focus my exploration of women as individuals on their conceptions of experiences and meanings attached to 'independence'.

What is independence?

People are citizens of modern, autonomous, sovereign nation states. An independent nation state is administered by its own government and law; independence is related to understandings of the status of a state in relation to other states. Citizenship defines the relationship of those under the same government to the nation state. Like the state they are integrated into, formally free and equal citizens are independent. They are 'not dependent ... earning, also not needing to earn, one's own living; unwilling to be under obligation; not dependent on others for validity'.[1] This description is congruent with individuals seen as absolute. Modern citizens are independent, autonomous individuals, responsible for the course of their own lives. The emergence of western citizenship hinged on binary oppositions (Chapter 4), one of which is independent/dependent. Meanings attached to this binary opposition and its constituent parts have shifted historically from a characterisation of the position of groups in a particular social order to a description of traits of individuals (Fraser and Gordon, 1992), while meanings attached to the 'individual' also changed (Chapter 2). My aim is to explore 'independence/dependence', not as character traits, but as social, cultural and economic concepts. I begin by focusing on what independence is; second, I explore what is involved in attempting to establish independence, and third, I connect independence and individuality. In this exploration I proceed thematically, rather than searching for cross-cultural differences; on the basis of preliminary analysis no consistent variation on meanings attached to independence on the basis of structural or cultural positions was found.

Financial independence

In the process of industrialisation, independence/dependence was increasingly defined through wage labour. In the interviews a crucial, constantly mentioned aspect of independence relates to economic autonomy.

> Financially I'm totally independent ... I keep myself, and nobody pays bills or mends my car or anything. (*Betsy*, Bri)

> [*TG*: You said you're independent?]

> Very independent. I work for my living, I don't wait on anyone, I never been on welfare, never expect to be there ... I work for what I get and I try to use it wisely. (*Naomi*, Cal)

> [Independence is] earning one's own money and being able to use it as you want. (*Eila*, Fin)

That financial independence is crucial was evident in the importance attached to work by single women and in the emphasis on getting by with one's own salary (Chapter 4). An ability to participate in the labour market is central in single women establishing independence. When future plans and hopes were discussed, financial situation was frequently mentioned; women hoped to maintain or to improve their financial position. Not engaging in paid wage labour makes single women particularly vulnerable to impoverishment and dependence, which are readily connected with individual character traits.

Taking care of yourself

Single women have to make decisions alone and have to care for themselves by themselves. Though many do so in the context of social networks constructed over the years, the majority of women, no matter how important their friendships and contacts with relatives were, emphasised that they were, and *had to be*, their own primary caregivers.

> I am a very strong person. At least I give that impression. I give that appearance of being strong. I'm self-sufficient, I'm independent, I'm able to cope. (*Shirley*, Bri)

> [Being independent] means to rely on yourself to get things done and as I said, it's not that you would never consult a friend or cry on a friend's shoulder, but ... then you go home and you make yourself a cup of tea and you're fine. You know, that you have strength, you know, it builds self-esteem, to be independent, because you're not depending on any other person to give you something that you need to live. Because I can live myself, I can provide everything I need for myself, by myself. (*Kate*, Cal)

> Well you become fairly independent [as a single woman] – you have to be almost like a caretaker, and do all the chores at home, plumbing and whatever. So I don't have any worries if something goes wrong. (*Ursula*, Fin)

Single women often referred to a process of becoming increasingly skilled at taking care of themselves (in a broad sense). This was not thought to be typical for women; not something they had been brought up to do. For women who have limited capacity to take care of themselves (such as disabled women) depending on others can slip into dependence and lack of autonomy.

Being in control

Being able to take care of oneself means being in control of one's life.

> Now I can remember to think, 'What do you want, Caroline?', 'Do you want to do this? Do you want to go from here to that seat over there? Because don't go if you don't want to'. And I find my life is so easy because – – – I just say, 'I don't want to'. Nobody can argue with that [laughs]. (*Caroline*, Bri)

> I don't like being dictated to. (*Judy*, Bri)

> when I come home I can just, you know, kick my shoes off, put the TV dinner in the microwave oven, or go to the pool, you know, swim as long as I want. I don't have to worry about my kids or my husband to feed. ... I can do whatever I want, I can go out anywhere I want 'cause I'm alone, right? (*Shoshana*, Cal)

> I have learned to say no – to different things that I don't want to do, and I just don't. And I feel that my independence is increasing all the time – little by little. ... And my freedom. ... And all the time the opportunities to do all sorts of things, sort of choices, increase, so that I have different options, more and more. (*Minna*, Fin)

Some women have struggled to be in control because they wanted to; others, particularly divorced women, found that they *had* to learn to be in control.

> You're bound to be independent when you live on your own, because you just have to do things on your own, so it becomes second nature to you. ... You get used to doing what you want to do when you want to do it. (*Emily*, Bri)

For disabled women who cannot take care of themselves without assistance, being in control is crucial in their struggle to establish independence. Independence then starts from very practical matters – deciding what you wear, what you eat and so on.

Emotional independence

Emotional independence means being self-reliant, not only in terms of practical issues or in terms of decision making, but also in relation to interaction with others.

> Basically I don't see myself living my life through someone else, which is what I did at one time. I seem to have got away from that and I'm a lot happier for it. (*Tina*, Bri)

> I feel independent, I suppose, since my mother died, because ... this is a kind of psychic independence – I suppose there always ... was a kind of pressure, a kind of pressure of her disapproval. (*Eileen*, Bri)

> I feel that I don't depend on people much for their – – – emotional support. I mean I like it – – – I get that, but if I don't get it from them that's OK, too. (*Rachel*, Cal)

> That I can go it alone, that I can have a happy life living alone, that's what [independence] means to me ... there was a long time when I wasn't sure about that. ... And I think that I came to it almost emotionally before I came to that intellectually, that I realised, 'Hey, everything seems to be going OK! It's OK!' (*Michelle*, Cal) [Being independent] means not depending on anybody or anything. (*Kaisa*, Fin)

Though emotional independence was mentioned by several women, the majority of them questioned their own emotional independence, and the value and possibility of emotional independence. I shall discuss this in more detail below, as comments expressed on this issue highlight the complexity of meanings of independence and shifts in such meanings. I shall also explore dependence, constructed as the shadow-side of independence/dependence as a binary opposition.

Mental independence

By mental independence I refer to a strong sense of self – not being influenced by others in situations where one is conscious that one's own decisions are different from those of others, and may be disapproved of by others.

> I suppose I'm independent in my head really. (*Tina*, Bri)

> I don't live my life for other people. ... Well, I live for some other people but I don't live it for what people think of me. ... I'm not interested in being the norm 'cos that's not what I am. (*Liz*, Bri)

> I think independence is being sufficiently rooted in yourself to just be able to do what you – do your own thing, not worry too much about what people think. (*Celia*, Bri)

> I'm looking for myself ... an individual which is able to find their own destination, I could make my own future, I don't have to depend on a lot of people. (*Amy*, Cal)

> I try to grow to be more independent, so that I would not be dependent on people in a wrong way, and on their opinions – so that I could not develop myself in a way that I want myself. (*Lea*, Fin)

> I'm independent in a sense that I think through my own brains, and nobody is saying to me that you are doing something right or wrong, or that I am stupid or intelligent; I have to decide it myself. And if I'm stupid, or if I've bungled, I have to swallow it myself. (*Rosa*, Fin)

Establishing such an independent mental attitude is not necessarily easy. Many women, when reflecting on why they are independent, referred to their upbringing. Some said they had been independent as long as they could remember; as soon as *Frances* (Cal) could talk, she said 'My do it!' Others remembered the encouragement of independent role models. Mental and emotional independence are individual character traits: single women try to be independent in their heads and hearts at the very least. Such character traits and their attribution are, however, *socially and culturally* constructed.

Being alone

Independence was often connected with being alone. Though not all the women lived alone, the number of those who lived with people other than their children was small. None of them said they lived in a particularly integrated or enmeshed manner.

It is the capacity to be alone without feeling as if, you know, you're missing something all the time, you're not fulfilled. Whether it's children or, you know, ... you have to have another person in order to be full. I mean I don't know what that says about people, that you need another person to be complete. (*Ella*, Bri)

I suppose I mean independent in the sense that I love being on my own, I love my own space. (*Tina*, Bri)

There's being independent and there's lonely, those kind of all exist at the same time, in a sense, perhaps different emphases at different points, they coexist, don't they? (*Frances*, Cal)

Whenever I went to visit friends that were married, I thought thank goodness I don't have to put up with that. I was glad to be going home alone and I saw it in some sense a strength, being single rather than being dependent on someone. (*Susan*, Cal)

I think it is sometimes a sort of obsession for me, I have to get by alone everywhere. (*Laura*, Fin)

Spinsters in the nineteenth century were unlikely to live alone; being located in other people's households meant that it was difficult to cultivate independence in a way that women living alone today can. But for these women independence is not merely something they *can* cultivate; it is also something they *have to* cultivate.

Independence: possibilities and limitations

Limitations of independence were experienced acutely by many women. Interviewees were asked to talk about negative and positive aspects of independence. Discussions about the negative meaning of independence included words such as stubbornness, aggression, burden, hardship, struggle, obsession, inflexibility, loneliness and conflict. Possibilities connected with independence were described through positive meanings such as challenge, strength, women's capacities, freedom, options and alternatives, being in control, defining oneself, having one's own lifestyle, not being dependent on a man, being complete and being a human being. For single women the process of establishing themselves as independent, and maintaining independence, was wrought with tensions and contradictions.

Becoming independent is a *learning process*; in several contexts single women referred to having to learn how to live their lives, and how to achieve a measure of satisfaction in their lives. That many of them had done so is indicated in a large proportion of them being voluntary singles. Some women felt that they had become independent through their upbringing; others had to establish their independence.

> I think it's something you have to grow into. (*Ella*, Bri)

> I don't have a terribly strong sense of myself and I've never been overly sort of confident and so on, but for me, what I've learnt from [having felt suicidal] is that if I can survive that, I can survive anything. On my own ... I mean it gives me a lot of strength, that, the strength of being independent. (*Celia*, Bri)

For some single women becoming independent was a particularly clear learning process, because they were very close to their parents and found it difficult to establish the 'rite of passage' to adulthood (Chapters 4, 5 and 7). They described their relationships to their parents as mutually supportive and emotionally rewarding.

> I was very dependent for a long time on my parents ... I didn't really achieve any autonomy until this last job that I've got now. (*Tina*, Bri)

> Even though I was out there doing whatever I had to do, I knew that if things got really bad I could always go to [my parents] for help. That's not – that option isn't there anymore. I have to depend on me – – – And I had to come to terms with that. It was hard. (*Inez*, Cal)

Inez had to develop new ways of coping after her parents' death. *Tina's* parents are still alive and, although she refers to having become more independent, she still 'dreads' the death of her parents.

That establishing independence is a learning process is particularly clear when focusing on divorced women, for whom the need to construct a single life is a great deal more sudden than it is for an unmarried woman.

> In my generation of women – what I've seen and what I've heard is that women were taught that they're nothing – they're not fulfilled in life unless they have a man. And that's a dependency problem for them, that they must outgrow to become independent. It would be like learning a typing system and then having to unlearn that ... I'm having to make ... my way in life in a different way without relying on another person ... I'm creating my own life ... I wasn't brought up that way. (*Jody*, Cal)

> I don't need somebody else to define myself. ... I can make decisions, ... I can handle business affairs, ... I can live my lifestyle and be happy. That's a fairly recent thing. (*Dorothy*, Cal)

> I have woken up to the need to be independent very late. (*Ritva*, Fin)

Learning to be independent involved hardship and struggle for those who did not perceive themselves as 'always' having been independent.

> It's something that I realise that I need to work at. It's not something that comes naturally to me. That I need to be aware that I am not as independent as I would like to be. (*Martha*, Cal)

> Learning to live alone has been a tough process, but it's been good, and I'm quite satisfied ... in some things I hope I'd be even more independent. (*Sanna*, Fin)

Highly educated single women of colour felt that they had had to struggle particularly hard to achieve independence and to balance interaction with predominantly white colleagues and their own ethnic groups. Other women of colour emphasised working hard not in order to be independent, but in order to maintain their financial position, especially if they had children. Independence to these women is a self-evident, though nevertheless valued, aspect of their lives. Having had to learn to look after oneself (and one's children) reduces the attraction of marriage; therefore the claim that black women's low marriage rates do not reflect economic independence, but problems of black men (Chapter 3), is a *partial* interpretation.

Having established an independent lifestyle, single women worked to maintain it. Always having to do everything for themselves by themselves was considered demanding by many women.

> Sometimes I do think to myself, you know, I wish I had somebody else to do this for me. (*Judy*, Bri)

> Being independent is a burden ... on you, because it tends to isolate you from the world, in the sense that because you're independent the rest of the people say, 'Oh gosh, she's so independent, she doesn't need anything'. (*Isabella*, Bri)[2]

Increased independence of single women, when observed by those around them, is connected with the modern stereotype of them (Chapter 7) and can provide new pressures. The coexistence of traditional and modern stereotypes has led to difficulties in categorising single women: 'I think the negative aspects of [independence] are that when you live in society people don't know what to make of you if you're on your own' (*Shirley*, Bri). In the context of traditional codes of femininity, women, *even when taking care of others*, are construed as dependent. Women are less likely to be viewed independent as 'women' than men are as 'men'.

Women often described both positive and negative aspects of independence. For example, *Peggy* (Cal) talked about the 'joys of being independent', but added that independence 'carries a very big price-tag'. The price was typically connected with loneliness, and difficulties in obtaining help and support when it was needed, or being able to ask for or receive support when it was available. Being independent can mean that there is little space for vulnerability; the veneer of strength can become a straitjacket to be worn at all times. Therefore connections with others are constructed, by many single women, through *being supportive* rather than being supported.

Independence and partnerships

The price of independence was particularly acutely felt in relation to establishing partnerships. Though there were some women who felt that relationships where both parties are independent were possible, and could think of examples, more commonly maintaining independence in relationships was considered difficult, if not impossible. Independent women are 'too strong' for men (*Greta*, Bri). Men consider them a threat: 'That's the kind of women that they would rather not be associated with' (*Clara*, Bri). Women who are more prepared to be submissive are thought to be preferred by men. Men are tempted to try to put independent women 'down' (*Laura*, Fin); they should not be 'too independent' (*Bridget*, Cal). For women who are used to being in control it 'seems more difficult to maintain a relationship' (*Sue*, Cal). If women do not need to depend on a man, can take care of themselves and are used to being in control, close partnerships seem to require giving up a lot.

> As I become more independent ... it frees me paradoxically from the need for ... a close relationship with a man ... as much as I still want it, it makes it more difficult because I have these independent notions and ideas which run counter to the facts of a conventional relationship. What I would like is an unconventional relationship. Independence for both parties. (*Dorothy*, Cal)

The more I was growing as an independent person – – – the less men were interested in me. (*Christine*, Cal)

It is interesting to consider whether women who have married are less independent than single women. The suggestion of single women that independent women are not wanted by men implies so. The modern ideal of a companionate marriage, a symmetrical partnership where both parties are equal, runs counter to the conceptions of many of the single women in this study. Feminists have argued that women are subordinated within the family, and the sexual division of labour is reproduced within it. Powerful arguments support this claim; domestic violence occurs in many families (see Wilson, 1983), many wives are raped by their husbands (10 per cent according to a study by Russell, 1990). Women do make compromises within marriages and families (see Coward, 1992; Hochschild, 1989) which curtail their independence. Skeggs (1991) argues, that though women are perfectly capable of challenging masculinity, they do not do so in relation to men who are important to them. Compromises that women make cannot be explained by their independence/dependence as personal characteristics, but are socially constructed. Women's challenges and compromises take place in the context of weighted balance of power, even though the particular balance of specific marriages is subject to variation (see O'Connor, 1991).

Difficulty in forming partnerships is not only connected with whether men are willing or able to accept an independent woman: women themselves had come to put a high value on their lifestyle and noted that they were reluctant to make compromises.

I can come and I can go as I like. Nobody questions me, more or less ... I've got my own independence and I don't think I want to part with that. It would be a hard step now, to part with something like that. Now I couldn't. (*Sylvia*, Bri)

A couple of times I met ... old-fashioned type [of men] who want to just take care of you and support you and everything else. But I felt really uncomfortable with it, even though that's what I thought I wanted. I just didn't feel comfortable with it. ... I know there's no way I could cope with it now, because I've been too independent for too long. ... I get really annoyed if a man tries to help me deal with my car or something, because I know how to [do it] – you just become so independent that you ... you're very aware of men patronising you, and it really puts my back up. So I think ... I don't stand a chance really [laugh]. (*Emily*, Bri)

Emily's comments indicate that her problems in forming relationships are a result of a mixture of her aversion to attitudes of men and a begrudging value she places on her lifestyle, despite her dissatisfactions with it. She also notes her insecurity, which is partly connected with her concern about her children. If she was not 'needy', and looking for someone to 'complete' her, establishing a positive partnership with a man would be easier in her view.

> I consider myself independent. I consider myself too independent, actually. And that is connected to me being a single woman. Because – I don't dare to be dependent on another person. Since I was a child I have been developing ways of coping, so that I would be independent and responsible ... and I have somehow taken that too far, so that there has been no room for a man there. ... I have always avoided commitment in my relationships with men.
> (*Hanna*, Fin)

If a woman has learned to cope on her own, it is difficult to alter that and share the coping with someone else. *Hanna* makes no reference to experiences with men who have expected her to compromise and submit – at least not explicitly; that does not rule out implicit assumptions which she may have encountered without giving those experiences conscious expression. That is speculation; there were, however, several women who talked about being 'too independent'. But there was a further strand in the responses of women: a fear of dependence was often connected with fears of their own propensity towards dependence.

Fear of dependency

Issues of independence/dependence in relationships are not only related to expressed attitudes and expectations of women themselves, or the requirements and demands of men they have been involved with. Independence, for the majority of women, was something they had established, something they had learned, something they had worked hard to gain. Their learning processes take place within the framework of their structural and cultural location and their biographies. We are influenced by our social positioning, and our psychic structures develop through interactive processes that take place with significant others in the context of a cultural environment which is shaped if not determined, by social divisions of inequalities.

We receive explicit messages and more amorphous hidden messages; these messages are likely to be contradictory. For example, there is an emphasis that girls should work and be capable of looking after themselves, but marriage and motherhood are still widely taken for granted. Girls are told that they are individuals who should realise their personal capacities, but processes of socialisation they experience are likely to be different from those of boys; girls are kept closer to parents, their needs are interpreted differently and they are consequently related to differently than boys (for example, Statham, 1986). Children have limited power in relation to adults; many of their learning experiences are connected with a realisation that they have erred. To avoid making mistakes they try to read both the open and the hidden messages; gender differences are part of both (see B. Davies, 1989). Dependency and submission are characteristics that most girls encounter as being aspects of femininity, but not of masculinity. Single women working to establish independence have internalised some of these messages.

In the interviews this internalisation was reflected in women recounting their experiences of dependency in relationships, and their fears that despite their independence they would lapse into similar patterns.

> I was pretty crazy in that relationship really – totally dependent. (*Greta*, Bri)

> If I had a relationship ... I would become so dependent on a man. (*Shoshana*, Cal)

> I have a fear that I'm an extremely dependent personality. Now this is my fear that what happened with this boyfriend, the last one, ... it was like my real nature came out. I mean there's all this independence I have in my life, in my day-to-day life – it's all a show and that ... given a man, I want to become like my mother and I'll be totally dependent on the man. (*Sue*, Cal)

Sue thought that her dependence was not connected with the expectations of her boyfriend:

> He thought I was this tough, independent woman and then when I got involved with him he found that I was just like all of his other women and became very dependent on him.

Michelle, similarly, explains that her ex-husband was uncomfortable with her dependence.

> I did not know what he meant. I know what he means now. ... I was dependent upon him for seeing that we had a good time, you know, that I was very dependent on him emotionally. I needed him to be there and he found that hard. ... I don't think I'd ever be that ... dependent again. (*Michelle*, Cal)

Laura relates her fear of dependence to psychic constellations shaped in the context of family relationships.

> It is in a sense true what one of my ex-boyfriends said, that I'm lacking in independence – perhaps I am still looking for some sort of father figure ... a man who would look after everything. I mean it would be nice [laugh] not to have to do everything yourself, and alone. (*Laura*, Fin)

Though establishing independence as a single woman was considered hard work, it was thought to be even harder to do so in the context of a partnership.

Fear of dependency was not simply connected with men and their expectations. Some women also experienced fear of dependency generally in relation to people: 'Maybe I am even a bit too neurotic about not being dependent on others' (*Ulla*, Fin). Tensions of dependence and independence in relationships were also recounted by lesbian women. *Sanna* (Fin) questioned whether she was too submissive in her relationship to a married woman. *Christine* (Cal) recounted having been too dependent on a man and then having recreated this pattern in lesbian relationships, but this time women were dependent on *her*. She had resolved this problem by becoming celibate; she lost her interest in cultivating sexual relations. While patterns of submission/domination exist in lesbian as well as heterosexual relationships, there is a further problem more prevalent in lesbian relationships: women can become enmeshed and experience fusion to the degree that neither partner retains independence.

> There's a kind of autonomy that is ... very important ... so that you don't become totally enmeshed and lose your own purpose and centre. ... It's been hard for me to centre that and I think that's part of the reason I don't stay in [relationships] a really long time or, rather, I think what happens is, I get to the point of two or three years down the road with somebody and I have lost my strength. (*Maxine*, Cal)

By stating that patterns of dependency do not only take place in relationships with men, I am not suggesting that such patterns are inherently typical for women. There is little doubt, on the basis of feminist research on family, marriage, relationships and sexuality, that codes of femininity are enforced by an unequal sexual division of labour, and the establishment of the sexual difference. I am suggesting that codes of femininity are internalised, and the learning processes typified by hard work and struggles for single women striving to establish independence are symptomatic of such internalisation.

A great many of the codes of femininity and masculinity, and the sexual difference, are communicated to us through our cultural environment and structures of power constructing it, but they are also communicated through interaction in families, as those who have tried to bring their children up in a non-sexist way realise (see Statham, 1986; Gordon, 1990). In Chapter 3 I noted the significance of fathers. As little research has been conducted into father–daughter relationships, my comments must remain speculative. There were indications in these interviews that fathers were important, in their presence or absence, and in positive and negative ways, in determining how successfully their daughters become autonomous, independent persons.

First, fathers can encourage independence by helping their daughters to form their own opinions, and to seek their own directions. Second, fathers can also encourage independence in a negative way; by exerting undue control they instil a desire in their daughters not to need to submit to such control again – they become imbued with a capacity and willingness to fight. Such daughters could become very independent, but at the same time have little space for relying on others and forming relationships. Third, fathers whose control is more complete and who manage to foreclose any possibility of fighting back bring up daughters whose independence is on shaky ground, who fear dependence and have experiences of having recreated patterns they have internalised in their interaction with their fathers or by observing the submissiveness of mothers in relation to their dominant husbands. Fourth, fathers seemed significant even though they were absent or had died; in a familist society those whose experiences are not congruent with the ideology of a nuclear family may come to experience a lack which cannot be directly 'read' from their household constellations. Some of the single mothers in this study had children who seemed to experience similar problems in relation to an absent father; they did not necessarily miss a particular person (they may not have known their fathers well or at all), but they missed a father figure: a completion of the familial unit.

The way in which relationships between daughters and fathers in relation to independence/dependence were constructed in different social groupings in this study was interesting. White women from middle-class backgrounds often had fathers who encouraged independence in a negative way. Women from working-class origins often had fathers who allowed no fighting back and hindered independence. Women from all social groups were included among those whose relationships with their fathers were characterised by close attachment, which hindered independence. Women whose fathers positively encouraged independence were mostly from ethnic minorities and poor economic circumstances. Strongest encouragement was reported by *Clara*, a daughter of a labourer in a shanty town in Chile, and *Carlotta*, a daughter of a Chicano labourer.

I have emphasised that establishing independence is not easy for single women; there are tensions and contradictions in the process. Women recount positive and negative aspects of independence. These are connected with broader societal patterns and with psychic patterns on the level of subjectivities of women. Independence is therefore a joy and a liberation, but also hard work: women seem to need to be on guard against dependence. In the case of individual women the emphases vary; their experiences have been shaped in different ways, in different structural, cultural and biographical locations. I shall now try to disentangle different strands of independence/dependence. The exploration of these strands allows us to detect changes and continuities in the position of single women. It also allows us to see that on the level of lived experiences single women are still involved in the process of pushing back the boundaries, as they were in the nineteenth century (Chapter 1).

Strands of independence

In the interviews many women emphasised the independence of single women, but there were different strands in this emphasis. The first strand is that of *positive* implications of independence and the possibilities it contains.

> All I know is like I turn my own key in my door and when I go in I don't have to answer to anybody about my life, you know. (*Gloria*, Bri)

The second strand views independence as a *necessary* factor in the lives of single women. Autonomy and ability to cope are essential in order to construct a satisfactory life out of the raw materials available; they are not luxuries.

> You're bound to be independent when you live on your own, because you just have to do things on your own, so it becomes second nature to you. (*Emily*, Bri)

In the third strand *negative* aspects of independence are raised:

I don't really believe in this thing about independence being great and all that. I don't think it's good to have to be that strong. Why take everything upon yourself? It's silly. (*Lorna*, Bri)

In the fourth strand independence is considered *in relation to dependence*.

Independence is an illusion. It's the biggest illusion, I think, of our age. ... Independence is a myth. ... There are periods of freedom, which prepares for the next period of dependence. I think my next period of dependence – – – is gonna be old age. (*Molly*, Bri)

I think if one's not careful, dependence is seen as a negative thing. But dependency, I think also, if it's used in a careful way – like if you're in some sort of crisis – doesn't have to be a severe crisis, it can be a minor crisis – it's learning to be open and to share and create a bond and you can be so independent you can't do that. It stops you from doing the give and take in a real meaningful way. (*Irene*, Cal)

These reflections challenge modern meanings of positive/negative connected with independence/dependence as binary opposites.

The fifth strand is the most interesting in the context of the theme of women constructing their individualities. Here independence is discussed in relation to *interdependence*.[3]

I feel I'm a very people-centred person, although I'm very independent and I can keep people at a distance – – – I'm independent, but – – – interdependence I long for. (*Gwen*, Bri)

I am independent. – – – I see my future as being interdependent, not just independent. (*Caroline*, Bri)

Interdependence was referred to particularly when emotional aspects of independence were discussed. Many women said they were independent in terms of being in control of their own lives, taking care of themselves, and in terms of mentally being relatively uninfluenced by other people's judgements and attitudes. But in terms of emotional independence most qualifications were offered.

Independence I always use in terms of finance. I don't think you can be emotionally independent. That is rubbish in my view ... You're dependent on good relationships ... in which you can extend yourself. (*Valerie*, Bri)

I feel independent, but I'm not positive that that's true. I prefer the word 'interdependent' more. ... I do a lot of things with other people and get support and, you know, I don't know that anybody is totally independent. (*Rachel*, Cal)

I don't think I'm overly independent. Like I would never want to be without other people, I'm very dependent on my friends and very dependent on my work with children, you know. But – um – this is all a matter of degree 'cause you can't be in the world without other people, you'd go crazy. (*Kate*, Cal)

I feel I'm independent. But independence doesn't mean not recognizing how other people can help you. (*Carlotta*, Cal)

I am fairly independent, but part of the lifestyle I live – relationships with people are part of that. And in some way – I am dependent on these relationships and on maintaining them and looking after them, sort of. (*Lea*, Fin)

I used to think that to be independent in everything was a good thing, but it's not like that in life, I mean you are almost always – I mean you're not independent anyway. And it's not such a bad thing. ... For example in relations with others. (*Harriet*, Fin)

Independence is also taking other people into account. (*Else*, Fin)

Women needed their important people. Their independence was structured on the basis of a safety network they had constructed. Within these networks many women were able to receive some intimacy, some support and, most commonly, sharing of experiences and a possibility of locating themselves in a social and cultural map that usually reinforced the validity of their lifestyle.

In most women's responses several strands were evident. Not many of them would have experienced themselves as independent solely in terms of separateness. When the women talked about what one of them referred to as 'learning a new script', they explored a process of tensions and contradictions in assuming an independent status and lifestyle as a woman. They were also attempting to move beyond absolute/relative individuality as well as independence/dependence. Interdependence does not refer to absolute individuals, but neither does it refer to 'others' constructed in subordinate relations of power relative to men. Interdependence means taking others into account; not *being* an 'other'. It challenges negative interpretations of dependence which transform interpersonal and social depending on to a personality trait of being dependent on. This distinction is crucial in the way we view children, the elderly, the disabled, the chronically ill and so on.

Conclusion

Single women continue to push back boundaries of individuality and to assert their own status as individuals. They try to construct a type of independence wherein relative individuality becomes a strength rather than a weakness. Single women tend, if not always in explicitly articulated ways, to move beyond traditional femininity and established sexual difference, whereby women are defined relative to others. But those who said they had borrowed from traditional masculinity had found it wanting and tried to move away from 'aggressive independence' (using others selfishly). Single women, in the course of their day-to-day lives, try to balance out their need for intimacy and independence. If interdependence is a way of pushing back boundaries, it means that perhaps modern single women in metropolitan areas are moving towards being 'complete without a complement', not as isolated heroes of their own lives, but in interaction with others. There are difficulties in this: in crises *women often rely on themselves rather than turning to others* (Chapter 5); women fear lapsing into negative dependency; they are often support persons (Chapter 6); and their emphasis on the responsibility of individuals bears traces of absolute individuality (see Chapter 7) separated from the social context. Nevertheless single women in this study strive for both independence and connections in symmetrical relationships. As *Rosa* (Fin) claimed, they try to be, above all else, 'human beings'.

9

Marginality

Multiple marginalities

I started by asking if 'relativity' still defines women as individuals, and if single women who cannot be defined in relation to men are 'others' for whom filling the space of an 'individual' is difficult. If so, single women would tendentially still be marginal. I wanted to explore whether there were continuities in the position of single women. I was also interested to find out whether changes in family formations had eroded the marginality of single women. Their location and status as outsiders may have altered as more people live in formations different from the familist ideal of a nuclear family. Moreover people shift in and out of categories more than they used to; marriage is more likely to lead to divorce, remarriage and so on. I noted in Chapter 2 that my initial use of 'marginality' did not problematise the concept. I realised that, if I wanted to use marginality as an analytical tool and not as a descriptive term, I would need to rethink what is understood by marginality. The term is frequently used and tends to refer to people on the sidelines, powerless and dominated. Though this understanding is countered by an emphasis on *challenge* from the margins to the centre, this is also simplistic. Marginality is not a place, it has no boundaries. Marginalisation as a process does not produce homogeneity and many members of groups who are on the edge do not consider themselves marginal. Power is constituted in different ways, and marginalities are also multiple (C. Davies, 1991).

The complexity of this discussion is indicated in the different types of analyses of family formation, singleness and single motherhood among women of colour. On the one hand, single mothers of colour are considered a pitiful, deprived group, who pass on their deprivation to their children. On the other hand, they are considered matriarchal towers of strength, amazons who contribute to the problems of men of colour, who find it difficult to establish their masculinity. There are large groups of black women in the USA and in Britain who are oppressed and who struggle with hardship caused by economic, social and cultural effects of racism. But single black women are not a homogeneous group: social class and biographical aspects intersect 'race' and gender. Labels of amazonian women and pitiful welfare mothers are both oppressive constructions which contribute to marginalisation. Family formation among women of colour has been flexible in the face of adversity;[1] women who have supportive networks of relatives and friends, based on shared responsibility in the struggle to construct daily lives, are in a different position from those who are alone and isolated and dependent on state welfare services. It is questionable to argue, as Staples (1981) does, that singlehood among black American women must be explained in terms of negatives pushes, rather than positive pulls. Naming groups as marginal depends on the vantage point; often that vantage point can be one of economic and cultural power of the structurally privileged. Family formations of different ethnic groups have been studied with the ideal of a nulear family as a normative starting point (Zinn, 1990; Taylor et al. 1990; Collins, 1990). Hence black women have been viewed as under-married, and Asian women have been seen as over-married (Chandler, 1991, p. 36). Views from the 'margin' may be different; what is 'central' is altered. A British Muslim woman of Asian origin explains:

> I come from a culture where the women are the centre of that culture; actually they are much more highly regarded, if you like, than in Western culture, where they are on the periphery looking in. (Gordon, 1990, p. 95)

Collins (1990) refers to the 'outsider-within' status of black women which contains limitations, but also enables unique standpoints to be developed (see hooks, 1984).

Throughout this book I have attempted to convey several narratives. My 'voice' resonates as the one which has analysed and selected what voices of the women I interviewed are heard, but the research stance and methodological approach I have adopted have been framed by an attempt to enable the narratives of the women to question the starting-points formulated by the theoretical concerns of this study. 'Marginality' is more my narrative than, for example, 'independence' (though there were women who introduced this narrative in the interviews in the context of other themes, before I had raised it).

To avoid naming and thus reinforcing marginality, rather than asking whether single women are marginal, it is more useful to ask what the implications of being *marginal to marriage* are. Chandler (1991) in her study of women without husbands argues that there are continua of marriage along which women are placed, being 'more or less marginal to marriage, more or less connected to men' (p. 3). Marriage, Chandler claims, 'casts a long shadow' on all women. It is a central institution which also influences those who are not married; this point is made by many researchers (see Barrett and McIntosh, 1982). To explore the implications of marginality to marriage, I shall discuss single men before turning to the question of marginality of single women in this study.

Marital status and gender

Though there are more single men than single women, there has been less research on them. Historically single men have been considered less of a problem than single women; the term 'bachelor' does not have evocations similar to 'spinster' or 'old maid'. Changes in the position of women have been greater than changes in the position of men, but men may nevertheless have been negatively influenced by challenges to the sexual division of labour at home and at work. Evidence seems to point to single men being particularly marginal: 'A man's single status is usually acceptable up to age of thirty, after which he is considered emotionally unstable, alcoholic, or homosexual' (Levine, 1981, p. 269).[2] Studies of physical and mental well-being indicate that single men are over-represented among those who experience least well-being; single women tend to be 'superior to single men in terms of education, occupation and mental health' (Macklin, 1980, p. 907)

Single women on single men

Single women were frequently described in positive terms in the association lists (in this research): independent, free, strong and so on. Single men were described in more negative terms: selfish, lost, drunkard, gay, partner hunters, strange, leeches and so on. Twenty-five women used the term 'independent' in association with single women, only three in association with single men. Sixty-two of the descriptions of single men were wholly negative, or included both negative and positive descriptions. Only 11 associations were positive and 27 were neutral (for example, 'no thought about this'). Finnish women were most negative about single men. Finnish women are less likely to suffer from severe poverty; the welfare state has improved the position of vulnerable groups such as single mothers, and the relatively high educational standards and full-time participation in the labour market have improved their opportunities. There is a gender-gap in physical and mental well-being; men are over-represented among alcoholics, the homeless, and those who commit suicide.[3] Equality of opportunity between the sexes is established state policy and so-called 'state feminists' in Finland and in other Nordic countries have used state institutions in their attempts to tackle inequalities. But this process of improvement in the position of women is characterised by tensions. Current cuts in public spending are going to have an adverse effect on the position of women; the neo-conservative backlash contains strong concerns about boys and men, and frequently the blame for problems they experience is laid at the door of women (Gordon, 1992).

The views that emerged on single men in the interviews were more complex. There were negative descriptions of single men:

> Some men ... expect a woman to wait on them hand and foot, the washing, the cooking, the fetching and carrying. If they don't get these things done, then they will tell you they have life difficult. But if they can get these things done with being single at the same time, it's all right for them, I suppose. (*Gloria*, Bri)

> The single men I've met [are] mostly oddballs, of one kind of another. (*Peggy*, Cal)

> I think that a large proportion of social drop-outs are single men. I mean – I think that it's a lot harder thing for a man, singlehood that is, than it is for a woman. (*Saara*, Fin)

There were traces of the old maid stereotype – men are single because nobody wants them: 'If [a man] is a bit older, and he's unmarried, it immediately crosses my mind – well, what's wrong with this geezer?' (*Ursula*, Fin). Divorced men are seen to jump into new relationships without sorting themselves out first; divorced men are, indeed, more likely to remarry, and to remarry sooner, than divorced women (MacLean, 1991).

But single women also thought that single men *have an easier life because they are men*, and enjoy prestige and privileges that maleness and masculinity confer. In particular, educated, professional, middle-class white men are thought to be thriving, if in somewhat dubious ways.

> [People have] more positive attitude to single men than single women. ... It's always – it follows the same thing ... that men decide what they do and women wait, the women are on the shelf. Men are never on the shelf. It's that whole bit about – a man must have decided but a woman is just like not wanted. (*Lynne*, Bri)

> I really think it's a man's world. ... I think single men, in a sense, are more welcome. Their presence has less of a sexual connotation. (*Carlotta*, Cal)

> Single men are either sort of pitiful creatures who long for somebody to look after them, or they are successful, independent, and freedom is important to them. (*Laura*, Fin)

Single men were thought to enjoy greater freedom, acceptability and better financial resources, and to be in a better position to find partners (because of demographic imbalances). Several descriptions divided single men into two: those who were pitiful and those who were doing just fine. Besides the financial resources and occupational level of the man, 'race' was also considered to make a difference; this difference was raised by women of colour.

> White men I suppose have more choices open to them. It always seems much easier for them to sort of then hitch up with a woman. ... Black men, they seem to have a harder time, just getting to know themselves, and their relationships with black women and women generally. (*Gwen*, Bri)

> The mentality a lot of the [black] single men seem to have is, the world owe 'em something because they're black and they been held back and all that. They use that as an excuse instead of getting it themselves. Everybody owe 'em something. (*Bridget*, Cal)

Bridget had little tolerance; she was the 'backbone' of her whole extended family, an unwilling 'matriarch' who gave support and did not obtain much of it when she needed it herself. She was also a political activist in an organisation aiming to involve black women in politics.

Her biography, and her determination in the face of difficulties she had experienced, led her to have little sympathy for men looking for somebody else to take care of them, instead of taking care of themselves. Though their gender confers greater privileges on single men, being single cuts across that – single men were also seen to have problems similar to those of single women. Single men 'confront the same emotional difficulties', have 'a really hard time', are 'lonely' and 'look for partners'. Being married confers power. Richardson (1988) notes that married men, in liaisons with unmarried women, are in a powerful position; but a married woman having a liaison with an unmarried man can exercise more power than an unmarried woman with an unmarried man.

As women marry 'up' and men marry 'down' (Chapter 3), men in an unfavourable structural, cultural and social position are more likely to remain single than men who are more favourably positioned. Thus there are fewer educated, well earning professional single men than similar single women. As there is an imbalance of power based on a sexual division of labour between women and men, and masculinity is more highly valued than femininity, even those men who do not represent hegemonic masculinity (see Connell, 1987) benefit from the patriarchal sex-gender system. But masculinity is also characterised by competition as well as solidarity; men are forced to place themselves in a hierarchy of masculinities; losing in this game can have considerable repercussions. That single women see single men as both miserable losers and successful city singles is consistent with what is known about men from a gender perspective.

It is nevertheless interesting to note that women's descriptions of single men evoke traditional and modern stereotypes of single women; single men are seen not to have been able to find a woman, or not having wanted one. More research is needed in order to establish what the experience of singlehood is like for men; I do not doubt that there are men who have experienced problems, *and* men who have been successful and able to sidestep many issues that single women have to deal with. But people's lives are more complicated than such generalisations suggest. Less successful men may not be uniformly miserable; successful city singles may not be uniformly happy-go-lucky. There are undoubtedly single men who fall between these two extremes.[4] Studies of single men from critical gender perspectives would tell us more of the length of the shadow that marriage casts upon them, for example through the operation of homophobia (see Segal, 1990).

Marriage and family are important institutions producing and maintaining sexual difference; those who are single are marginalised as outsiders in relation to marital norms. *Marital status cuts across gender.* But there are differences and similarities in the way such a process influences women and men of different ethnic groups, of different social classes, of different ages and of different geographical locations (metropolitan/rural).

Are single women marginal?

It is not surprising that no one answer can be given to the question of the marginality of single women. The women interviewed were a heterogeneous grouping in three different countries. It is difficult, through interview data, to make a distinction between structural marginality in relation to economic, political, social and cultural power, and marginality as a subjective experience. Two women with roughly similar structural positions may have different experiences in relation to their status; is the one who does not experience herself as marginal less marginal than the one who does? What do we make of many women claiming that they did not experience any marginality, but that single women are marginal? Discussing a concept like 'marginality' is difficult in interviews; women in a cross-cultural study are likely to understand and interpret it in a variety of ways. The differences relate to their broader world-views and, in particular, how explicitly political their world-views are. Differences also relate to age, 'race' and sexual orientation. But because marginality is an amorphous structural/cultural/subjective positioning, meanings attached to it vary, so that in this research clear differentiation between various groupings did not emerge, except that the more multiple indices of marginalisation applied to a woman, the more likely she was to cite experiences of marginalisation, to point to societal processes connected with power that produced those, and their effectiveness on a subjective level. Nevertheless the cross-cultural nature of this study is important in analysing the complexity of marginality (see C. Davies, 1991).

'I am marginal'

There were women who said that they, or single women generally, were marginal:

> I do [feel marginal]. I really don't know quite where I belong. Yes, I do actually, very much. I'm very much outside of things. ... I'm quite frightened of being isolated, I suppose. (*Lynne*, Bri)

Often single people are just not included. ... Mainstream and social acceptability – I think that the single people are on the fringes of that. ... I think single people, because they are out of the mainstream, are questionable: why is that person out of mainstream? (*Peggy*, Cal)

I guess I see myself as a misfit. And it would be nice if I didn't. ... The world is made for couples, I think. And not for people who are single. (*Sue*, Cal)

I see myself on the edge. I see the mainstream as being sort of typical, family structure, wife, husband, two kids, that sort of thing. I don't see myself as being part of this group. (*Susan*, Cal)

I have this sense ... of difference and deviance. ... I sometimes experience myself as fairly detached. (*Helka*, Fin)

These women did not add further qualifications; for them marginalisation of single women was generalisable.

Marginality was typically related to social situations: being excluded, forgotten and invisible, being made to feel uncomfortable, or experiencing discomfort regardless of other people's reactions in a particular situation. This was often explained in terms of couples and families socialising with others in similar positions. But broader references to 'couples society' can be read as references to familism. This is particularly evident in comments by women who said that they did not experience a sense of marginality personally, even though they generally considered single women to be marginal.

I don't feel odd. But I think it's because I am with other people and a lot of people I know are in the same position. I think if most of my friends were couples I'd feel much more peculiar. (*Betsy*, Bri)

I don't feel odd one out being single in Berkeley. (*Michelle*, Cal)

I haven't experienced [marginality] myself really. But it could be – yes – I think it's dependent on your surroundings and your job and – what you identify yourself with, and how many similar ones there are. Yes I think it could be very easy to end up like that. (*Laura*, Fin)

There were constant references to women's own personal networks, or broader alternative sub-cultures. Being located in these was a form of protection from a *sense* of marginality, if not from marginality itself. These networks and sub-cultures provided women with a safe haven from negative experiences instigated by others. They do not have a sense of 'lack' or difference which they are likely to feel when coming across family structures and coupled social interaction.

Protective networks were typically connected with location. Women thought that being single was relatively easy in these three metropolitan areas where the interviews were conducted. Particularly in London, there were further refences to specific locations; for example: 'This is the end of the sort of [North London] bedsit-land kind of area which is full of rather peculiar, odd people.' But the size of London also posed difficulties in the construction of everyday lives. In the San Francisco Bay Area, alternative networks were considered more amorphous and there were fewer references to particular locations. In Helsinki, the contrast was mainly between Helsinki and rural areas; there were fewer references to differentiation within Helsinki.

The locations of these women served to protect them from socictal pressures; their own networks, often deliberately and consciously constructed over the years, operated as buffer zones providing further safety. But the protection is not complete and those particularly whose single status is not voluntary stable experience problems when they come across mainstream values and find it difficult to construct their own orientation in relation to these values. *Lorna*, who considers herself 'abnormal', described a crisis she went through in her early thirties; singleness played a significant part in that, but was interconnected with other facets of her life (see p. 47).

> [I had] no proper job, no husband, no property. ... I'm still not sure whether it only bothered me because I could see other people living in a different way, or whether it actually ought to bother me. ... But I've just so arranged my life that I avoid [societal pressures]. ... you realise that most of the time you are actually just avoiding the way of life most people live. ... [I have] chosen the hardest way. ... But ... I've arranged it so that people around me feel pretty much the same way. (*Lorna*, Bri)

Singleness cannot be isolated as an especially significant factor in marginality among women who experience a sense of being marginal and give several reasons for it. As there is not one margin, but multiple marginalities, one person can be located in several of these.

Social class

Greta, like *Lorna*, is a member of alternative networks in North London. She can be described as having 'sidestepped' mainstream society. She has done this relatively successfully; this was indicated in her description of a traditional wedding she observed in the countryside – she expressed amazement that such customs and traditions still exist. She lives in short-life housing, her income is very small, she is outside 'proper society' and interacts with 'fringe people'. She explains her choices:

> In the sort of mainstream society I could have become a very successful member – – – [but] I went into sort of slum housing conditions ... I had a headstart anyway – I could take that freedom, you know ... all these risks I've taken, I've always had a safety net which is I've had a good education. ... It's certainly all done from a middle-class position. (*Greta*, Bri)

Greta has maintained some advantages acquired through her middle-class background, while forsaking others. *Harriet* (Fin) has not enjoyed such advantages. She thinks of herself as marginal, and has always thought that she is different, and an outsider, for many reasons. One of them is her working-class background, the significance of which she explains to be particularly pronounced because she is a Swedish-speaking Finn. For historical reasons, Swedish-speaking Finns, though not entirely homogeneous, have contained a powerful, wealthy elite; this added more poignancy to the isolation *Harriet* experienced because of her working class background. For her, marginality is less a matter of choice than it is for *Greta*.

'Race' and ethnicity

Single women of colour and members of ethnic minorities were generally very conscious of being part of marginal and marginalised groups.

> I'm black first, and a woman second, and I come from humble origins. ... if I weren't black then I would fall in and be assimilated. But because I'm different I'm treated differently, and therefore I have to recognise that and respond to that in a positive way. And nobody's gonna pull me up when they're pushing me down. (*Valerie*, Bri)

Even though women thought they were members of groups that were discriminated against, their personal sense of marginality was not necessarily greater than that of women from ethnic majority groups. Their protective social networks were constructed along ethnic lines and thus provided protection from racism as well as from uncomfortable experiences in relation to singlehood.

> I think the black community, I think they are more tolerant of their own ... they would rather sometimes ignore the fact that you're not married and try

to, you know, give you the support, than let you go drifting about outside into the unknown. (*Gloria*, Bri)

Those between different cultures found their situation more of a problem. For example, *Ella* considered herself marginal in relation to English people, but also in relation to her own community. Many women managed to negotiate their multiple locations fairly comfortably. Particularly in cultures where family orientation is strong, it is relatively easy to interact with different groups, and to be located in predominantly white society in the context of work, but to maintain close connections with one's own ethnic group.[5]

Being located between two cultures can also be considered a strength. *Rosa*, a Romany gypsy, left home at the age of 13, in order to avoid being brought up into 'the system', although she has maintained her ties with Romany culture. She explains her own variety of outsider-within standpoint:

> I know quite a lot about both cultures. ... I have created my own path for myself. ... I don't consider myself as being in-between, but that I have found my very own road that I travel along. I don't veer to the left or the right, but stay in the middle of the road, and this gets stronger the older I get. So it is more about finding yourself than belonging to any clan ... I think it's important to find your own road, through yourself. (*Rosa*, Fin)

There were women who had experienced more bitter and direct racism and were less able to sidestep it: for example, *Miriam* (Bri), who is Jewish and has a mixed-race child whose father is Afro-Caribbean, and *Judy* (Bri) who lives in a council flat with racist white neighbours who 'always complain about little things', so that she feels like 'a sort of prisoner'. Most of the highly educated women of colour recount experiences of discouragement and discrimination, and the considerable determination and struggle required to reach their positions.

Immigration

Ambivalence about one's cultural location was experienced also by many who are not members of ethnic minorities, but who are located in a cultural setting different from their original one. For example, *Simone*, who is French and lives in California, *Galina*, who is Eastern European and lives in Finland and *Shirley*, who is American and lives in Britain, experience ambivalence and a degree of detachment; processes of cultural exclusion can apply to those who are not native to the country of residence. Many of them also experience varying degrees of discrimination. It is possible that experiences of migration increase the likelihood of remaining unmarried or becoming divorced.

Women with disabilities

The disabled are particularly likely to experience marginality and a sense of invisibility. Disability is a 'social malady'; the disabled are marginal outsiders (Murphy, 1990) and social relations between them and the able-bodied are difficult (Morris, 1991). Disabled women are particularly invisible, often ignored and devalued (Lonsdale, 1990). Lonsdale argues that this is possible because it is more acceptable for a woman to become disabled as 'passivity, docility and dependency are more compatible with the female sex role' (p. 42). For disabled women, getting out of the marginal status, whether they are married or not, requires resources and reorganisation. Generally women suffering from ill-health are more likely to remain single or, if they become ill or disabled after marriage, they are slightly more likely to experience divorce than men (Lonsdale, 1990, pp. 73–6). Disabled women are a heterogeneous group too, and their experiences of processes of marginalisation and personal sense of marginality vary according to the resources that are available and to the degree of their disability. *Nina* (Fin) connected the question of marginality with inequalities experienced by single women. *Hanna* (Fin) connected it more with social situations where she tries to 'dive in' and 'take her place', though in situations which she has preselected, to avoid ones where her disability and singleness combined lead to experiences of exclusion. Overall, equality for disabled people is 'still a dream' (*Nina*, Fin).

Lesbian women

Lesbians felt strongly marginalised; not all the lesbians interviewed had come out, and those who had not led double lives. Lesbians were particularly unlikely to be able to take their own lifestyles for granted. Even those who had come out felt they were on the sidelines in social interaction and discriminated against on the societal level. Though lesbians thought that homosexuality had become more acceptable, there are still

processes of marginalisation operating on many levels. Liberal attitudes pose problems too; saying that people's sexual orientation is a personal matter contributes to a process of exclusion by ignoring homophobic attitudes and discrimination against lesbians and gays.
The marginality of lesbians was particularly strong if it was combined with other social factors which confirmed it. Thus *Harriet* (Fin), who felt she was different because of her working-class background, also felt different because she is a lesbian. *Gwen* gave examples of the way difference leads to an outsider status in multiple contexts:

> I don't fit the stereotype really. I've always ... felt like I'm in a group that is marginalised ... it was like within the women's movement, being a black woman, and you know, the black women's feminist movement, being on the edge as a lesbian, and – yeah, I'm used to operating in the margins and I like it. (*Gwen*, Bri)

Single women without partners were thought to be marginalised among lesbians:

> I'm not into one of these strong couples scenes, which are ... quite common in London. It becomes to me too reminiscent of some heterosexual circles, where people are only welcomed if they're part of a stable couple. Other people are seen with suspicion. (*Eileen*, Bri)

Jeffreys (1985) argues that the right for women to remain single is crucial; marginalisation of lesbians is connected with the marginalisation of all women who live independently of men. Lesbianism poses a challenge to heterosexuality. Sexual love between women contradicts the entrenched idea of complementarity between women and men and thus potentially erodes sexual difference.

Biographies and personal characteristics

There were a few women who considered themselves marginal because of particular biographies or characteristics they possessed. For example, two very tall women considered themselves as outsiders partly because of their height. There were also a few women who said they were 'different', without any clear-cut explanation for that difference. 'Being different', that is crossing a subtle and ambivalent borderline from acceptable individualistic variations to a more total distinctness, leads to a social stigma which is not easily defined. In everyday life this process is clearer when applied to those who, for example, outrageously flout codes of dress, but it is less clear when applied to those who are, for example, quiet, introvert, not seeking approval, dressing 'down' in an understated way and so on. Additionally being 'different' may be derived from, for example, having been a member of the Salvation Army; one woman explained how a label had been attached to her, which after some decades had not been forgotten. It is possible that those who are 'different' are more likely to remain unmarried; it may also be that, as they remain single, they feel in control and see no pressing reasons to alter their appearance or conduct.

'I am not marginal'

A small number of women stated that they experienced no sense of marginality and made no qualification to that by referring to particular networks or sub-cultures which might have reduced a sense of marginality. No structural and cultural characteristics were shared by this group; for example they were not uniformly privileged middle-class women in well-paid jobs. They included a black and a white-working class woman, a director and a retired woman. Two have children. Common features were that they are all extrovert, find it easy to make contact with people, and their work involves a great deal of social interaction.

There were also women who did not consider themselves and single women in general marginal, or who at least played down this possibility. *Kaisa* (Fin) stated that she thought single women were not marginal as a direct answer to a direct question, but said in another context that she thought that single women were discriminated against. I considered that an indication of marginality. I have interpreted indices of marginality broadly. A more stringent interpretation would have come up with more women who bore no traces of marginality. My interpretation can be supported by several points: (1) those who find it relatively easy to construct networks and to be sociable, and who are less likely to experience loneliness and existential angst are also less likely to consider themselves marginal; (2) single women are concerned to control and construct their own lives – they have often struggled in the past to do so and have undergone learning processes through which their lives seem relatively comfortable and problem-free; (3) many single women emphasise that important changes take place on the level of the

192 *Single Women*

individual – thus marginality, for them, may be located 'in the head' or 'between the ears' of a single woman, and changing the perception one has of oneself is sufficient to eradicate a sense of marginality; (4) women make references to tendencies which push them into the margins, but also their own resistance to that; playing down marginality in an interview may reflect this – I stated earlier (Chapter 2) that naming particular groups 'marginal' is a problem, because by doing so it is possible that one contributes to their marginalisation.

Margins as the centre?

A significant theme in relation to marginality was defiance. It consisted of several modes of action and thought. Constructing supportive networks was the first mode of action which challenged marginality. Even if these single women are marginal, a *sense* of marginality was nevertheless conquered. Second, women struggled to pull themselves out of the margins. If they thought there were processes of marginalisation affecting them because of their singlehood, or singlehood combined with other dimensions of difference, women resisted this process, for example 'in their heads' or by ignoring exclusion in social situations.

> Well, I don't know – if I have been pushed [onto the edges] then I have furiously scrambled out of there, I have not consented to being there [laughs]. I am sure that sort of thing exists. (*Minna*, Fin)

Thirdly, women *made their margins their centres*; this is implicitly done in the first course of action, but others also did this explicitly – they did not want to be in the maintream.

> I'd far rather be different than like one of the crowd. ... I just cannot see myself as being one of a crowd, you know, one of a sort of accepted type of person. I mean, I go out of my way to be perverse half the time, because I can't bear being stuck in with everyone else, and being the same as everyone else. ... I think a lot of it is that I spent so many years of being laughed at and teased for being different in a way that I couldn't help that I've almost gone the opposite way. ... I quite enjoy it. (*Tina*, Bri[6])

> I have no desire to be in the mainstream. (*Celia*, Bri)

> A single woman – we are dealing with labelling that goes on in our society, we're dealing with stereotypes of who we are and what we are. ... But I also feel strongly that we've got to take an active ... role to redefine it and change

it and stop letting society control how we define ourselves, some of the values they put on us. (*Carlotta*, Cal)

It ... has made me think in a different way than if I'd have just followed the flow. (*Harriet*, Fin)

The strongest statement of challenge and transformation of a margin to a centre is given by *Gwen*, a black lesbian woman. She 'quite likes being on the margin'. She has not chosen to be there, but has been 'rejected' by mainstream society. She has turned this rejection into something positive: 'If I didn't I'd be dead [laughter]'. She explains:

> It's like they say, all right, you're only worth this little piece in the corner, and like I say, let me look at this piece and see what I can fashion out of it, you know, that's got me in it. And that's fine, 'cos, you know, they leave you alone. It's nice to be on the margin. ... I'm there anyway, I might as well enjoy it. (*Gwen*, Bri)

Power can be exercised in many ways, in many locations. The power of *Gwen* is not the same as the power of an influential, wealthy male middle-class business executive, politician, member of the judiciary and so on. But dominant power in society has not eclipsed her, has not determined her, and has not foreclosed her opportunities. Making the margins one's centre is hard work, but it has given *Gwen* scope to try to structure her life without being submissive and conformist. Grand solutions offered, for example, by socialist politics have not worked; people have not formed a united front to resist their oppression. But neither have people necessarily given their consent and buckled under. They may struggle and challenge structures and cultures that dominate them. Single women have, for a long time, been among those people who have not accepted limitations placed on them, and have explored possibilities and delved into oppositional spaces, but they have not done so according to the dreams of radical politicians. They have, instead, made a virtue of quiet, everyday oddness, they have tried to behave as though limitations are not there, and they have taken the raw materials available and tried to construct the best possible life out of them. On the simplest level this is indicated by the fact that the majority of these women are voluntary singles in what many of them consider to be a couple- and family-oriented society.

Their acts are often everyday rebellions; they may not give explicit, coherent political explanations for them; while struggling to extend what 'a woman' is, they may not accept feminist theorising of it. Singleness, though a different experience for women and men because of the greater economic, cultural and social resources of the latter, cuts across gender. Many women have experiences of other women marginalising them, excluding them and relating to them as though they are a threat.

> I think what annoys me is that women in Finland still control themselves and other women, too much, more than men even. (*Laura*, Fin)

This kind of observation makes single women critical of feminism and reduces their sense of solidarity with women in general terms. It can be argued, however, that women have been placed in the situation of being controlled and controlling simultaneously by the sexual division of labour. For example, in the context of semi-professions women participate in a process of regulation, whilst the framework within which they operate is set by predominantly male professionals at upper levels of the hierarchies (Walkerdine and Lucey, 1989). Women have been granted a power of prohibition (Gordon, 1992) and placed in positions where they have to exercise it within limited frameworks; it is not by any means easy to do so wisely.

It is not useful to idealise marginalisation, or to adopt a simplistic liberal approach emphasising the tolerance and permissiveness of pluralist modern societies, or to argue that there is no basis from which to be marginal in postmodern societies (see Yudice, 1988). Marginality is not in a mechanic relationship to *a* centre; marginality is not single but multiple; marginality is neither a weakness nor a strength in any simple sense; but marginality is structurally and culturally produced: a *social positioning* as well as a subjective experience.

Changes in the position of single women

There are continuities in the position of single women. Women not defined in relation to a man can still be considered a threat and be looked at askance: why have they not married? People find it difficult to categorise them, and veer between stereotypes of old maids and city singles. In the labour market they are first and foremost women and, like other women, disadvantaged in relation to men. Single women still do not find it easy to have active, satisfactory sex lives. If they are single mothers, they have to struggle with financial difficulties and often with poverty. If they do not have children, it is difficult for them to make the decision to become lone parents. Childcare is organised in such a way that a wide responsibility is exercised in nuclear families by mothers and fathers, with the latter tending to share at least some of the responsibility. Families have monopolised children; it is generally assumed that a family, defined precisely as a nuclear family, is the best and most secure place for children to grow up. That is at least partly true, because familist ideology and policies support such a form of childcare.

Family has also monopolised a great deal of intimacy and at least a sense of companionship, if not the reality of it. The experiences of single women in this study indicate that in many ways families do 'work'. Though there are those who have had painful experiences in their childhood, and a majority have experienced at least some ambivalence in relation to their parents, siblings and other relatives, for many of them, members of their family of origin have been an important source of support. But because family ties in terms of responsibilities towards aging parents have relaxed, single women have had more space to develop their friendship networks and to explore possibilities for support and intimacy, particularly with other women. Being single has also become an *opportunity*, not simply fate. Education and participation in the labour market have afforded women a degree of financial independence which makes the option of remaining unmarried or getting divorced more feasible than in the nineteenth century or in the 1950s. But single women are still unlikely to take their lifestyle for granted at all times; they may learn to do so, but the majority have to reflect on their single status, usually around the age of 30. Marriage still does cast a long shadow.

Though a few women in this study resisted the identity of 'single woman', none of them would have been likely to say that being single is simply a 'statistical category', as *Marina*, a young single in her twenties, stated. Two young singles were interviewed: *Marina* lives in the San Francisco Bay Area, *Sirkku* in Helsinki; *Marina* is 23, *Sirkku* 27. Both are voluntary temporary singles; they hope not to remain single.[7] Singleness is most typically a phase (or phases) in a woman's life. Women who never marry are still a minority. The increase in singleness is largely due to delaying marriage. Young women are often 'still' single, or 'not yet' married. *Sirkku* and *Marina* enjoy their exploration, but if they are still single in their thirties, on the basis of their present reflections, they will reach a point when they want to 'settle down'. They will need to review their current outlook if they 'settle down' as single women. In particular they will both need to consider how they are going to deal with their expressed desire to have children.

Conclusion

This is a cross-cultural rather than a comparative study, therefore comparisons between the different countries are not particularly conclusive. There were features which could be detected in all: in none of the countries could singleness be sidestepped and ignored when women organise their lives, or when they reflect on their lives; moreover, in all three locations of the study, women thought that it was easier to be single there than in other parts of the country. Singleness for Finnish women is somewhat easier because historically the proportion of single women has been relatively high. In the United States the increase in singleness is most recent, but in the San Francisco Bay Area ease of singleness was particularly connected with networking. Being a single parent is least difficult in Finland, but there are cuts in public spending and, as the welfare state diminishes in significance, their position is likely to deteriorate. Finnish women were less likely to point to severe difficulties connected with singleness. Partly this is due to a way of talking formed in a cultural context (see Tannen, 1992, p. 202). Finnish women were less likely to cry, but they were also less likely to laugh. Alternative networks are not as significant in Helsinki as in London or the San Francisco Bay Area – thus Finnish women have sought incorporation more. San Francisco has been described as the cultural capital of family change (Stacey, 1990). In the USA the increase of singleness is relatively recent. Because the welfare state has been weak, women have been more dependent on men. Single-parent families headed by women have increased, but a large proportion of these live in poverty. The conservative administration refused to tackle this problem by strengthening the welfare state. (The writing of this book was almost completed by the time President Clinton was elected.) In Britain proportions of single women have been higher than in the USA, and lower than in Finland. The welfare state has been stronger than in the USA, and was established earlier than the Finnish welfare state. The British welfare state has been based on more familistic assumptions than the Finnish welfare state. Familial ideology and rhetoric have emphasised wifehood and motherhood more than in Finland, but less than in the USA. Inequalities between different social groups are less pronounced in Britain than in the USA, and more pronounced than in Finland, but women living in London, like their San Fransisco Bay Area counterparts, are more likely to be able to build their own networks in the context of greater cultural diversity than in Helsinki. Single women who challenge limitations of absolute individuality and attempt to balance independence and intimacy do so in a societal framework where individuals as citizens are placed in a particular relationship to the state. Formal, political citizenship is most clearly defined through individualism. Social citizenship is also determined by individualism, in theory; in practice, familism is also significant in defining social citizenship. Finland, like other Nordic welfare states, has made social citizenship more accessible to women than have Britain and the USA, where familism more explicitly frames social services (see Lewis, 1991; Barrett and McIntosh, 1982). In particular, single mothers (unmarried or divorced) benefit from provisions which facilitate engaging in paid work. Debates about Nordic welfare states have contained conflicting views on how fundamental are the shifts involved (for example, Siim, 1987; Hernes, 1988; Haavio-Mannila *et al.*, 1985; Julkunen, 1990). Walby (1990) makes a distinction between public and private patriarchy. In Finland the shift from private to public patriarchy is more advanced than in Britain or the USA. Combined with an ideology of equality of opportunity, public patriarchy has provided women with more opportunities for economic independence. This has afforded single women more scope in determining the course of their lives, but the apparent gender neutrality of the Finnish welfare state assumes gender specificity when neutral principles are translated into practice.[8] I agree with Walby that patriarchy, by becoming more public, has partly been reduced in degree and has partly altered its form.

Constructing an independent life, reaching the status of 'the individual' and obtaining full social citizenship are still areas of struggle. Women are developing 'individuality' where relative/absolute distinctions are diminished through efforts to achieve interdependence. Single women are still marginalised in familist societies and many of them experience multiple marginalisation. But they also challenge marginality and develop 'outsider-within' standpoints. There have been considerable changes in the position of single women since the nineteenth century and a great deal of improvement has taken place during the last three decades. But the rise of neo-conservatism has posed a challenge to opportunities which have been opening up for women. Constant, steady progress in the position of single women is unlikely. The proportion of singles is likely to rise, but this may be increasingly due to 'pushes': economic circumstances frame the possibilities of building families which are safe havens for all the members. Forming a unit approximating to the middle-class nuclear family is difficult for those dealing with problems associated with poverty. The ideal of equal symmetrical relationships is particularly unattainable in the context of increasing inequalities. But there are also 'pulls'; in this study women, *regardless* of social class, ethnic group, sexual orientation and age *valued independence*, even if some were reluctantly single.

Tensions between separateness and connectedness, and between independence and intimacy, pose a tightrope for single women. I wanted to explore how single women deal with pressures towards marriage and maternity. Sidestepping pressures towards marriage involves gains and losses. Pressures towards maternity are not experienced by women as single. On the contrary, they have to deal with pressures *not* to have children. Those single women who would like to have children are likely to experience sadness. Single women who have children are likely to experience material and social problems.

Single women are faced with processes of marginalisation *and* incorporation. Singleness is not a misfortune, though it can be, if combined with poverty and isolation. For women to achieve full citizenship, the needs of most vulnerable women must be met (Sarvasy, 1992) through a welfare state which does not uphold sexual difference or familism. Singleness offers possibilities, but those possibilities contain tensions and contradictions. *Molly* (Bri) explains that there is 'a sense of free spirit involved in being single'. One of the benefits is that 'I can actually do, you know, within my own limitations, whatever I decide to do'. But, she adds 'it's a big wide world out there, and it could become hostile, it could become lonely – I could find that I'm, you know, all alone and sinking'. Nevertheless she associates her image of a single woman with a horse running free.

Appendix: the interviewees

Name	Status[1]	Children[2]	Age	Occupation	Other
London					
Greta	NM	—	41	Freelance potter	Central European
Liz	S	—	40	Social worker	
Lorna	NM	—	35	Freelance cabinet maker	
Lynne	NM	—	41	Social worker	
Ella	NM	—	39	Psychotherapist	Southern European
Gina	NM	—	46	Social worker	Lesbian
Betsy	NM	—	35	Freelance painter/signwriter	
Tina	NM	—	35	Administration	
Judy	NM	17, 14	35	Freelance painter/decorator	Afro-Caribbean
Isabella	NM	—	44	Head of Department, Further Education	Chilean
Roberta	NM	—	43	Valuer	
Shirley	D	—	53	Painter	American
Molly	NM	—	49	Psychotherapist	Lesbian
Caroline	D	22	47	Lecturer, Further Education	
Jill	D	21, 20, 18	47	Lecturer, Further Education	
Gwen	NM	—	35	Freelance Photographer	Lesbian Afro-Caribbean
Sylvia	D	5 adults	55	Health worker	Afro-Caribbean
Clara	D	4 adults	46	Community worker	Chilean
Gloria	NM	12, 5	38	Community worker	Afro-Caribbean
Valerie	NM	3, 1	37	Legal adviser/secretary	Afro-Caribbean

Name					
Miriam	NM	20 1 child has died	42	Unemployed	Jewish
Celia	NM	—	55	Administrator	Lesbian
Eileen	NM	—	60	Clinical manager	Lesbian
Emily	D	13, 10	41	Nurse	

San Francisco Bay Area

Name					
Rebecca	NM	—	68	Retired nurse	Jewish
Simone	S	2 adults 1 child has died	61	Administrator	French
Jody	D	—	40	Administrator	D twice
Peggy	NM	—	52	Administrator	
Violet	D	1 adult	43	Entrepreneur	
Bridget	S	28, 25	48	Secretary/ instructor	African– American
Frances	D	2	50	Part-time property dev.	
Shoshana	D	—	41	Office work	Iranian
Sue	NM	—	42	Doctor	Japanese– American
Rachel	NM	—	40	Physician's assistant	Jewish
Dorothy	D	3 adults 1 child has died	67	Art student	
Inez	NM	—	46	Consultant	Chicana
Norma	S	—	38	Administrator	
Michelle	D	—	54	Social worker	
Rita	D	35	54	Consultant	
Christine	D	—	51	Professor	Lesbian
Amy	D	12, 8	40	Administration	Chinese– American
Kate	D	—	51	Teacher	
Maxine	NM	—	44	Musician	Lesbian
Naomi	NM	38	61	Nurses' assistant	African– American
Carlotta	NM	—	34	Researcher	Chicana
Irene	D	—	47	Art admin	Chicana
Martha	NM	—	69	Administration	
Susan	NM	—	48	Administration	British

Helsinki

Name					
Anni	NM	—	57	Laboratory	
Eila	NM	—	49	Research assistant	
Sanna	NM	—	37	Social worker	Lesbian

The interviewees 201

Name	Status	Children	Age	Occupation	Other
Lea	NM	—	44	Teacher of disabled children	
Ursula	NM	—	45	Nurse	
Helka	NM	—	64	Retired nurse	
Minna	D	—	44	Office work	
Laura	D	—	42	Freelance reporter	
Taina	NM	—	37	Caretaker	
Reija	NM	—	42	Freelance graphic artist	
Soili	NM/S	13	44	Freelance art admin	
Helena	NM	—	56	Office worker	
Mari	D	25	45	Office worker	Sami
Ritva	D	6, 13	41	Social worker	
Rosa	NM	—	35	Freelance artist	Romany
Kaisa	D	21	45	Cleaner/seamstress	
Harriet	NM	—	41	Social worker	Lesbian
Else	D	—	49	Croupier	
Saara	NM/S	—	36	Art admin	
Eeva	D	2 adults	65	Retired shopkeeper	
Ulla	NM/S	—	36	Manager	
Nina	NM	—	43	Organiser, voluntary association	Disabled
Hanna	NM	—	45	Retired office worker	Disabled
Galina	D	35	52	Office work, interpreter	Eastern European

Notes
1. NM = never – married; D = divorced; S = married but separated; NM/S = separated after cohabitation
2. The ages of children, or number of adult children are stated.

Notes

Introduction

1. Thomas Bulfinch (1981) *Myths of Greece and Rome*, Penguin, Harmondsworth.
2. The name she used herself was Jehanne la Pucelle (Warner, 1983, p. 41).

Chapter 1: From spinsters to singles

1. Wacklin, Sara (1966) *Sata muistelmaa Pohjanmaalta*, WSOY, Porvoo, pp. 76–82.
2. The position of upper-class single women was comparable to that in Britain and the USA.
3. Friedan, Betty (1963) *The Feminine Mystique*, Dell, New York.
4. Cf. M. Young and P. Wilmott (1973) *The Symmetrical Family*, Routledge & Kegan Paul, London.
5. Thornton concentrates on America; research by Nummenmaa in Finland and Holland in Britain indicates similar expectations of young girls.
6. Sources: England and Wales – percentages calculated from 'Marriage and Divorce Statistics', Series FM2, No. 2, London, HMSO; Finland – percentages calculated from data in 'Structure of Population and Vital Statistics 1988', Central Statistical Office of Finland, Population 1191:7; USA – US census, *Population Characteristics*, Current Population Reports, series P. 20, no. 433.
7. The average age at marriage for women was 24.1 in Britain in 1986 (*Social Trends*, 1988).
8. Sources: Finland – Ritamies (1988); Britain – *Social Trends* (1988); USA – L.L. Bumpass and J. Sweet (1989). Accurate up-to-date figures on cohabitation are difficult to find; see for example discussion in Bumpass and Sweet (1989).

Chapter 2 : Individuality, autonomy and women

1. The percentage for London is calculated from census figures; the percentage in California is calculated from *Current Population Survey*, California State Census Data Center, 1988; the percentage for Helsinki is calculated from the *Statistical Yearbook of the City of Helsinki*, 1989.

Chapter 3 : The making of a single women

1. Young singles would be an interesting group to study, as singleness has particularly increased among them, but it would have been difficult to combine studying those who are more likely to consider themselves temporarily single with those who are more likely to remain single, and have been single for some time. Two young singles, however, were interviewed (Chapter 9).
2. The Sami traditionally live in Lapland and keep reindeer.
3. 'Semi-profession' is a term used to indicate that jobs such as teaching, social work and nursing fulfil some criteria of professions, but not all of them. They are based on expertise, but do not enjoy a high status or include autonomy from external control. Typically 'professions' with a large proportion of women are termed 'semi-professions'.
4. That Sinikka Aapola participated in interviewing was useful. This provided opportunities for cooperation in discussing the interviews, comparing our assumptions and preconception (Sinikka is a single woman in her late twenties) and checking the 'hunches' that were worked on. Sinikka also found some of the Finnish interviewees.
5. Women were asked to list ten people whom they considered important in their lives, without the interviewer setting more precise criteria than that. I shall describe these lists more fully in Chapter 5, where the networks of the women are discussed.
6. The names of the women have been changed. Abbreviations are for California, Britain and Finland, respectively.
7. In the extracts from the interviews ... indicates that a section has been omitted; ___ indicates that the section is inaudible on the cassette.
8. I went through all the interviewed women on the basis of choice, voluntariness, permanence, and contentment with single status. Sinikka Aapola than went through the same process. When we compared our notes, we were surprised to discover that our categorizations overlapped in the majority of cases. I rechecked and reconsidered those cases where our judgements had differed, and made revisions in some. Though categorisations were difficult, there was a great deal of information in the data which facilitated this process.
9. US Census, Current Population Reports, series P. 20, no. 433 Population Characteristics.
10. She was the only woman in the study who, having agreed to be interviewed, at the beginning of the interview stated that she did not think she was single after all. As she did not live with a partner, and did not spend a considerable amount of time with her partner, I judged her to be single woman who had a girlfriend.

Chapter 4 : Excursion into the public sphere

1. Of the 23 women who had children, 14 had adult children, two had children under school age and five had children under the age of ten, and 2 had children aged between 10 and 18.

2. 'Ambition' was not covered in all the interviews here.
3. In the U.S.A, median weekly earnings of full-time employees were 468 dollars for men and 328 dollars for women (source: *Statistical Abstract of the United States, 1991*, US Department of Commerce, Bureau of the Census). In Britain the median gross weekly earnings of men were £258 for men and £178 for women (source: Tom Griffin (ed.) *Social Trends*, Central Statistical Office, HMSO, 1992). In Finland in 1991 the average monthly earnings for men were 10 128 Fin Marks, and for women 8143 Finn Marks (source: Central Statistical Office, *Hinta – ja palkkatiedote*, 1992).
4. One parent (most often the father) had died or parents had difficulties in their own relationships: alcoholism, large families, poverty, recovery from war and geographic dislocation. However not all families characterised by any of these features were unable to pay attention to their children.
5. Such solutions are merely apparent for married mothers in paid labour.

Chapter 5: Excursion into the private sphere

1. Women were asked how much time they spent at home; accurate information was difficult to obtain, as women often said that their patterns varied according to the situation at work, illness, financial situation, time of the year and so on. About two-thirds were out several evenings a week. Over a fifth spent more evenings out than in. Retired women spent more time at home, even though they were also involved in many activities outside the home.
2. These activities were obtained from lists of hobbies and 'out-of-work' activities filled in during the interviews.
3. Many women acquired their homes at a time when the housing market was easier to enter than during later periods when house prices and/or interest rates were more prohibitive.
4. Married women do not (intrinsically) enjoy housework either: Ann Oakley (1974) *The Sociology of Housework*, Martin Robertson, Oxford.
5. There were some interviews where this area was not discussed.
6. Their smaller homes and kitchens are not well equipped for this.
7. This is particularly typical of Finnish women. The fact that the majority of women work full-time has contributed to the emphasis on provision of nutritious subsidised meals at work-based refectories.
8. These were mainly carried out by Sinikka Aapola.
9. Allardt in her study of 25 single women in Finland also found that their networks consisted mainly of other single women. Allardt, Monica Storstadens '"Swinging Singles" eller stackars gammalpigor?', undergraduate dissertation, Department of Sociology, University of Helsinki.

Chapter 6: Partnerships and sexuality

1. The research I referred to is British, but the need to safeguard sexual morality applies also in the USA (see Rose and Frieze, 1989) and Finland (see Hukkila, 1992).

2. Women were told that some of the questions in the interviews would be personal and that it was up to them to decide if there were questions they did not want to answer, or they could decide how much they were willing to say on the subject. Many women brought the subject of sexuality up themselves, before any questions had been asked.
3. The length of celibacy varied a great deal; for example, more than ten years, or one year some time in the past.

Chapter 7: On being single

1. In a research project students studied representations of single people in popular culture; they discovered positive representations of singleness, but found that these were marginal in relation to mainstream representations relying on traditional stereotypes (*Itselliset: Vanhoja piikoja ja poikia vai meneviä sinkkuja*, Department of Sociology, University of Helsinki, 1991).
2. For example, Christine *Gorman*'s article, 'Sizing up the Sexes' in *Time* magazine, 20 January 1992. The cover illustrates a young boy checking his arm muscles, whilst a young girl looks one. The caption reads: 'Why Are Men and Women Different? – It isn't just upbringing. New studies show they are born that way.'
3. For example, in a Finnish survey of women, 57 per cent agreed completely, and 24 per cent agreed to some extent with the statement, 'A single woman may have a child even though she does not want a steady relationship with a man': Timo *Nikander* (1992) *The Woman's Life Course and the Family Formation*, Central Statistical Office of Finland, Population 1992: 1.
4. Studies using different criteria are not consistent (see Zollar and Williams, 1987; Ball and Robbins, 1986; Coleman *et al.*, 1987).

Chapter 8: Independence

1. *Pocket Oxford Dictionary* (1961) Clarendon Press, Oxford.
2. Though I have only quoted British women here, similar themes were found in American and Finnish interviews. But women often talked about demands of independence by giving long examples and so on, so it is difficult to extract quotations.
3. Only a small number of women used the term 'interdependent'; I have included in my analysis of interdependence responses that questioned independence/dependence as a binary opposition to which positive/negative meanings were ascribed.

Chapter 9: Marginality

1. The effects of slavery, colonisation and immigration have impaired the opportunities of family formation for racial–ethnic minority groups. Familism has

emphasised that 'the family' as a central unit must be reinforced through social policies and legislation, but family formation among racial–ethnic minority groups has not received such reinforcment (see Glenn, 1986; Bhavnani and Coulson, 1986).
2. This would apply particularly to unmarried (rather than divorced) single men.
3. Tough this over-representation of men is typical in all countries studied, especially in suicide rates the gender distinction is considerably greater in Finland: Markku Javanainen (1989) *Convergence of Life Styles and Sex Ratio in Suicide Mortality in Finland*, Department of Sociology, University of Helsinki, Working Papers, No. 46.
4. Darling (1981) studied bachelors who have married late, and concluded that their late marriage is connected with situational conditions; they were 'buffered from the effect of marital norms because of their integration into personally significant societies' (p. 36).
5. For example, the three Chicana women in the San Francisco Bay Area and one Sami woman in Helsinki maintained close and supportive interaction with their families in particular, but also with other members of their ethnic groups and organisations concerned to promote the economic and cultural position of their particular ethnic groups.
6. Tina is very tall.
7. Neither is ready for a committed relationship, though *Sirkku* has a boyfriend and *Marina*, critical of monogamy, juggled between three men at the time of the interview. Both wanted to develop their work and have new experiences. In the future, when they are ready, they would like to meet a man to whom they can be committed, though *Marina* is not interested in marriage. Both want to have children. *Marina* has thought of how to bring up children, if a close relationship with a man does not materialise: she would like to live with friends and share childcare with them. Neither *Marina* nor *Sirkku* experience existential angst. *Marina* does not think of herself as a single woman, but is conscious of a range of stereotypes about single women and notes that she is reaching an age where there are few role models for her. In the context of counter-cultures she is exploring how to live in interaction with her friends. Both women feel that their future is open and full of possibilities. *Sirkku* talks more like older single women. 'Single woman' is associated with 'independent' in her list; she is aware of her singleness in situations where there are couples, and people have started to ask her why she is not married. *Sirkku* is getting used to living alone – she may find it difficult to compromise the independence she is building. She considers her present lifestyle 'wonderful', but would not have energy to sustain it in the future.
8. In Gordon, Lahelma and Tarmo (1991) we discuss how gender-neutral principles are transformed into gender-specific practices in the education system.

Bibliography

Aapola, Sinikka (1991) *Ystävyyden keinulauta: helsinkiläistyttöjen ystävyyskulttuurista*, Sosiaali- ja terveysministeriö, Sarja D. Naistutkimusraportteja 2/1991, Helsinki.
Abercrombie, Nicholas, Hill, Stephen and Turner, Bryan (1986) *Sovereign Individuals of Capitalism*, Allen and Unwin, London.
Adams, Margaret (1976) *Single Blessedness: Observations on the Single Status in a Married Society*, Heinemann, London.
Allen, Katherine (1989) *Single Women/Family Ties: Life Histories of Older Women*, Sage, London.
Anderson, Michael (1984) 'The Social Position of Spinsters in Mid–Victorian Britain', *Journal of Family History*, Winter, pp. 377–93.
Arber, Sara and Lahelma, Eero (1992) 'Women, Paid Employment and Ill-Health in Britain and Finland', paper presented at the British Sociological Annual Conference.
Baker, Luther G. (1968) 'The Personal and Social Adjustment of the Never-Married Woman', *Journal of Marriage and the Family*, Vol. 30, no. 3, pp. 473–9.
Baker, Niamh (1989) *Happily Ever After? Women's Fiction in Postwar Britain 1945–60*, Macmillan, London.
Ball, Richard and Robbins, Lynn (1986) 'Marital Status and Life Satisfaction Among Black Americans', *Journal of Marriage and the Family*, no. 48, May, pp. 389–94.
Ballaster, Ross, Beetham, Margaret, Frazer, Elizabeth and Hebron, Sandra (1991) *Women's Worlds: Ideology, Femininity and the Woman's Magazine*, Macmillan, London.
Barrett, Michèle (1980) *Women's Oppression Today*, Verso, London.
Barrett, Michèle and McIntosh, Mary (1982) *The Anti-Social Family*, Verso, London.
Bellah, Robert, Madsen, Richard, Sullivan, W.M., Swidler, A. and Tipton, S.M. (1988) *Habits of the Heart: Middle America Observed*, Hutchinson, London.
Bernstein, Basil (1975) *Class, Codes and Control*, vol. 3, Routledge and Kegan Paul, London.
Bhavnani, Kum-Kum and Coulson, Margaret (1986) 'Transforming Socialist-Feminism: The Challenge of Racism', *Feminist Review*, No. 23, pp. 81–92.
Birkett, Dea (1989) *Spinsters Abroad: Victorian Lady Explorers*, Basil Blackwell, Oxford.

Boose, Lynda E. (1989) 'The Father's House and the Daughter in It: The Structures of Western Culture's Daughter-Father Relationship', Boose, Lynda E. and Flowers, Betty S. (eds) (1989) *Daughters and Fathers*, Johns Hopkins University Press, Baltimore.

Boose, Lynda E. and Flowers, Betty S. (eds) (1989) *Daughters and Fathers*, The Johns Hopkins University Press, Baltimore.

Breen, Jennifer (1990) *In Her Own Write: Twentieth-Century Women's Fiction*, Macmillan, London.

Brenner, Johanna and Laslett, Barbara (1991) 'Gender, Social Reproduction, and Women's Self-Organisation: Considering the U.S. Welfare State', *Gender and Society*, vol. 5, no. 3, pp. 311–33.

Brittan, Arthur (1989) *Masculinity and Power*, Basil Blackwell, Oxford.

Brittan, Arthur and Maynard, Mary (1984) *Sexism, Racism and Oppression*, Basil Blackwell, Oxford.

Brönte, Charlotte (1974) *Shirley*, Penguin, Harmondsworth.

Bryan, Beverley, Dadzie, Stella and Scafe, Suzanne (1985) *The Heart of the Race: Black Women's Lives in Britain*, Virago, London.

Bumpass, Larry L. and Sweet, James A. (1989) 'National Estimates of Cohabitation', *Demography*, vol. 26, no. 4, pp. 615–25.

Butler, Julie (1990) *Gender Trouble: Feminism and the Subversion of Identity*, Routledge, London.

Campling, Jo (1981) *Images of Ourselves: Women with Disabilities Talking*, Routledge and Kegan Paul, London.

Carter, Erica (1988) 'Intimate Outscapes: Problem-Page Letters and the Remaking of the 1950s German Family', in Roman, Leslie G., Christian-Smith, Linda K. and Ellsworth, Elizabeth (eds) *Becoming Feminine: The Politics of Popular Culture*, Falmer Press, London.

Chambers-Schiller, Lee (1984) *Liberty, A Better Husband: Single Women in America: the Generations of 1780–1840*, Yale University Press, Newhaven.

Chandler, Joan (1991) *Women without Husbands: An Exploration of The Margins of Marriage*, London, Macmillan.

Chapman, Rowena (1988) 'The Great Pretender: Variations on the New Man Theme', in Chapman, Rowena and Rutherford, Jonathan (eds), *Male Order: Unwrapping Masculinity*, Lawrence and Wishart, London.

Chapman, Rowena and Rutherford, Jonathan (1988) *Male Order: Unwrapping Masculinity*. Lawrence and Wishart, London.

Chatters, Linda M., Taylor, Robert J. and Neighbors, Harold W. (1989) 'Size of Informal Helper Networks Mobilized during a Serious Personal Problem Among Black Americans', *Journal of Marriage and the Family*, no. 51, pp. 667–676.

Chisholm, Lynne (1987) *Gender and Vocation*, working paper, Post-Sixteen Centre, University of London Institute of Education.

Chodorow, Nancy (1978) *The Reproduction of Mothering: Psychoanalysis and the Sociology of Gender*, Berkeley, University of California.

Chodorow, Nancy (1986) 'Toward a Relational Individualism: The Mediation of Self through Psychoanalysis', in Heller, T.C., Sosna, M. and Wellbery, D.E. (eds), *Reconstructing Individualism: Autonomy, Individuality, and the Self in Western Thought*, Stanford University Press, Stanford.

Chow, Esther Ngan-Ling (1987) 'The Development of Feminist Consciousness among Asian American Women', *Gender and Society*, vol. 1, no. 3, pp. 284–99.

Christian-Smith, Linda K. (1988) 'Romancing the Girl: Adolescent Romance Novels and the Construction of Femininity', in Roman, Leslie G., Christian-Smith, Linda K. and Ellsworth, Elizabeth (eds) *Becoming Feminine: The Politics of Popular Culture*, Falmer Press, London.

Cockburn, Cynthia (1988) 'Masculinity, the Left and Feminism', in Chapman, Rowena and Rutherford, Jonathan (eds), *Male Order: Unwrapping Masculinity*, Lawrence and Wishart, London.

Cocks, Jean (1989) *Oppositional Imagination: Feminism, Critique and Political Theory*, Routledge, London.

Coleman, Lerita M., Antonucci, Toni C., Adelmann, Pamela K. and Crohan, Susan E. (1987) 'Social Roles in the Lives of Middle-Aged and Older Black Women', *Journal of Marriage and the Family*, 49, November, 761–71

Collins, Patricia (1990) *Black Feminist Thought*, HarperCollins, London.

Connell, R.W. (1987) *Gender and Power: Society, the Person and Sexual Politics*, Polity Press, Cambridge.

Cooney, Teresa M. and Uhlenberg, Peter (1989) 'Family-building Patterns of Professional Women: A Comparison of Lawyers, Physicians and Postsecondary Teachers', *Journal of Marriage and the Family*, vol. 51, no. 3, pp. 749–58.

Coward, Rosalind (1992) *Our Treacherous Hearts: Why Women Let Men Get Their Way*, Faber and Faber, London.

Darling, John (1981) 'Late-Marrying Bachelors', in Stein, Peter (ed.), *Single Life: Unmarried Adults in Social Context*, St Martin's Press, New York.

Davidoff, Leonore and Hall, Catherine (1987) *Family Fortunes: Men and Women of the English Middle Class, 1780–1850*, Hutchinson, London.

Davies, Bronwyn (1989) *Frogs and Snails and Feminist Tales: Preschool Children and Gender*, Allen and Unwin, Sydney.

Davies, Carole Boyce (1991) 'Writing off Marginality, Minoring and Effacement', *Women's Studies International Forum*, vol. 14, no. 4, pp. 249–63.

Davies, Diane E. and Astin, Helen S. (1990) 'Life Cycle, Career Patterns and Gender Stratification in Academe: Breaking Myths and Exposing Truths', in Stiver Lie, Suzanne and O'Leary, Virginia (eds), *Storming the Tower: Women in the Academic World*, Kogan Page, London.

Davis, Angela (1981) *Women, Race and Class*, Random House, New York.

De Beauvoir, Simone (1972) *The Second Sex*, Jonathan Cape, London.

Delamont, Sara (1992) 'Can a Woman Be an Intellectual? Can an Intellectual Be a Woman?', in Kauppi, Niilo and Sulkunen, Pekka (eds), *Vanguards of Modernity: Society, Intellectuals and the University*, Publications of the Research Unit for Contemporary Culture, University of Jyväskylä, Finland.

Devor, Holly (1989) *Gender Blending: Confronting the Limits of Duality*, Indiana University Press, Bloomington and Indianapolis.

Donzelot, Jacques (1980) *The Policing of Families*, Hutchinson, London.

Doudna, Christine and McBride, Fern (1981) 'Where Are the Men for the Women at the Top?', in Stein, Peter (ed.) (1981) *Single Life: Unmarried Adults in Social Context*, St Martin's Press, New York.

Eisenstein, Zillah (1988) *The Female Body and the Law*, University of California Press, Berkeley.
Faludi, Susan (1992) *Backlash: The Undeclared War Against Women*, Chatto and Windus, London.
Fraser, Nancy and Gordon, Linda (1992) 'A Genealogy of "Dependency": A Keyword of the US Welfare State', paper presented at the American Sociological Association Conference.
Garcia, Alma M. (1989) 'The Development of Chicana Feminist Discourse 1970–1980', *Gender and Society*, vol. 3, no. 2, pp. 217–38.
Gatens, Moira (1988) 'Towards a Feminist Philosophy of the Body', in Caine, Barbara, Grosz, E.A. and Lepervanche, Marie de (eds), *Crossing the Boundaries: Feminism and the Critique of Knowledge*, Allen and Unwin, London.
Gilligan, Carol (1982) *In a Different Voice: Pscyhological Theory and Women's Development*, Harvard University Press, Cambridge.
Girls and Occupational Choice Project (1987) *Hidden Messages: An Equal Opportunities Teaching Pack*, Basil Blackwell, Oxford.
Gittins, Diana (1985) *The Family in Question: Changing Household Ideologies and Familiar Ideologies*, Macmillan, London.
Glenn, Evelyn Nakano (1986) *Issei, Nisei, Warbride: Three Generations of Japanese American Women in Domestic Service*, Temple University Press, Philadelphia.
Gordon, Tuula (1986) *Democracy in One School? Progressive Education and Restructuring*, Falmer Press, Barcombe.
Gordon, Tuula (1988) 'Progressive Education, Oppositional Spaces and Gender', in Green, A. and Ball, S. (eds) (1988), *Progress and Inequality in Comprehensive Education*, Routledge, London.
Gordon, Tuula (1990) *Feminist Mothers*, Macmillan, London and New York University Press, New York.
Gordon, Tuula (1992) 'Citizens and Others: Gender, Democracy and Education', *International Studies in Sociology of Education*, vol. 2, no. 1, pp. 43–56.
Gordon, Tuula, Lahelma, Elina and Tarmo, Marjatta (1991) 'Gender and Education in Finland – problems for research', *Nordisk Pedagogik*, no. 4, pp. 210–17.
Greenblatt, Stephen (1986) 'Fiction and Friction', in Heller, Thomas C., Sosna, Morton and Wellbery, David E. (eds.) *Reconstructing Individualism: Autonomy, Individuality, and the Self in Western Thought*, Stanford University Press, Stanford.
Grimshaw, Jean (1986) *Feminist Philosophers: Women's Perspectives on Philosophical Traditions*, Wheatsheaf Books, Brighton.
Gullestad, Marianne (1984) *Kitchen–Table Society*, Universitetsforlaget, Oslo.
Haavio-Mannila, Elina *et al.* (eds) (1985) *The Unfinished Democracy: Women in Nordic Politics*, Clarendon Press, Oxford.
Hamacher, Werner (1986) '"Disgretation of the Will": Nietzsche on the Individual and Individuality', in Heller, Thomas C.,Sosna, Morton and Wellbery, David E. (eds) *Reconstructing Individualism: Autonomy, Individuality, and the Self in Western Thought*, Stanford University Press, Stanford.
Heater, Derek (1990) *Citizenship: the Civic Ideal in World History, Politics and Education*, Longman, London.

Henriques, Julian, Hollway, W., Urwin, C., Wenn, C. and Walkerdine, W. (1984) *Changing the Subject*, Methuen, London.
Hernes, Helga (1988) 'Scandinavian Citizenship', *Acta Sociologica*, vol. 31, pp. 199–216.
Heron, Liz (ed.) (1985) *Truth, Dare or Promise: Girls Growing up in the Fifties*, Virago, London.
Higginbotham, Elizabeth (1981) 'Is Marriage a Priority? Class Differences in Marital Options of Educated Black Women', in Stein, Peter (ed.) (1981) *Single Life: Unmarried Adults in Social Context*, St Martin's Press, New York.
Hill-Miller, Katherine S. (1989) 'The Skies and Trees of the Past: Anne Thackeray Ritchie and William Makepeace Thackeray', in Boose, Lynda E. and Flowers, Betty S. (eds), *Daughters and Fathers*, The Johns Hopkins University Press, Baltimore.
Hilton, Gillian L.S. (1991) '"Boys Will Be Boys – Won't They?": the attitudes of playgroup workers to gender and play experiences', *Gender and Education*, vol. 3, no. 2, pp. 311–13.
Hochschild, Arlie with Machung, Anne (1989) *The Second Shift: Working Parents and the Revolution at Home*, Viking, New York.
Holdsworth, Angela (1988) *Out of the Doll's House: The Story of Women in the Twentieth Century*, BBC Books, London.
Holland, Janet (1987) 'Girls and Occupational Choice: in search of meanings', Girls and Occupational Choice Project, University of London Institute of Education, working paper no. 10.
Holland, Janet, Ramazanoglu, Caroline and Scott, Sue (1990) 'Managing Risk and Experiencing Danger: Tensions between Government AIDS Education Policy and Young Women's Sexuality', *Gender and Education*, vol. 2, no. 2, pp. 125–46.
Hollway, Wendy (1987) '"I Just Wanted to Kill a Woman." Why?: The Ripper and Male Sexuality', Feminist Review (ed.), *Sexuality: A Reader*, Virago, London.
hooks, bell (1982) *Ain't I a Woman? Black Women and Feminism*, Pluto Press, London.
hooks, bell (1984) *Feminist Theory from Margin to Centre*, South End Press, Boston.
Houseknecht, Sharon K., Vaughan, Suzanne and Statham, Anne (1987) 'The Impact of Singlehood on the Career Patterns of Professional Women', *Journal of Marriage and the Family*, 49, May, pp. 353–66.
Hukkila, Kristiina (1992) 'Seksi ja Se Oikea. Tyttöjen ensimmäiset kokemukset ja käsitykset seksistä', in Näre, Sari and Lähteenmaa, Jaana (eds), *Letit Liehumaan: Tyttökulttuuri murroksessa*, SKS, Helsinki, pp. 56–68.
Jalland, Pat (1988) *Women, Marriage and Politics 1860–1914*, Oxford University Press, Oxford.
Jallinoja, Riitta (1983) *Suomalaisen naisasialiikeen taistelukaudet*, WSOY, Porvoo.
Jallinoja, Riitta (1986) 'Independence or Integration: The Women's Movement and Political Parties in Finland', in Dahlerup, Drude (ed.) *The New Women's Movement*, Sage, London.

Jeffreys, Sheila (1985) *The Spinster and Her Enemies: Feminism and Sexuality 1880–1930*, Pandora Press, London.
Jewish Women in London Group (1989) *Generations of Memories: Voices of Jewish Women*, Women's Press, London.
Jones, Kathleen B. (1990) 'Citizenship in Woman-Friendly Polity', *Signs*, no. 41, pp. 781–812.
Joseph, Gloria (1981) 'The Incompatible Ménage à Trois: Marxism, Feminism and Racism', in Sargent, Lydia (ed.), *The Unhappy Marriage of Marxism and Feminism: A Debate on Class and Patriarchy*, Pluto Press, London, pp. 91–107.
Julkunen, Raija (1990) 'Women in the Welfare State', in Setälä, Päivi (ed.), *The Lady with the Bow: The Story of Finnish Women*, Otava, Keuruu, pp. 140–60.
Julkunen, Raija (1992) *Hyvinvointivaltio käännekohdassa*, Vastapaino, Tampere
Kauppinen-Toropainen, K., Haavio–Mannila, E. and Kandolin, I.(1984) 'Women at Work in Finland', in Davidson, M.J. and Cooper, C.L. (eds), *Women at Work*, Wiley, London.
Keith, Pat M. (1980) 'Two Models of Singleness: Managing an Atypical Marital Status', *International Journal of Sociology and the Family*, vol. 10, no. 2, pp. 301–10.
Kerber, Linda K., Greeno, Catherine C., Maccoby, Eleanor, Luria, Zella, Stack, Carol B. and Gilligan, Carol (1986) 'On *In a Different Voice*: An Interdisciplinary Forum', *Signs*, no. 2, pp. 304–33.
Kessler, Suzanne J. and McKenna, Wendy (1978) *Gender: an Ethnomethodological Approach*, University of Chicago Press, Chicago.
Kirk, Ilse (1987) 'Images of Amazons: Marriage and Matriarchy', in Macdonald, Sharon, Holden, Pat and Ardener, Shirley (eds), *Images of Women in Peace and War: Cross-Cultural and Historical Perspectives*, Macmillan, London.
Lees, Sue (1986) *Losing Out: Sexuality and Adolescent Girls*, Hutchinson, London.
Leigh, Barbara C. (1989) 'Reasons for Having or Avoiding Sex: Gender, Sexual Orientation, and Relationship to Sexual Behaviour', *The Journal of Sex Research*, vol. 26, no. 2, pp. 199–209.
Levine, Martin P. (1981) 'Employment Discrimination Against Gay Men', in Stein, Peter J. (ed.) *Single Life: Unmarried Adults in Social Context*, St Martin's Press, New York.
Lewis, Jane (1991) 'Back to the Future: A Comment on American New Right Ideas about Welfare and Citizenship in the 1980s', *Gender and History*, vol. 3, no. 3, pp. 326–36.
Lonsdale, Susan (1990) *Women and Disability: The Experience of Physical Disability Among Women*, Macmillan, London.
Lukes, Steven (1973) *Individualism*, Basil Blackwell, London.
Luukkonen-Gronow, Terttu (1987) 'Naisten mahdollisuudet yliopistouraan Suomessa 1980-luvulla', in Rantalaiho, Liisa and Saarinen, Aino (eds), *Working Papers*, No. 22, Department of Sociology and Social Psychology, University of Tampere.
Maclean, Mavis (1991) *Surviving Divorce: Women's Resources After Separation*, Macmillan, London.

Macdonald, Sharon, Holden, Pat and Ardener, Shirley (eds) (1987) *Images of Women in Peace and War: Cross-Cultural and Historical Perspectives,* Macmillan, London.

Macklin, Eleanor (1980) 'Nontraditional Family Forms: A Decade of Research', *Journal of Marriage and the Family,* vol. 42, no. 4.

Marcus, Leah S. (1989) 'Erasing the Stigma of Daughterhood: Mary I, Elizabeth I, and Henry VIII', in Boose, Lynda E. and Flowers, Betty S. (eds), *Daughters and Fathers,* The Johns Hopkins University Press, Baltimore.

Marcus, Maria (1987) 'Women, Success and Civil Society', in Benhabib, Seyla and Cornell, Drucilla (eds), *Feminism as Critique,* University of Minnesota Press, Minneapolis.

Markkola, Pirjo (1990) 'Women in Rural Society in the 19th and 20th Centuries', in Setälä, Päivi (ed.), *The Lady with the Bow: The Story of Finnish Women,* Otava, Keuruu.

Martin, Emily (1987) *The Woman in the Body,* Open University Press, Milton Keynes.

McLanahan, Sara and Booth, Karen (1989) 'Mother–Only Families: Problems, Prospects, and Politics', *Journal of Marriage and the Family,* 51, August, pp. 557–80.

McPherson, C.B. (1962) *The Political Theory of Possessive Individualism,* Clarendon Press, Oxford.

Meese, Elizabeth A. (1986) *Crossing the Double-Cross: The Practice of Feminist Criticism,* University of North Carolina Press, Chapel Hill and London.

Miles, Rosalind (1989) *The Women's History of the World,* Paladin, London.

Morris, Jenny (1991) *Pride Against Prejudice: Transforming Attitudes to Disability,* Women's Press, London.

Morris, Jenny (ed.) (1992) *Alone Together: Voices of Single Mothers,* Women's Press, London.

Murnen, Sarah K., Perot, Annette and Byrne, David (1989) 'Coping with Unwanted Sexual Activity: Normative Responses, Situational Determinants, and Individual Differences', *Journal of Sex Research,* vol. 26, no. 1, pp. 85–106.

Murphy, Robert (1990) *The Body Silent,* W.W. Norton, New York.

Nachman, Gerald (1989) *The Fragile Bachelor: Perilous Adventures in the Single Life,* Ten Speed Press, Berkeley.

O'Connor, Pat (1991) 'Women's Experience of Power within Marriage: an inexplicable phenomenon', *Sociological Review,* vol. 39, no. 4, pp. 823–42.

Outinen, Hellevi (1992) 'Häpeästä nautintoon. Seksuaalisuus tyttökirjoissa 1920-luvulta 1980-luvulle', in Näre, Sari and Lähteenmaa, Jaana (eds), *Letit liehumaan: tyttökulttuuri murroksessa,* Suomalaisen Kirjallisuuden Seura, Helsinki.

Paredes, Raymund A. (1989) 'The Evolution of Daughter–Father Relationships in Mexican–American Culture', in Boose, Lynda E. and Flowers, Betty S. (eds), *Daughters and Fathers,* The Johns Hopkins University Press, Baltimore, pp. 136–56.

Pateman, Carole (1988) *The Sexual Contract*, Polity Press, Cambridge.
Pearlin, Leonard I. and Johnson, Joyce S. (1981) 'Marital Status, Life Strains, and Depression', in Stein, Peter (ed.) (1981) *Single Life: Unmarried Adults in Social Context*, St Martin's Press, New York.
Pohls, Maritta (1990) 'Women's Work in Finland 1870–1940', in Setälä, Päivi (ed.), *The Lady with the Bow: The Story of Finnish Women*, Otava, Keuruu, pp. 55–73.
Räisänen, Arja–Liisa (1991) 'Avain uuteen rakkaudentaivaaseen. Aviopuolisoille suunnatun populäärilääketieteellisen opaskirjallisuuden (1865–1906) seksuaalikäsityksiä', *Naistutkimus–Kvinnoforskning*, no. 3, pp. 5–17.
Ribbens, Jane (1989) 'Interviewing Women: an "Unnatural Situation"?', *Women's Studies International Forum*, vol. 12, no. 6, pp. 579–92.
Richardson, Laurel (1988) 'Secrecy and Status: The Social Construction of Forbidden Relationships', *American Sociological Review*, vol. 53, April, pp. 209–19.
Riddiough, Christine (1981) 'Socialism, Feminism and Gay/Lesbian Liberation', in Sargent, Lydia (ed.), *The Unhappy Marriage of Marxism and Feminism: A Debate on Class and Patriarchy*, Pluto Press, London, pp. 71–89.
Riessman, Catherine (1987) 'When Gender is Not Enough: Women Interviewing Women', *Gender and Society*, vol. 1, no. 2, pp. 172–207.
Riley, Denise (1988) *'Am I That Name?': Feminism and the Category of Woman in History*, Macmillan, London.
Ritamies, Marketta (1988) 'Yksin olevat: Ei naimisissa olevien ja yksin asuvien tarkatelua', Väestotutkimuslaitoksen julkaisusarja D, No. 23/1988, Helsinki.
Rose, Suzanna and Frieze, Irene Hanson (1989) 'Young Singles' Scripts for a First Date', *Gender and Society*, vol. 3, no. 2, pp. 258–68.
Russell, Diana, E. H. (1990) *Rape in Marriage*, Indiana University Press, Bloomington and Indianapolis.
Rutherford, Jonathan (1988) 'Who's That Man,' in Chapman, Rowena and Rutherford, Jonathan (1988) *Male Order: Unwrapping Masculinity*, Lawrence and Wishart, London.
Sarvasy, Wendy (1992) 'Beyond Difference versus Equality Policy Debate: Postsuffrage Feminism, Citizenship, and the Quest for a Feminist Welfare State', *Signs*, vol. 17, no. 2, pp. 329–62.
Sayers, Janet (1989) 'Melanie Klein and Mothering – a Feminist Perspective', *International Review of Psychoanalysis*, vol. 16, part 3, pp. 363–76.
Segal, Lynne (1990) *Slow Motion: Changing Masculinities, Changing Men*, Virago, London.
Segura, Denise A. (1989) 'Chicana and Mexican Immigrant Women at Work: The Impact of Class, Race, and Gender on Occupational Mobility', *Gender and Society*, vol. 3, no. 1, pp. 37–52.
Setälä, Päivi (ed.) (1990) *The Lady with the Bow: The Story of Finnish Women*, Otava, Keuruu.
Sharpe, Sue (1984) *Double Identity: The Lives of Working Mothers*, Penguin, Harmondsworth.

Shields, Rob (1991) *Places on the Margin: Alternative Geographies of Modernity*, Routledge, London.
Siim, Birte (1987) 'The Scandinavian Welfare States – Towards Sexual Equality or a New Kind of Domination?', *Acta Sociologica*, vol. 30, nos 3/4, pp. 255–70.
Siltanen, Janet and Stanworth, Michelle (1984) 'The politics of private woman and public man', in Siltanen, Janet and Stanworth, Michelle (ed.), *Women and the Public Sphere*, Hutchinson, London.
Silverstolpe, Fredrik (1989) 'Äktenskap mellan kvinnor under 1600– och 1700– talen', *lambda nordica*, no. 1, pp. 188–204.
Simon, Barbara L. (1987) *Never Married Women*, Temple University Press, Philadelphia.
Simonen, Leila (1991) *Contradictions of the Welfare State, Women and Caring*, Avebury, Aldershot.
Skeggs, Beverley (1991) 'Challenging Masculinity and Using Sexuality', *British Journal of Sociology of Education*, vol. 12, no. 2, pp. 127–39.
Smith, Dorothy (1988) *The Everyday World as Problematic: A Feminist Sociology*, Open University Press, Milton Keynes.
Smith, M.B. (1951) *The Single Woman Today: Her Problems and Adjustment*, Watts, London.
Sokoloff, Natalie J. (1981) 'Early Work Patterns of Single and Married Women,' in Stein, Peter (ed.) (1981) *Single Life: Unmarried Adults in Social Context*, St Martin's Press, New York.
Spelman, Elizabeth (1990) *Inessential Woman: Problems of Exclusion in Feminist Thought*, Women's Press, London.
Stacey, Judith (1986) 'Are Feminists Afraid to Leave the Home? The Challenge of Conservative Pro-family Feminism', in Mitchell, Juliet and Oakley, Ann (eds), *What Is Feminism?*, Basil Blackwell, Oxford.
Stacey, Judith (1990) *Brave New Families: stories of domestic upheaval in late twentieth century America*, Basic Books, New York.
Stanko, Elizabeth (1985) *Intimate Intrusions: Women's Experience of Male Violence*, Routledge and Kegan Paul, London.
Staples, Robert (1981) 'Black Singles in America', in Stein, Peter (ed.) *Single Life: Unmarried Adults in Social Context*, St Martin's Press, New York.
Statham, June (1986) *Daughters and Sons: Experiences of Non-Sexist Childrearing*, Basil Blackwell, Oxford.
Stein, Peter (1978) 'The Lifestyles and Life Chances of the Never-Married', *Marriage and Family Review*, no. 1, pp. 1–11.
Stein, Peter (ed.) (1981) *Single Life: Unmarried Adults in Social Context*, St. Martin's Press, New York.
Stiver Lie, Suzanne (1990) 'The Juggling Act: Work and Family in Norway', in Stiver Lie, Suzanne and O'Leary, Virginia (eds), *Storming the Tower: Women in the Academic World*, Kogan Page, London.
Sulkunen, Irma (1989) *Naisen Kutsumus: Miina Sillanpää ja sukupuolten maailmojen erkaantuminen*, Hanki ja Jää, Helsinki.

Sulkunen, Irma (1990) 'The Mobilisation of Women and the Birth of Civil Society', in Setälä, Päivi (ed.), *The Lady with the Bow: The Story of Finnish Women,* Otava, Keuruu, pp. 42–53.

Summers, Yvonne (1989) 'Women and Citizenship: The Insane, the Insolvent and the Inanimate?', paper presented at the British Sociological Association Annual Conference.

Tannen, Deborah (1992) *You Just Don't Understand: Women and Men in Conversation,* Virago, London.

Taylor, Robert J., Chatters, Linda, Tucker, Belinda and Lewis, Edith (1990) 'Developments in Research on Black Families: A Decade Review', *Journal of Marriage and the Family,* no. 52, November, pp. 993–1014.

Theweleit, Klaus (1987, 1989) *Male Fantasies,* vols 1 and 2, Polity Press, Cambridge.

Thorne, Barrie and Yalom, Marilyn (eds) (1982) *Rethinking the Family,* Longman, London.

Thornton, Arland (1989) 'Changing Attitudes toward Family Issues in the United States', *Journal of Marriage and the Family,* vol. 51, no. 4, pp. 873–93.

Turner, Bryan (1984) *The Body and Society: Explorations in Social Theory,* Basil Blackwell, Oxford.

Vega, William A. (1990) 'Hispanic Families in the 1980s: A Decade of Research', *Journal of Marriage and the Family,* 52, November, pp. 1015–24

Vicinus, Martha (1985) *Independent Women: Work and Community for Single Women 1850–1920,* Virago, London.

Wakil, S. Parvez (1980) 'To Be Or Not to Be Married', *International Journal of Sociology of the Family,* vol. 10, no. 2, pp. 311–18.

Walby, Sylvia (1990) *Theorizing Patriarchy,* Basil Blackwell, Oxford.

Walkerdine, Valerie and Lucey, Helen (1989) *Democracy in the Kitchen: Regulating Mothers and Socialising Daughters,* Virago, London.

Wallace, Michele (1990) *Black Macho and the Myth of the Superwoman,* Verso, London.

Warner, Marina (1983) *Joan of Arc: The Image of Female Heroism,* Penguin, Harmondsworth.

Warner, Marina (1985a) *Alone of All Her Sex: The Myth and Cult of Virgin Mary,* Picador, London.

Warner, Marina (1985b) *Monuments and Maidens: The Allegory of the Female Form,* Weidenfeld and Nicolson, London.

Watkins, Susan C. (1984) 'Spinsters', *Journal of Family History,* Winter 1984, pp. 310–25.

Weiss, Robert S. (1981) 'The Study of Loneliness', in Stein, Peter (ed.), *Single Life: Unmarried Adults in Social Context,* St Martin's Press, New York, pp. 1015–24.

Wheelright, Julie (1989) *Amazons and Military Maids: Women Who Dressed as Men in Pursuit of Life, Liberty and Happiness,* Pandora, London.

Williams, R. (1961) *The Long Revolution,* Penguin, Harmondsworth.

Willis, Paul (1977) *Learning to Labour: How Working Class Kids Get Working Class Jobs,* Saxon House, Farnborough, Hants.

Wilson, Elizabeth (1983) *What Is To Be Done About Violence Against Women?,* Penguin, Harmondsworth.

Wood, Julian (1984) 'Groping Towards Sexism: Boys' Sex Talk', in McRobbie, Angela and Nava, Mica (eds), *Gender and Generation*, Macmillan, London.

Woodhouse, Annie (1989) *Fantastic Women: Sex, Gender and Transvestism*, Macmillan, London.

Yudice, George (1988) 'Marginality and the Ethics of Survival', in Ross, Andrew (ed.), *Universal Abandon? The Politics of Postmodernism*, Edinburgh University Press, Edinburgh.

Yuval–Davis, Nira (1991) 'The Citizenship Debate: Women, Ethnic Processes and the State', *Feminist Review*, Special Issue no. 39, pp. 58–68.

Zavella, Patricia (1987) *Women's Work and Chicano Families: Cannery Workers of the Santa Clara Valley*, Cornell University Press, Ithaca and London.

Zinn, Maxine Baca (1990) 'Family, Feminism and Race in America', *Gender and Society*, vol. 4, no. 1, pp. 68–82.

Zollar, Ann Creighton and Williams, J. Sherwood (1987) 'The Contribution of Marriage to the Life Satisfaction of Black Adults', *Journal of Marriage and the Family*, no. 49, pp. 87–92.

Index

Aapola, S. 40
Abercrombie, N., Hill, S. and Turner, B. 26, 31
Achilles 2
Adams, M. 22
adoption 154
AIDS 116, 123
Allen, K. 21, 22, 23, 35, 73, 74, 98
Amazons 2–4, 5, 6–7, 13, 51, 155, 179
  see also single women, and Amazons
Amy 52, 85, 90, 122, 139, 154, 164
Anderson, M. 9, 11, 12
androgyny 4
Anni 98, 101, 128, 133
Annikki 45
Antiope 2
Arber, S. and Lahelma, E. 151, 157
Athenian society 2

bachelor 180
Baker, N. 16, 18
Barrett, M. 19
Barrett, M. and McIntosh, M. 18, 19, 106–7, 180
Bellah, R. et al. 25, 29
Bernstein, B 126
Betsy 45, 90, 91, 100, 104, 113, 114, 121, 135, 161, 185
Bhavnani, K. and Coulson, M. 19
binary opposites 26, 160
  public/private 5, 65, 82, 83, 104
  women/men 4, 111
Birkett, D. 13–14
black people 24, 27
  see also black women; familism, and black people; family, black; men, black
black women 30, 50–1, 129, 179
  and colonialism 12
  educated 52
  and marriage and maternity 23
  sexualisation of 14

and slavery 12, 13
stereotypes of 3, 18
see also single women, black
Blackwell, Emily 4
body 7, 32, 89, 125
  distinction between mind and body 27, 119
  and gender 5
  and reproduction 15
  of women 14, 27
Boose, L. 58
Brenner, J. and Laslett, B. 35
Bridget 43, 68, 85, 104, 111, 121, 141, 168, 182
Britain 9, 20, 34–5, 50, 81, 99, 147, 151, 154, 157, 179, 196–7
  see also family, nuclear; single women, British; spinsters, in America; women, in Britain; welfare state, in Britain
Brittan, A. 28
Brontë, C. 30
Bush, Kate 3
Butler, J. 4, 5, 29, 42

Campling, J. 53
Carlotta 55, 68, 79, 88, 90, 103, 124, 149, 174, 176, 182, 192
Caroline 62, 93, 111, 121, 125, 134, 162, 175
Carter, E. 17
Celia 134, 138, 142, 145, 164, 192
celibacy 123–6, 172
Chambers-Schiller, L. 4, 11, 12, 14, 15, 25, 31
Chandler, J. 30, 49, 73, 92, 96, 126, 127, 179, 180
Chapman, R. 138
Chapman, R. and Rutherford, J. 28
childlessness
  involuntary 149
  voluntary 148–9

Chisholm, L. 1
Chodorow, N. 28, 29, 62
Chow, E. 51
Christian-Smith, L. 17
Christine 72–3, 75, 76, 78, 101, 110, 124, 135, 148, 169, 172
citizenship/citizens 5, 8, 25, 27, 36, 159, 160, 197
  and women 25, 198
city-singles *see* stereotypes, of single women
Clara 45, 79, 112, 152, 168, 174
class 21, 27, 184
  see also family, middle-class; marginality, and social class; single women, middle-class, upper-class, working-class; women, middle-class, working-class
Cockburn, C. 28, 111, 116
Cocks, J. 4
cohabitation 22, 38, 49, 45, 53
colonialism 13, 27
Collins, P. 19, 179
companionate/symmetrical marriage/partnership 19, 110, 126, 169, 198
complementarity, between women and men 15, 16, 28, 51, 111, 115, 177, 190
Connell, R.W. 27, 28, 183
Cooney, T. and Uhlenberg, P. 21, 50
Coward, R. 71, 111, 169
courtly love 31
cross dressing 4, 6, 7, 8, 25

Davidoff, L. and Hall, C. 11
Davies, B. 4, 171
Davies, C. 178, 184
Davies, D. and Astin, H. 67
Davies, A. 13
De Beauvoir, S. 1
Delamont, S. 15
dependence 10, 170–2, 175, 176
Devor, H. 4
disability 27, 176, 189
  see also single women, disabled
division of labour
  gendered 28
  sexual 172, 183
  social 26
divorced women
  statistics on 22
  see also men, divorced; single women, divorced

domestic violence 169
Donzelot, J. 20
Dorothy 152, 167, 168
Doudna, C. and McBride, F. 49

education 56, 57, 167, 195
  boarding schools 11
  gender and 1
  and opportunities for women 31–2
  progressive 1
Eeva 61, 72, 141
Eila 32, 134, 139, 161
Eileen 163, 190
Eisenstein, Z. 4, 28
Elizabeth I 7–8
Ella 75, 76, 110, 119, 137, 139, 149, 165, 166, 188
Else 91, 176
Emily 43, 91, 117, 154, 162, 169, 174
ethnic groups 184
  see also family, and ethnic groups; single women, and ethnic groups
existential angst 143–7, 152

Faludi, S. 21, 132
familism 19, 103, 110, 137, 147, 151, 173, 185, 197
  and black people 23, 154
family 15, 18–21, 106, 108–9, 144, 169, 178, 184, 195, 197
  black 19, 154
  changes in formation 20–1
  criticism of by feminists 19
  and ethnic groups 51–2
  forms of 1, 19–20, 159
  middle-class 19
  nuclear 28, 151, 173, 198; in Britain, Finland and the USA 20
  patriarchal 31
  single parent 196
  women in the 1
fathers 13, 147
feminism and feminists 16, 28, 32, 33, 65, 79
  and single women 32
femininity 1, 14, 57, 105, 113, 168, 172, 173, 177, 183
feminist mothers 1, 42, 70–1, 146, 150
Finland 10, 15, 16, 20, 31, 33–5, 50, 66, 81, 99, 147, 151, 157, 181, 196–7
  see also family, nuclear; single women, Finnish; women, in Finland; welfare state, in Finland

Index

Frances 56, 103, 110, 118, 119, 141, 152, 154, 164, 165
Fraser, N. and Gordon, L. 160
French-Sheldon, M. 13
Friedan, B. 16

Galina 79, 120, 142, 188
Garcia, A. 19, 51
Gatens, M. 27
gender 5
  constitution of 4
  social construction of 1
gender blenders 4
Gilligan, C. 29
Gina 110
Gittins, D. 18, 19
Glenn, E. 19
Gloria 174, 181, 188
Gordon, T. 1, 26, 38, 70, 147, 154, 173, 179, 181, 194
Gordon, T., Lahelma, E. and Tarmo, M. 1
Greenblatt, S. 4
Greta 107, 114, 120, 128, 134, 159, 168, 171, 186, 187
Gullestad, M. 85
Gwen 45, 56, 108, 133, 141, 150, 175, 182, 190, 193

Haavio-Mannila, E. *et al.* 36, 197
Hamacher, W. 29
Hanna 62, 68, 104–5, 109, 128, 170, 189
Harriet 121, 142, 176, 187, 190, 193
health 21, 156–7, 180, 189
Helena 78, 100, 134, 135
Helka 91, 103, 141, 185
Helsinki 2, 36, 121, 139, 186, 195, 196
Henriques J. *et al.* 26
hermaphrodites 3, 4, 5
Hernes, H. 36, 197
Heron, L. 18
Higginbotham, E. 52
Hill-Miller, K. 10
Hilton, G. 57
Hochschild, A. 111, 169
Holland, J. *et al.* 125
Hollway, W. 116
homophobia 183
hooks, b. 3, 13, 18, 51, 179
Houseknecht, S., Vaughan, S. and Statham, A. 50
Hypatia 31

immigration 188–9
independence 28, 198
  aggressive 177
  and being alone 163
  emotional 163, 175
  financial 160, 167
  mental 163–4
  negative aspects of 165, 174–5
  positive aspects of 165
  strands of 174
  and taking care of oneself 162–3
  and women 2
  and work 70, 73–4
individual 1, 27, 160, 178
  as absolute 25, 26, 197
  as gender specific 25, 26
  as a masculine construction 2, 25
  women as 26
individualisation 26
individualism 26, 29, 42
individuality 26, 28, 29, 90
  and women 31–3
industrialisation 32, 160
Inez 79, 133, 166
interdependence 175–6, 197
Irene 71, 79, 89, 156, 175
Isabella 155, 167

Jalland, P. 9, 10, 11, 32
Jallinoja, R. 14, 32
Jeffreys, S. 9, 14, 15, 32, 116, 126, 190
Jill 94
Joan of Arc 5, 6–7, 25, 29
Jody 107, 142, 166
Judy 72, 80, 135, 152, 162, 167, 188
Julkunen, R. 19, 35, 197

Kaisa 55, 110, 163, 191
Kate 56, 93, 108, 137, 138, 141, 161, 176
Kerber, L. 29
Kessler, S. and McKenna, W. 4
Kirk, I. 2–3

Laura 47, 60, 98, 112, 113, 117, 123, 129, 133, 165, 168, 172, 182, 185, 194
Lea 99, 131, 137, 138, 155, 164, 176
Lees, C. 116
Leigh, B. 119
lesbians 15, 39, 52–3, 75, 79, 101, 172
  and motherhood, 150–1
  see also marginality, and lesbians; single women, lesbian

Levine, M. 180
Lewis, J. 197
lists
  Top Ten People 49, 95–7, 99
  word association 40, 108, 142, 160, 180
Liz 43, 48, 79, 90, 128, 131, 132, 135, 164
London 2, 36, 121, 139, 186, 196
Lonsdale, S. 53, 189
Lorna 47, 54, 60, 73, 88, 98, 99, 100, 107, 109, 119, 133, 142, 145–6, 175, 186
Lukes, S. 26
Luukkonen-Gronow, T. 67
Lynne 62, 93, 111, 113, 117, 124, 128, 136, 138, 149, 182, 184

Maclean, M. 156, 181
Macklin, E. 21, 180
Marcus, L. 7
Marcus, M. 71
marginality 1, 8, 33–4, 83
  and biographies 1901
  and disability 189
  and ethnicity 187–8
  and immigration 188
  indices of 191
  and lesbians 189–90
  as multiple 178, 186
  and 'race' 187–8
  and social class 186–7
  see also single women, and marginality
Mari 52, 77, 152
Marina 195
Markkola 12
marriage 1, 2, 14, 28, 29, 108, 110, 144, 171, 180, 183, 184, 195
Martha 78, 102, 113, 118, 167
Martin, E. 15, 32
masculinity 28, 31, 147, 173, 177, 183
  hegemonic 27, 183
  subordinated 28–9
matriarchy 3
Maxine 46, 75, 76, 91, 172
McLanahan, S. and Booth, K. 151
Meese, E. 4, 5
men 5, 181
  associated with culture 3, 26
  black 3, 50, 51
  and citizenship 25
  of colour 51
  divorced 181
  as a norm 1, 25
  problems of 28–9
  and sexuality 116
  unmarried 183
  white 27
  see also single men
methodology 41, 159, 179
  comparative research 2, 41, 196
  cross-cultural study 2, 196
  interviews 38, 40–1, 159–60, 184
  snowball method 39
  theoretical sampling 39
Michelle 54, 62, 73, 144, 163, 171, 185
Miles, R. 31
Minna 88, 92, 111, 156, 162, 192
Miriam 79, 111, 117–18, 141, 188
Molly 80, 94, 100, 110, 124, 141, 175, 198
Morris, J. 152
motherhood 1, 14, 29, 171, 196
mothers 13, 28, 73
  see also feminist mothers; single mothers
Murphy, R. 189

Naomi 43, 121, 128, 161
neo-conservatism 181, 197
never-married women 22, 23, 44, 46
New Right 21, 28, 116, 132
Nina 90, 189
Norma 45, 61, 71, 74–5, 86, 97, 128, 142, 146

O'Connor, P 169
old maids see stereotypes, of single women
otherness 1, 3, 13, 19, 25, 27, 33, 133, 159, 176
Outinen, H. 17

Paredes, R. 51
Pateman, C. 25, 26, 27
patriarchy 2, 3, 197
Pearlin, L.I. and Johnson, J. 157
Peggy 58–9, 68, 112, 123, 128, 144–5, 168, 181, 185
Penthesilea 2, 6
Pisan, Christine de 31
Pohls, M. 12, 16
postmodern societies 194
Potter, Beatrice 10
power 120, 126, 173, 178, 183, 193

psychoanalysis 15, 28, 58
public/private *see* binary opposites
'race' 27, 182
  see also marginality, and 'race'
Rachel 45, 59, 90, 119, 138, 163, 176
racism 12, 13, 27, 29, 51, 154, 187
Räisänen, A. 116
rationality 27, 28
Rebecca 48, 57, 113, 123
Reija 69, 71, 90, 113, 118, 125, 136, 141
religion 31
  and single women 121–2, 123, 144
reproduction 15, 32
Ribbens, J. 41
Richardson, L. 104, 126, 183
rights, legal, civil, political 26
Riley, D. 4, 5, 31
Rita 111, 117
Ritamies, M. 10
rite of passage 73–4, 98, 133–4, 166
Ritva 167
romantic love 1, 16
Rosa 52, 75, 76, 103, 110, 121, 139, 164, 177, 188
Russell, D. 169
Rutherford, J. 147

Saara 47, 88, 137, 181
San Francisco Bay Area 2, 36, 121, 134, 139, 186, 195, 196
Sanna 79, 167, 172
Sarvasy, L. 35, 198
Sayers, J. 58
Segal, L. 18, 183
sexual contract 26
sexual difference 2, 4–5, 6–7, 15, 26, 27, 28, 111, 172, 173, 184, 190
sexuality 16, 116, 119, 120, 122, 125, 126
  see also celibacy; black women, sexualisation of; men, and sexuality; single women, and sexuality; women, sexualisation of
Sharpe, S. 66
Shields, R. 33, 34
Shirley 72, 120, 134, 138, 156, 161, 168, 188
Shoshana 54, 91, 118, 132, 135, 162, 171
Siim, B. 36, 197
Siltanen, J. and Stanworth, M. 65
Silverstolpe, F. 4

Simon, B. 22, 43, 44, 46, 66, 68, 74, 96, 98, 116
Simone 62, 153, 188
Simonen, L. 19, 35
single men 180–4, 183
single mothers 38, 44, 50, 68, 92, 94, 108, 143, 147, 151–5, 173, 178, 198
single women
  and Amazons 3, 17
  and ambition 70–1
  American 44, 63, 81, 82, 92, 97
  black 50, 52, 56, 72, 191, 193
  British 44, 63, 81, 82, 92, 97
  caring for parents 74, 98–9
  changes in the position of 194
  and children 108
  of colour 79, 167, 179, 182, 187
  conception of self as 43–4
  and depression 91, 112
  disabled 39, 53, 94, 114, 123, 148, 162, 162 189
  divorced/separated 48–9, 55, 73, 87, 92, 97, 100, 112, 114, 148, 155–7, 166, 189
  educated 52, 69, 79, 167
  and ethnic groups 39, 50–2, 53, 68, 72, 100, 129, 139–40, 153–4, 167, 174, 187–8
  and families of origin 97–9
  and fathers 58–61, 96, 173–4
  and feminism 80–2, 193, 194
  and financial position 80, 153
  Finnish 44, 63, 81, 82, 84, 92, 97, 181, 196
  and food 87–9
  and friends 96, 99–104, 107
  homes of 84–6
  and housework/cooking 87–9
  incompleteness of 14
  and intimacy 17, 106–8, 117–18, 176, 198
  involuntary 46, 48–9, 50, 127, 135, 142
  lesbian 100, 114, 125, 189–90, 193
  and loneliness 89–92, 152
  and marginality 20, 24, 34, 198
  and men 103, 114–15, 168
  middle-class 21, 52, 56, 68, 72, 96–7, 173, 187
  and mothers 58, 61–3, 96, 134
  and parents 55–63
  on partnerships 60, 74–6, 107, 109–15, 168–74

and politics 80–2
professional 50
and public places 93–5
and relatives 107
and sexuality 115–26; and casual sex 119; and sexual morality 120
and social networks 95–7, 129, 186, 192, 195
stable 46, 48
statistics on 21–2
and therapy 92
as support persons 104–5, 168
temporary 46, 48
as 'third sex' 3, 6, 13, 53, 136, 159
unmarried 15–18, 55, 73, 92, 97, 183
upper-class 73
voluntary 45, 46–8, 50, 108, 112, 127, 135, 166, 193, 195
white 50, 56, 72, 173, 191
and work 66–79, 85, 144
working-class 21, 23, 35, 56, 68, 722, 96–7, 173, 187, 191
young 195
as young girls 54–7
see also feminism, and single women; never-married women; religion, and single women; single mothers; stereotypes, of single women
singleness
and choice 44–6
as deviant 22
and ethnic groups 50
negative aspects of 112, 143–7
positive aspects of 140–2
Sirkku 195
Skeggs, B. 169
slavery 13
Smith, M.B. 16
social contract 25, 26, 119
Soili 102, 118, 152
Sokoloff, N. 66, 73
Spelman, E. 4, 29
spinsters 9–15, 25, 30, 31, 126, 136, 180
in America 9–10, 11, 12, 14
in Britain 9, 11–12, 14
in Finland 10, 12, 14
Stacey, J. 15, 18, 80, 81, 196
Stanko, B. 94
Staples, R. 50, 179
Statham, J. 171, 173
Stein, P. 14, 46, 53, 66
stereotypes, of single women 3, 42, 44, 112, 128, 137, 138, 167–8, 183
city singles 44, 131–2, 135, 183
old maids, 44, 15, 17, 22, 112, 126, 128–31, 134, 137, 180, 181
Stiver Lie, S. 67
subjectivity 26
Sue 43, 49, 52, 60, 69, 99, 100, 110, 114, 139, 140, 168, 171, 185
Sulkunen, I. 16, 31
Summers, Y. 36
Susan 48, 102, 131, 144, 165, 185
Sylvia 142, 154, 169

Taina 80
Tannen, D. 196
Taylor, R., Chatters, L., Tucker, B. and Lewis, E. 19, 179
Thackeray, Anne 10
Thackeray, W.M. 10
Theweleit, K. 27, 116
Thorne, B. and Yalom, M. 18
Thornton, A. 21
Tina 60, 62, 85, 94, 98, 11, 130, 135, 163, 164, 165, 166, 192
transsexuals 4
transvestites 4
Turner, B. 31

Ulla 75–6, 85, 121, 140, 172
unmarried women *see* single women, unmarried
Ursula 43, 78, 101, 104, 119, 162, 181
USA 9–10, 15, 16, 18, 20, 34–5, 50, 81, 99, 147, 151, 154, 179, 196–7
see also family, nuclear; single women, American; spinsters, in America; women, American; welfare state, in the USA

Valerie 56, 94, 97, 109, 120, 175, 187
Vega, W. 51
Vicinus, M. 11, 14, 15, 25, 32
Victorian lady explorers 13–14, 26, 32
Violet 120, 152

Wacklin, S. 10
Wakil, S. 34
Walby, S. 35, 197
Walkerdine, V. and Lucey, H. 19, 194
Wallace, M. 3, 18, 51
Warner, M. 3, 4, 6–7, 25, 27, 31
Watkins, S. 9, 10
Weiss, R. 90

welfare state 33, 35–6, 74, 99
  in Britain, Finland and USA 99,
    196–7
  early stages 5, 14
  and family 19
  Western democracies 25
  see also social contract
Wheelwright, J. 3, 4
Willcox, Toyah 3
Williams, R. 25
Willis, P. 116
Wilson, E. 116, 169
Wittig, M. 5
women 5
  associated with nature 3, 26
  Athenian 2
  in Britain 12, 16, 17, 67
  with children 66
  of colour 51, 182
  in Finland 12, 16, 17, 67
  in USA 12, 17, 67
  married 41, 101, 102, 104, 111, 132, 146, 169, 183
  middle-class 21, 30
  professional 21, 23

sexualisation of 14, 27
and suffrage 12
white 12, 20, 27, 29, 30
and work 10, 11, 12, 16, 17, 18, 32
working-class 12, 20, 21, 23, 30
see also black women; body, of women; citizenship, and women; divorced women; education, and opportunities for women; family, women in the; individual, and women; individuality, and women; never-married women; single women
women's movement, the 15, 32
Woodhouse, A. 4
Wood, J. 116
work see independence, and work; single women, and work; women, and work

Yudice, G. 198
Yuval-Davis, N. 25, 27

Zavella, P. 19, 51
Zinn, M. 19, 50, 179